CUT-THROAT

THE VICIOUS WORLD OF ROD McLEAN –
MERCENARY, GUN-RUNNER AND
INTERNATIONAL DRUG BARON

CUT-
THROAT

WAYNE THALLON

MAINSTREAM
PUBLISHING
EDINBURGH AND LONDON

First published in Great Britain in 2005 by
MAINSTREAM PUBLISHING COMPANY (EDINBURGH) LTD
7 Albany Street
Edinburgh EH1 3UG

ISBN 1 84018 975 4

Reprinted 2005

A catalogue record for this book is available
from the British Library

Maps on pages 8 and 10 © Gilles d'Amecourt

Typeset in Badhouse and Caslon

Printed and bound in Great Britain by
William Clowes Ltd, Beccles, Suffolk

'Abandon all hope, ye who enter here.'
Dante Alighieri, *Divine Comedy*

CONTENTS

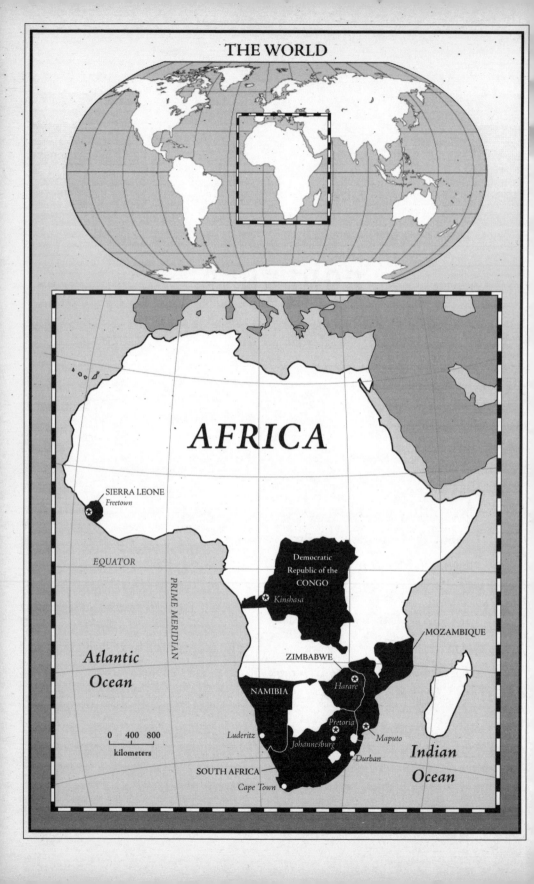

PROLOGUE

The first eight chapters of the Rod McLean story have been written through his own eyes, in his own words and by his own hand. Assembled from his writings at sea, his diaries in prison, and from nothing but the scribbles on the back of cigarette packets when necessary, this is his last will and testament and it pulls no punches.

The ninth chapter, 'Out With the Laundry!', however, was written after his death, with the help of an anonymous few.

The final chapter is yet to be finished!

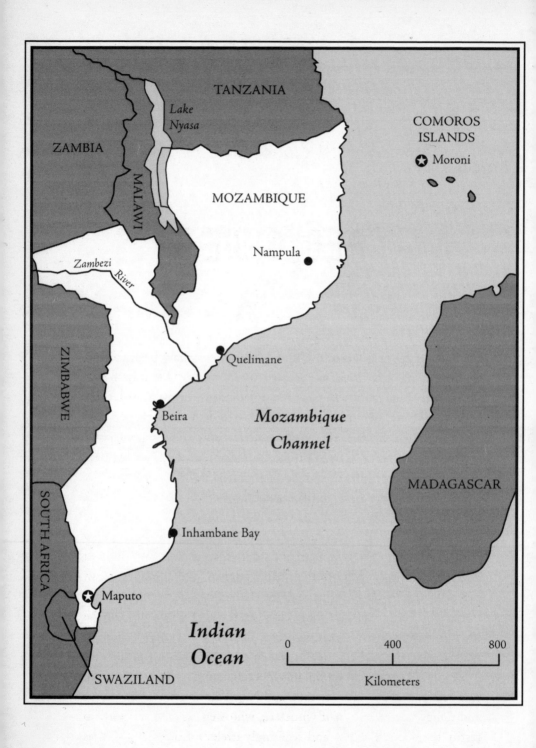

INTRODUCTION

A SHOWER OF BASTARDS

By 20 February 1997 our trial was over. It had lasted a total of 56 days. Every morning a large-scale police operation had swung into action, ferrying me and the eight other defendants to the High Court, sitting in Dunfermline, from HMP Saughton in Edinburgh. This commotion, overseen by both Lothian & Borders and Fife Constabulary, consisted of traffic divisions, armed-response vehicles and 'secure' vans containing armed guards, while the security at the Court was of the highest profile, reminiscent of the Old Bailey's IRA trials, and certainly out of the ordinary in Scotland. To enter the courtroom, it was necessary to pass through a search area manned by armed police, while the courtroom itself was guarded by at least a dozen burly policemen with their batons drawn. What nobody knew, especially the impressionable jury, was that as little as three days prior to the start of the trial, all the accused were being transported in the usual manner – a court van with a civilian driver and one unarmed police officer. How different this was to the stage show that followed.

Beyond the misinformation, misdirection and, at times, fabrication, this trial by ordeal over Christmas and New Year boasted an enormous and unnecessary number of witnesses, who were brought forward to testify to the most minor and seemingly irrelevant details, as well as

11

those which were very complex in nature. In the end, after two female jurors had requested to leave, as they had been unnerved by all the guns around the court, eight of us nine were found guilty. I was charged with contravening section 170(2)(b) of the Customs and Excise Management Act 1979, namely that of drug importation, for which I received 14 years, and attempting to defeat the ends of justice, for which I also received 14 years – to run consecutively. Bastards!

But that wasn't all – the gloves were off. Fearing my escape, they branded me a supergrass, fabricated an elaborate plot to kill me and layered a plot-line so thick that the story soon had a life of its own. Well, grass, my arse! What kind of grass gets 28 years? And while I could tell you a James Bond tale like the one they've suggested, that me – Rod McLean – a sneaky Customs informer, was part of an international sting operation to snare Jan van Rijs, the global big shot and leader of 'Octopus', the Dutch mafia, I won't. This is for two reasons: firstly, because it's pish, and secondly, because the real story is far, far better – The Rod McLean Story!

CHAPTER I

THE BLOODY CONGO

I was just a kid when I landed in the Congo. Probably the youngest white mercenary they'd seen. Standing next to the rest of the battle-hardened hired guns, I was nothing. I would have argued that point back then, but I know better now. I entered this world at 19 and, believe me, there's nothing more dangerous than a 19-year-old Scot who's convinced he's immortal, with a machine gun and a bag of grenades. Like my granddad had said after war in the trenches, the thing that the Germans feared most was a Jock with a half-brick and a bottle of whisky. That was me.

After three years of active service, most of it in Kenya mopping up the Mau Mau, I was ready to fight, a trained killer with sweeties in my pocket. Although I was reluctant to become a mercenary, it seemed an obvious way out of a hole. I'd just got married, and life was difficult scraping about for the first rung on the ladder. You know what they say: 'When poverty comes through the door, love flies out the window.' So when a mate of mine from the Scots Guards, Andy – that's not his real name, but he knows who he is – talked about a few months' work in the jungle, I thought fuck it. After all, how bad could it be?

I knew little about the conflict, even less about the country. I knew

I was going to conduct counter-insurgency operations to 'purge the freedom-loving people of the Congo from their communist aggressors'. But, in reality, I was there for a fat pay cheque and a few laughs. I knew there would be trouble, that's why we were there, but I'd seen it before with the Guards, and I knew I could stomach it. I'd volunteered for the Congo and went with my eyes wide open. I calculated the odds of survival and tried to increase them by taking to heart the sacred laws of combat drilled into our thick skulls by our superiors in the British Army: stay down, fire and move, never be third on a match when lighting your smoke, only drink bottled water and don't talk to strangers. Well, the last two came from my wife, Susan, but they still applied to the Congo.

I was brash and self-confident when I landed at Leopoldville one hot and muggy morning in late '64. I thought I knew what to expect – a sea of smiling faces on a flower-waving populace. Instead it was a silent indifference from a bewildered minority. Less than an hour later we were walking along the dusty clay road towards the processing centre when a Belgian Army truck came tearing round the corner and hit our point man head-on. The impact belted him a fucker, 50 ft through the air and another 50 along the road, before his body came to rest just inches away from my shiny new corps boots. I couldn't believe a man so badly mangled could still be breathing. A couple of the older lads started to break out their field dressings, but even a shiny new hospital wouldn't have saved him. He gasped for air like a fish out of water, then died staring straight into my eyes. Seeing a man killed on my first day gave me the shits. I took it as a bad omen. For three in our small group, it was.

Within a few minutes we moved on and joked to mask our shaken nerves, each man trying to outdo the other with demonstrations of just how little that scene had affected him. I think I said something like, 'He never knew what hit him.' But when we finally entered the barracks, each man found a quiet place. Later that afternoon I was issued with an M2 carbine and a stack of rounds – as many as I could carry. I took a lot. As I loaded the 30-round magazines, the reality of being in a war zone sank in. I loved it. That evening, we gathered in the bunkers and heard about the war. The CO of our detail was a retired British officer. He had a particular disfigurement, which if I share will probably identify him. I'll call him Colonel Green, a classic ex-public-school adventurer, made of the stuff that built the Empire, and more than content to be neck-high in shite.

Our outfit was a loose collection of nationalities: British, American, Belgian, but mainly South African. I didn't know any of them before I joined, but I did have a mate already working here. He'd come out the month before and I hoped to meet up with him soon. The Colonel said that we were here to quash the second rebellion in as many years. This one had been sparked by some guy called Pierre Mulele, who'd been trained by the Chinese in guerrilla warfare, and whipped up by another, Gaston Soumialot, who in January 1964 was sent to Burundi by a left-wing political movement based in the former French Congo, with the mission of organising it. Soumialot was able to recruit thousands of dedicated supporters in eastern Kivu, along the border with Burundi. The rebellion was fuelled by a general hatred of the Congolese government. Many of the rebels clung to ancient animist religious patterns, and many genuinely believed that 'magic water' dispensed by witch doctors could make a warrior immune to government bullets, transforming the warrior into a 'Simba' (Swahili for lion). Consequently, the Congolese rebellion came to be known as the Simba rebellion.

The Simba rebellion quickly gained ground and before they knew it, it had taken the government stronghold of Stanleyville. Equipped with armaments left by the defeated Congolese National Army units, the Simbas pushed on north and west of Stanleyville, eventually penetrating as far west as Lisala on the Congo River. By September that year they'd proclaimed a revolutionary government in Stanleyville, and almost half of the Congo and seven local capitals out of twenty-one were in rebel hands. If that wasn't bad enough, the Colonel informed us that discipline amongst the Simba, in some parts, was all but gone and that serious acts of violence and terror were increasing, so we should expect no quarter given if captured.

Although we didn't know it at the time – well, I should speak for myself and say I didn't give a fuck – the Soviet Union and the United States were at it as usual. The US had committed their support to the central Congolese government, our side, and so the CIA began to organise a small air force to support the Congolese ground forces and to raise a force of mercenaries to provide 'much-needed leadership for the conduct of military operations'. Basically, we were to spearhead attacks against rebel strongholds. Sitting tight, cramped in our bunker under a low-watt light bulb, as the Colonel steadily painted a shite storm before our very eyes, it suddenly began to dawn on me that somehow I'd managed to stumble into a major fucking war. But in my youthful naivety, I was up for it.

After a few days' orientation I was assigned to a squad. I wasn't thrilled. They weren't thrilled with me either. By the looks I received, you'd have thought I'd come straight from a cow's arse. I was now in a man's world. The mean age of my squad was 30. I'd expected the Congo to be a lot like Kenya, but it couldn't have been further away. My squad were serious professional soldiers, who, for one reason or another, had opted into a life which was, as yet, near impossible for me to understand. Soldiering until now had been like a normal job. You got up and did your work, then knocked off at teatime, providing you weren't on exercise, and got pissed, chased birds and had a laugh. These guys trained all day, then slept, then got up and trained some more, and apart from reconnaissance patrols and the training of the Congolese forces (the Armée Nationale Congolaise, or ANC – not to be confused with the other ANC) we hadn't really joined the war yet. I was bored, out of my depth and alone. This wasn't what I'd seen in the brochure.

The guys' only recreation seemed to be the catching of rats and other assorted nasties. Personally, I never had a problem with rats. They were just big mice and I liked them. I knew a bird in London who had a pet mouse that would run all over her suntanned body. It would run up her trouser legs and nest in her blouse, giving me the opportunity to stare at her chest under the guise of rodent-watching. The first time I saw a rat in my hut, I tried to befriend it. Then, over the period of a week, I managed to have it eating from my hands. At night, it would negotiate our bergens and scurry along the makeshift skirting from the far end of the hut, to where I'd feed it from under my mosquito net. I named him Archie after my father-in-law. He was a small rat with long whiskers and big bug eyes. He was my friend. Becoming more detached from the man's world I now inhabited, I'd even fantasise about taming him and having a rat to keep watch for me at night, warning me of enemy ambushes.

My efforts at escapism were further encouraged when I got given a dog off the Colonel. I've always loved dogs, and this hairy mutt got all my attention. I'd get down on the floor and wrestle the day away. He'd chew my face with his razor-sharp teeth, then chew through the hut, which made the guys mad. But I didn't care. It gave me a sense of security and took me back, back to my youth. I'd felt alone then, too. I guarded that animal like a newborn child. I even took him to the shite-house when I was back in the hut, and everybody laughed at me. But I still wasn't bothered. I quickly fell in love with him and kept him for weeks. So when he disappeared, I fucking lost it. I ripped the camp apart looking for him, panicking like I'd lost a child. I tried to get the rest of the squad involved, but they couldn't have cared less. The locals then, so I thought, would help for a few tins of Spam, but they weren't about. Looking for them, I went round the back and found them huddled around a fire, and to my horror, I saw them cooking my dog on a stick. Bastards!

I turned pale and saw red. And before I knew it, I'd footed one of the coons up the arse so hard I swear I'd cleared him over the spit roast like a rugby ball. But just before I set about the rest of them in a frenzy, I was grabbed by two big Boers and thrown back on the ground. Standing up, I felt my 'friend' come to me – a feeling I get which I call my 'ace card'. When I get it, I know I'll never be beaten, because I'll either win or die fighting – either way is fine. I was ready to kill the Boers and the coons with my bare hands. But like when someone talks to you when you're asleep and they actually enter your dream, I heard a voice to my right: 'Rod, Rod, this isny your fight!' It was one of the boys from my squad. I staggered back to my hut, then straight on to the armoury, my haven. Once inside, I mounted a .30-calibre machine gun in a vice and pulled back on the cocking handle. I pulled the trigger, sending the bolt slamming against the empty chamber. I cocked and fired, cocked and fired repeatedly, until eventually someone burst in behind me. It was Tosh McKenzie, one of the 'ex-British NCOs'.

'Rod, one of the South African lads has gone to the Colonel. He seems to think you've lost it. What's the fucking problem?'

'There's no problem,' I snarled.

'Well, there is now. Get it sorted!'

I tried to mask my childish emotions, but they soon came out with the tantrum-like aggression of a four year old. 'What's there the fuck to sort? That bunch of wog bastards are cooking my fucking dog!' I quickly turned away and drew so hard on the cocking handle that I pulled the gun from the vice, which sent it clattering to the floor. At this, Tosh left.

A few minutes later someone else entered the makeshift armoury and hoisted himself onto the sandbag wall behind me. It was Allan Patterson. I concentrated on hiding my tears by keeping my head turned. Allan had been doing this sort of thing for years, so had seen more action than a hooker at a card table. What's more, this former SAS man had a brain to match his brawn. 'Listen, kid,' he said. 'I canny say I totally agree with the Colonel's wit, he's one sick fuck. But there'll be a tag on your toe before the sun's down if you dinny grow up fast.' He had my attention, but I was still too embarrassed to face him. He grabbed my shoulder, turned me, then thumped my chest over my heart, saying, 'This'll get you fucking killed. In case you've missed it, this isny square-bashing in Nairobi, it's the fucking Congo, the arsehole of Africa. You're goanna see shite here that you canny even imagine. Right? In Kenya, if it fucks up, we can always call the cavalry. Here, we're the fucking cavalry! And that's fucking that. See these cunts, they'll skin you alive and eat your fucking heart out – you understand? I've seen the Colonel do this before to make his point. Most cunts click after the first week. A few take two. You're the first that took three. That makes you the best doggy fattener we've had.' I tried to smile, but he didn't. 'You're a right tough bastard, Rod. You've got bottle and sense, and I'd hate to have to tell your missus you didny make it. Dying for your country's one thing, but dying for a few quid . . .' He paused. 'Well, it's no easy for family to get their heads round, right?' He was dead right on that. 'You've been here a good few weeks now, but more and more boys are arriving by the day, and that means that things are about to kick off.'

He hopped down and started for the door, pausing to add, 'Oh, about the coons. Coons eat dogs and any other fucking thing that's no varnished or stapled down. They're the top of the food chain here. Dogs are a delicacy; it's their pheasant. Dinny be holding hard feelings towards them. They thought you were doing them a favour.' He winked, and with a reassuring clout over the back of my head, left.

I passed the coons on my way back to my hut. They grinned and returned to their pheasant. Later that afternoon I sat on my bunk, thinking about Allan's words. Just before it was time to get my shit together for the nightly patrol, Archie came out for his snack. I calmly reached under the bed to draw my bayonet, and with one quick strike nailed that beady-eyed Simba rat bastard to the floor.

Though meant as a wind-up, the Colonel's puppy prank had served as a lesson that stayed with me for the rest of my life. The tears I shed that day were the last tears I shed for 33 years. I zipped close friends into body bags and shed no tears. I witnessed evil so extreme that it clung to my soul, and shed no tears. I was tortured and was a torturer, and shed no tears. In 1997, my eldest son was given a 12-year sentence in his prime; I knelt in my cell and, all alone, cried the tears of 33 years.

In the beginning I never got to see fighting in the Congo that resembled what I'd seen on TV, or in the odd skirmishes against the Mau Mau diehards in Kenya, though six weeks in the jungle had given me a real taste for the war. I learned that the enemy was an elusive bastard that you had to go looking for, and that once you found him, he'd try to run away. The coons we were with weren't looking very hard to begin with, and if, by chance, they stumbled upon the enemy, they were just as likely to shoot each other. Fighting in the Congo, so far, had a lot in common with a car crash. Sometimes two motors would smack head-on, while others got rear-ended or blindsided. The skirmishes would last for minutes that seemed like hours and, when asked, everyone would remember them differently.

Real fighting wasn't very visual either. With most scuffles happening at night or in heavy jungle filled with smoke and debris, sight was severely restricted, and with so many bangs and cracks that the wall of noise often became a blanket, hearing was soon to follow. In fact, of the five senses, touch, taste and smell played a bigger role than sight or hearing. Combat, then, has an acrid stench, a metallic, bitter taste that makes you gag as high explosives give off a toxic gas, while their energy rips through the ground and thumps your soul. And all the time, cracking like bullwhips around your head, rounds whiz by at supersonic speed, as their displaced air lashes against your skin – an experience that takes some getting used to. In the beginning I was paralysed, but army training and the basic instinct of self-preservation soon help you to find your rhythm. And so I abandoned 'spray and pray', which only scares the wildlife, and instead made headway with controlled single shots, short bursts, tear gas and everybody's favourite – white phosphorous.

As the time passed, we steadily eased ourselves into the war. We knew that sooner or later we'd be hitting the rebels head-on, but even though I was now on active patrols, the nature of the battles still seemed to lack a reality. Soon, though, I began to adapt to the life. I started to feel the part and gain a real confidence in myself as not only a soldier, but as a professional killer – a real mercenary. I was learning fast, and it was a craft I loved. One of the Boers who dragged me off the coons at the dog roasting was to become the new leader of my squad. His name was Craig Kruger. Craig wasn't his real first name, not because I'm hiding his identity, but because he was. Craig was German and had been in the Hitler Youth as a boy. He'd escaped death and capture and had made it to South Africa, where I assume he'd shed his past. He was in his early 40s but had the energy of someone half his age, and the head of someone double it. He took a liking to me. I like to think it's because he saw something of himself in me that day over the fire, but I can't be sure. He'd been wounded several times in his life, but had never known when he was beat: something I saw of myself in him. He was never a Nazi at heart and, as was obvious to me, he didn't need a cause to fight. He was just a warrior, and his only allegiance was to his men.

Kruger was an amazing man. In battle, he was without fear. He knew the enemy better than the enemy knew himself. In a firefight, he would often stand up in order to see clearly what was going on. He taught me how to read trails, how to survive a near hit from a 500-lb bomb, how to control a large group of men without radios and how to arm a 60 mm mortar round without dropping it down a tube. He was a fair and even-handed leader, and uncharacteristically for a 'South African ex-Nazi', treated the whites just as badly as the blacks.

The jungle was a sheer bastard to work in. The creatures that couldn't poison you simply swallowed you whole. Incessant rain, leeches, bats, rats, gnats and flora with an appetite for flesh all conspired to make a mercenary's life miserable. And, as if the environment wasn't bad enough, it was booby-trapped. The sneaky bastards might not have been up for a square go to begin with, but they had no qualms about taking your fucking legs off with a trip line. Still, like a bee sting on sunburn, these wee games helped to take our minds off the weather.

Talking of animals, now's a good time to mention another man in my squad. To be honest, I really hated the fucking sight of him from the start. From the minute I laid eyes on him, I could tell that he wasn't right in the head and was the closest thing to a human reptile I'd ever seen. His slight frame and cold, steely blue eyes, which never blinked, revealed little about the person inside: a sheer demon of a man. After a long life of villainy I can truthfully say that I've met a lot of bad men in my time, but none have ever come close to Ivan. Ivan the fucking terrible. Although, by this time, we'd all got to know each other pretty well, nobody really knew much about Ivan. And while we'd all discussed each other's pasts and future hopes, we knew fuck all about his. What we did know was that whenever we asked him if there was anywhere else he'd rather be, he'd say no, and that in itself was fucked up. On all of our patrols, I'd always made a point of being at the opposite end of the snake from Ivan; I'd always felt that, given half a chance, the sneaky weasel-faced bastard was as likely to put a fucking bullet in me as he was the Simbas. But it's a funny world, and little did I know that fate would ensure that both Ivan and myself would soon cement a bond that lasted a lifetime. That, however, was some time ahead.

By mid-October we were pushing along the Congo River basin after the taking of Lisala. We'd been in the thick of it for close to three days and had fought intermittent contacts, but nothing off the scale. By now it was the jungle more than the Simba which was taking its toll. Having said that, and given the option, I'd have happily gunned down our bunch of useless Congolese fucks before the jungle life trying to bite my ankles. Our band of merry men were mega-light infantry. Anything beyond a magazine to carry was a burden, and they'd leave a trail of equipment in our wake, not only giving the Simbas a road map to our location, but a steady supply of ordnance. Still, it was always nice of the Simbas to return what they found – usually with a bang! Back in the camp, I'd seen our lot use mortar rounds for fishing and the C4 from Claymore mines to cook with. If that wasn't bad enough, they stuck the Claymores back in the 'to use' pile. The result? Simbas with slight flesh wounds. As for giving them grenades, no fucking chance.

We were on our way to a rendezvous with another squad and we knew that the enemy were in the area. We could hear firing off in the distance, both small arms and some heavy thumps. To our right was a long-ridged rock formation which needed to be checked. Besides the usual foliage there were all sorts of nooks and crannies, and in one we found a wounded man. He appeared to be a Simba. He didn't have a weapon but there were a few grenades and rounds lying around him. He seemed to have been in this hole for quite a few days, which made no sense. One of his legs was broken in half and the maggots had already gotten in and were eating him alive. Everyone spread out and took a knee, while Xavier, an ex-Belgian Para, went over with one of the coons. They stood for a minute; the man was in serious pain and didn't look that happy. I had a problem with the situation. I don't know what it was, but the whole set-up looked wrong. Our coon was trying to speak to him, but he didn't get a word. No wonder. With 250 ethnic groups and 700 local languages, it was always going to be a long shot.

Watching this ordeal from my position on point, I began to feel the hairs on the back of my neck standing up, and soon my heart began to race so much that I could feel the thump pulling me forward. Looking about, the place had ambush written all over it. If it kicked off here, we'd have no chance. Peeling my tongue from the roof of my moistureless mouth, I tried to stabilise my breathing. I knew this feeling: it's a high, but one that's better enjoyed as a memory. I could hear the fighting getting closer and could swear a thousand eyes were on me. I picked a tree and took a firing position. I unhooked two MK2 fragmentation grenades and pulled the pins half out. I was straining to see through the trees and was convinced that some fucking thing was about to hit.

Impatiently, another of our squad, Jimmy Harrison, walked forward, taking his knife from his belt and saying, 'I'll fucking help him!' I knew what he was about to do. Just then, it happened – bang! I turned round to see a plume of smoke where the coons had been, and a second later, both Xavier and Jimmy came running out squealing like pigs. The Simba fuck had set off a white phosphorus grenade. It's a fucked way to go and no fun to watch. It delivers a chemical burn from particles frying at 5,000 degrees. They slice into flesh like a hot knife through butter and only extinguish when they've burned themselves out. Xavier took it right in the face. It burns for a full minute – that's a minute with your face being cooked, and there's fuck all anyone can do about it.

He ran one way, then another. He banged into trees, he fell down, he got up, he ran again. Like the macabre farce it was becoming, Jimmy, who had it all down his front, was doing the same – they even collided. While the suffering circus clowns performed in the ring, we, the powerless audience, sat gasping in shock. After the burn, the characteristic smell of garlic and the lingering white smoke started to clear, leaving the two heroic actors twitching uncontrollably. I ran over to Jimmy. I could see the hundreds of phos holes still smouldering away, crusty yellow rings now forming around each wound. I looked over to where Xavier lay, a perfectly intact body and a completely destroyed head; I'll never forget that. Looking back up, I saw Kruger, pistol in hand. He said nothing but gestured me away. No sooner had I turned my back than I heard two shots. What else could he do? They took the bodies and quickly buried them in the hole where we'd found the coon. Meanwhile, I waited for the ambush, which never came. I breathed a sigh of relief, but the adrenalin was still pumping. Both excitement and despair now charged the air. This was war. People died.

Back on the move, and the midday sun shattered on the canopy above and fell, fragmented, in a golden glow around me. The humid rainforest air was now a second skin which hugged us, moist and clammy, like a blanket of reality within the dreamlike jungle greenery. In the course of those hours my entire world had changed as, for the first time, there was no time. Now, there was only the trail behind and the trail ahead, a muddy brown streak that remained hidden except for chance appearances when we'd least expect it. The intensity of the morning, now just a haze, steadily disappeared over my shoulder, while still ahead lurked an all-too-uncertain future. The only thing that mattered now was finishing this patrol and getting back to base, alive and in one piece. In all, I was fucking sick of it, wading through the leech-infested streams, crossing cliffs by holding onto rotten tree roots, the 60-degree slopes, the 110 varieties of poisonous snake – and the rest. I wanted a fight. Then I wanted to fuck off. At that moment, I was thinking of strippers. I always hated strippers: what was the point? Spend your money to see some fanny, and still walk out with a hard-on! Better to see a hooker. Cost a bit more, but you'd leave all relaxed – up for a pint and a nice bit of dinner. Here, in this bedlam, I was in the front row of the world's longest strip show.

Cutting trail was a slow and tedious process. We kept starting and stopping, stopping and starting, as the point man hack-hacked his way through the triple-canopy undergrowth. By now, the temperature was fast reaching 45 degrees. Somewhere ahead and somewhere behind, the others were walking just like me – stealthily, crouched and pensive. Except for an occasional glimpse, I wouldn't even have known they were there. Gone was the banter that travelled our line the night before. Instead were the muffled tones of laboured breathing. Out here, silence was a utility. Taped down to make them as quiet as possible were the trappings of war we each carried, rubbing gently against our combat fatigues as the soft noise blended easily into the jungle around us. Between the intermittent adrenalin bursts, heat and fatigue, the jungle light created no end of illusions as jet-black shadows bounced between an evergreen background presenting us with a cinematic experience, almost like a frame-by-frame film shot through a drug-induced View Master.

Our destination was a location on a map, several miles north. That's where we were to hook up with the second squad before tabbing to the stage area and the rendezvous with the third. On the terrain map it looked like a starfish with a rounded body and five emanating ridges like legs that sloped down into ravines. We were sweeping round the ravines to the east. The second squad were cutting a direct route through the middle, while the third took the longer dogleg to the west. The idea was that we'd meet up and hit a rebel stronghold, a village whose name escapes me now, and then press on to link up with other white-led units in the area.

At around 1400hrs the heavens opened up. South of the Equator the rainy season lasts from October to May, and north of it, from April to November. Along the Equator itself, rainfall is fairly regular throughout the year, and that was us. Thunderstorms were violent, but seldom lasted more than a few hours, and for me, a few hours' break under a violent thunderstorm wasn't all bad. We formed a defensive perimeter, with two men in each makeshift bunker, and sat it out. With me was an American who called himself Mark. In fact, he was a Cuban exile, one of the many who'd escaped Castro to Florida, only to be mobilised in the Bay of Pigs plan of 1961. Mark was one of the many Cubans in the Congo that year. Since the Congolese had no trained pilots to fly the planes supplied by the CIA, ex-Cuban pilots were used. At first, they had a few T6 trainers, armed with gun pods and rocket launchers, before moving to more advanced T28s. Mark was a great guy. He was also our radioman. With a scar running over his right eye, and standing at over 6 ft 6 in. and weighing at least 18 st. of solid muscle, he was every bit the warrior, both with and without a tool. He'd arrived in the Congo on the same day as me, and by this time was probably as close to a mate as I was likely to get out there. Our banter was 90 per cent offensive humour. I'd say all sorts of things about his mum; he'd say all sorts of things about mine. He cracked jokes, usually at my expense, and I'd rip the fucking piss back, like only a 'wide-o' Scottish lad could. Not only would we do it in private but also in public, like we were in a slander competition. I liked that. I liked the look on people's faces when I'd say stuff so personally offensive that they thought he'd kill me. To them, I was yanking a lion's tail. To me, I knew he was just a pussy-cat. As those damp hours passed, we sat, we got wet, and we highlighted the promiscuity of each other's mother.

As the storm pissed itself dry, Kruger came round all the holes to bark his instructions. Before leaving us, he turned to Mark and said, 'Mark, I'm not happy with your camouflage. I want you to cover up better.'

Mark looked at Kruger for a moment with some bemusement, before replying in a really calm voice, 'Craig, I'm 6 ft 6. The radio antennae on my back is 4 ft 4. Tell me, what fucking good is a few bits of grass when I'm 11 ft tall?'

I swear the fucking Simbas could have dropped us all. We laughed so hard I took a hernia. Even Kruger, trying to keep a straight face, was now in the hole with us. It took him five minutes to get back out. As soon as we could stand, we were back on the trail, one nervous step at a time. Suddenly the stillness of the jungle was shattered by the tremendous roar of a jet turbine engine. Some minutes later we were to hear the thump of its ordnance. It rattled the trees and stirred the birds. It reminded us of just how close we were to contact. I dropped another foot when I walked.

At 1800hrs we hit a creek bed which, after the torrential downpour, had become a fast-flowing river. Crossing it was both dangerous and unnecessary. To the west and north-east was thick jungle growth, which sloped upwards to our direction of travel – not an option. After a pause for thought, Kruger made the decision to double back for a mile, then swing further east and around the ridge, which was blocking us. The only thing was we wouldn't be able to reach the second squad that day. But with no alternative, it had to be done. All set to retrace our steps, Kruger stopped us. We took a knee while he headed to the point. I don't know if he sniffed the air or held an ear to the ground, but Tonto wasn't happy. He sent out a recce, an all-black one. As four ANC boys disappeared, I took it upon myself to light a smoke. I sat on a rock and took a deep drag, then looked to my right, and I nearly shat myself. It was Mark. He'd decided to respect Kruger's camo order and was now looking like a walking hedge. What a fucking laugh! I won't offend the botanists by trying to cite the name of the plant, but he'd gone and got some kind of lily or some other plant with leaves the size of a table. He'd taken a leaf, cut out two eyeholes and wrapped it round his head, and was now jumping about, all 6 ft 6 in. of him, like a fucking nut. I'll never forget that. The laugh subsided and Mark sat down, but as we relaxed, the smiles stayed on our faces, and for that moment I really think we forgot where we were.

It was the beginning of the end of a very long day. The setting sun projected a sky so red that the forest began to pulse. The air seemed fresher, even cooler, and, like most of us, I started to find some peace, a break from the strain of staying alive. I decided that I'd make this a double smoke break. Lighting my new fag with the butt of my old one, I started to dream of Edinburgh, the city I called home. I hadn't had a chance to dream for days; it felt good. Everyone around me, even the ANC boys, were starting to dream as we sat together in Eden while our minds struggled to leave hell. It's a funny old world.

Just then, the silence of the jungle was interrupted by the unmistakable cold, sharp 'crack' of AK47 fire. Our hearts jumped, but our bodies froze. Then came the answer of an M16-A1 on full automatic. Silence. Then thumps, three altogether, and each one louder and closer. Boom, boom . . . boom! Then more automatic-weapon fire, then silence. Still frozen, like rabbits caught in the headlights, our hopelessness caused us to hope all the more. Hell had smacked us all for daring to leave, and this time – it smacked us hard. It was Kruger's voice that rang the end-of-dinner bell. 'Defensive perimeter!'

We didn't know what the fuck was going on. We braced for an attack, but again, none came. The minutes now passing seemed like hours as we waited for something, something which would certainly be terrible, but nothing happened and nothing continued to happen. But at that time and for the first time, I felt no fear, as I was completely saturated with anger – pure fucking anger! I hated those Simba fucks so bad I would have gone in after them all with a blade. 'C'mon, c'mon!' I was saying to myself over and over again, as I scanned through the trees for the slightest twitch.

'Identify it's not our boys coming back,' said Kruger, shouting in a whisper.

Personally, at that moment, I didn't give a fuck. Anyone showing his face was getting it. Still nothing. 'Oh, this isny real!' I said to myself, finger twitching on the trigger.

As I said that, Kruger jumped by my side. 'Right, we got to take it to them. You, Mark, Bill [another white mercenary from South Africa] and half our lot [meaning half the ANC troop], up the front. We'll swing round the flank. When you hear the sound of the thumper, it's us. We'll be on your right!'

The 'thumper' was the American-made M79 grenade launcher that had come into our possession.

With a surge of adrenalin I was off, tearing through the jungle, the boys behind me. Then I stopped like a dog on a leash as my body bolted back with a jerk. I almost stood on the bastard. It was one of the ANC boys, lying on the ground and looking more than a mess with both his knees bent at 90 degrees in the wrong direction and his fatigues littered with hundreds of holes. Through the holes, his arteries had pumped him dry, spurting the blood everywhere. As I took a knee, all hell broke loose.

Like the sound of a canoe paddle on the mud, a shot hit the upper arm of an ANC boy to my left and entered his side. He was bleeding in spurts. I fired two bursts, then ducked down and ripped away at his shirt with my knife and did him up. I got back up and tried to search for a target, but the scene was one of fucking chaos, each group firing blindly at the other. The fire was so intense that the shot-up leaves from the trees were being hit more than once before they touched the ground and were now dancing about like feathers in the wind, while so many rounds pelted the ground that it looked like heavy rain. In all, the whole fucking jungle was moving. And all the time, the noise and acrid stench of grenades thumping the dirt was filling the air.

Then, to my left again, another ANC boy screamed. A bullet had gone through his boot and taken off his toes. He was in agony and crying. Soon he was swearing and in shock. If I'd helped him then, I'd have been killed myself, as the Simbas now swarmed around us. 'At least I can see the bastards!' I shouted, as I crouched down to use the first ANC body as a sandbag. Just then, two Simba heroes came rushing through the brush. The first was cut down instantly from my right, while I fired at point-blank into the second one's face. His head literally disappeared.

I was still waiting on the thumps from the M79. I was going fucking mad because, without them, we'd essentially cut our numbers in half to attack an ambush. Not a wise move. I looked behind me to the left, to see our ANC line had retreated. I cursed the cowardly bastards then, but I can't blame them now, as we were seriously fucked. Left in my section was Mark, who was about 5 yards to my two o'clock, and an ANC boy a few yards further still. I put my head up and caught sight of him losing his. I put mine back down. Then I saw at least seven of them appear 10 yards beyond Mark, just as he was changing magazine. We were fucked. Mark played dead, so I jumped in a bush.

Three of the group started to set up a machine gun, while one of them used Mark as a seat. The fighting line, if there had ever been one, had now moved some 100 yards back down towards the creek. The wall of noise, now following the fight, passed over our heads like a moving tornado. Suddenly we were left in a wake of calmness. Even my breath seemed as loud as a gunshot. Now in the belly of the beast,

I stopped to breathe and tried to keep low, so low I could have rear-ended a snake's arse. If they'd even taken one more step, they'd have seen me. To make things worse, I was staring down the wrong end of a Browning .50-cal. machine gun. What the fuck was I going to do? Throw a grenade? Kill Mark? Fuck that!

Suddenly, M79 rounds began dropping out of the sky – the best thumps I've ever heard. The rounds hit, bringing the storm right back upon us, killing the Simbas, but wounding Mark. The shock from one of the blasts had also hit me, making me lose my bearings. When I came round, I was bleeding from my head and mouth. Unable to get on my feet, I crawled over the Simba bodies towards Mark. He was lying on his back and moving his arms and legs all slow like a bug in the water. When I reached him, I saw that his fatigues and shirt had been blown off and I saw grey guts hanging from his belly. What could I say? I knew he was fucked, and so did he. Five minutes later, my mate Mark died in my arms.

In my head, we'd been shafted because Kruger had taken too fucking long to get on the enemy's flank. Looking back, he'd actually done well, considering the type of ground he was covering and that he never knew where the bastards were. On top of that, he'd not only outflanked them, but had managed to convince them they were surrounded. The result was that they fucked off, so, even with their superior numbers, we'd given them a hiding. I liked that!

When the killing had stopped, it was Kruger himself who found me. I was lying on top of Mark. His gut was still in my hand where I'd made a futile attempt to stop him from dying. I'd obviously been passing in and out of consciousness, 'cause when he shook me, I was surprised to see where I was. He didn't say anything – he'd had a cunt of a time as well – but he got me to my feet and dusted me off. He looked at Mark. He looked at our radio. He looked pissed off.

Soon I realised that I was standing amongst a scattering of death. Still half-dazed, I walked around and stared at each body now lying around me. I saw the bastard who had sat on Mark. I stood over him for the longest time, just staring. He was an enemy hero, a lucky bastard and an unlucky one, all within the space of a minute. I felt no animosity. I didn't feel like spitting or kicking. He was just another dead hero on a jungle floor of heroes. I didn't cry. I didn't yell. My work was done. It was the ANC boys who had the privilege of burying the dead. In an ideal world, we'd have marched them out with us. Or, had it been the regulars, an airlift. But it wasn't the 'regs', and nothing here was ideal, so they spent eternity where they dropped.

As the sun began to set, Kruger began to rally the troops. In no uncertain terms, he got us going; not that we needed it! I was pumped. I'd taken death by the hand but it'd let me go. I'd become an animal in an animal's world, a hollow man, reduced to suffering and needs, without dignity or restraint. I had battled to save my body, but, like all of us, had lost my soul: eroded away, one bit at a time.

It had been a time to discover who I really was. And I did. It's all relative, of course. You don't need a bloodbath to know yourself, but it's all about stretching your comfort pocket and pushing your boundaries. And when you're on the edge, just about to snap, take a picture of yourself and have a good look. What will you see? What I saw defined me for the rest of my life. I invited pain into my life and it became my friend. When I welcomed its arrival, it became me and I became it. For that, I lived. I lived when I should have died. After that fight I divided humanity into two. There were those who, upon seeing their own blood, roll over, cry and beg for life. Then there were those who see their own blood but taste it, and, like wounded animals, attack. When I moved Mark's body, I saw he'd been shot, twice. Before he'd been forced to play dead, Mark, the crazy bastard, had been fighting like fuck with two bullets in his side. He enjoyed the taste.

Back on the hoof, we chopped our way for half an hour to make the ridge top, then descended, trigger-fingers at the ready, until after 200 yards the light finally went. Holding on to the guy in front, so we knew where to go, we walked on till it bottomed out. At this, Kruger ordered an NDP (night defensive perimeter). Unknown to us, we had moved to within 200 yards of the second squad and within 50 yards of another Simba ambush. But by us moving at night, a tactic that took a lot of getting used to, they couldn't be sure where we'd set up, and by opening fire, they'd have given their own position away from their muzzle flashes. The enemy waited.

When nightfall hits the jungle, it comes alive. It gets so dark that you can't even see a hand in front of your face. You hear the constant droplets of water falling from the trees, while everything that crawls crawls, everything that flies flies, everything that slithers slithers and, above all, everything that eats eats. It's shit being on the menu. All of this keeps you awake: good if you're on watch, but it sure plays tricks with your mind. To begin with, it does your head in, but in time it's fine, 'cause it's when you don't hear the jungle's natural sounds that you're fucked. During the early hours it went quiet.

I pulled the 0400hrs to 0600hrs watch, but between the constant rain and the leeches crawling up my legs, it was difficult to get much sleep. As dawn broke, the gaps in the canopy revealed an overcast sky, with a ceiling so low you could touch it, and all around was a fog just waiting to drop. As we readied the troops, Kruger sent out a recce. They came back in one piece, but told us how close we'd been to an ambush. Seems the Simbas had fucked off during the night. We set out, and advanced in formation through their abandoned positions. But with no radio, we had a new worry: being shot by our second squad. Kruger decided on a white-faced point. He decided on me.

As I took the front, the fog came down. The temperature dropped and the jungle was quiet. With every step I took, my legs got heavier. I looked round, to see an ANC face. For some reason he was staring right at me, rather than scanning the surrounding jungle. I think he felt death upon me as he hypnotically fixed on my movements. He was 20 yards back. I looked forward. I looked back again. I was alone. I paused, and within that breath the fog revealed its secret: a man, a white man, slumped against a tree. I approached to within 10 yards and looked straight into his eyes. He was dead. I didn't check his pulse – you don't need to: the dead look dead. He showed no sign of injury. I saw no blood. He was just dead. I looked at my feet and saw scatterings of spent 45 PC and Tupeolov 9 mm casings (the Tupeolov was a Russian-made pistol). The fighting here had been close. I heard a whisper. It was Kruger. We looked at each other. We looked around.

We were in a terrible place, and in that moment, with almost prophetic intuition, the reality was revealed to us: it was a fucking massacre.

Ten minutes later the rising fog lifted the horror-show curtain. We heard a voice to our right. It was Ivan. We ran over to see him standing with his hands on his hips and looking down. He was shaking his head as if he was being proved right. He gestured with his foot. 'That's no bullet wound.'

Kruger bent down. 'What the fuck?' he said, standing up again and looking to the next corpse. 'They're missing their hearts; they're missing their fucking hearts!'

'That's not all,' said Ivan, now placing two fists inside two neat kidney holes. 'I think you'll find they're all like that,' he said, jumping from body to body like a kid over stepping stones. 'Oh, and have a look at this!' He summoned us along like a tour guide. 'They must've run out of magic water,' he sniggered. 'They think eating organs makes them bullet-proof as well.'

'Oh, Christ,' said Kruger, standing in front of a tree. 'Bastards, evil fucking bastards.' It was the second Boer from the dog-grilling episode. He was tied to a tree, and, by the looks of it, had been eaten alive. Covered in bite marks, his flesh was ripped and devoured in what could only have been a frenzy. He hung like a pulped crucifix, with only the flesh around his eyes remaining, like a white Zorro mask. We stood in silence. We'd hacked and suffered our way through the jungle for days, hungry and exhausted, and we'd made it. We'd made it to an expected calm before the storm, but the storm had beaten us to it. Now that we were in it, it wasn't possible to sink any lower; no human condition was more miserable than this, nor could it be imagined so. If yesterday I'd entertained death, today I had an audience with evil.

In later life I've had many a discussion over the nature of evil. Not so long ago, in my new home of HMP Leyhill, a religious man told me that evil wasn't a created 'thing' but an absence of something. 'Darkness isn't a thing,' he said. 'It is the absence of light. Light's a thing, made up of particles and waves. Take away the created "thing" and the result is darkness or nothing. Temperature works the same way. Cold isn't a thing, but is the absence of heat. Take away the element of physical motion, which creates heat as we know it, and you are left with cold. Evil, then, is not a created thing, but is the absence of good.' I smiled at the time, but I knew this was piss. To tell him would've been like explaining colour to a blind man. If I could have dragged him back, to stand him in front of that tree, to see what we saw and feel what we felt, his view of evil through absence – well, would have been absent.

They ate that poor bastard; that's what they did. They ate him while alive. Each one lining up to take a bite. Did he die on the tenth bite, the twentieth bite, the hundredth bite? Like my peace made with death, that day I grasped the nature of evil. And it's not simply the absence of good. Evil's an action, and it can apply to us all. The Simba did what they did, but they were no more evil than us. It wasn't the Simba who invented white phos, it was us. To me, we're all evil, and we must opt out to be good.

For the third time in 24 hours, we buried the dead. I personally helped bury 20 – it took over an hour. The rest worked for two hours after that. By lunch-time the jungle came back to life. Soon it would reclaim the clearing once formed by slash-and-burn farmers, erasing all trace of the massacre from the landscape, but not from our minds. By now, Kruger had managed to find and repair second squad's PRC radio. It was like finding a wormhole through hell. He relayed our past 24 hours and what we'd found at first light. He spoke to third squad – they'd also had a bashing, but had fought off their attackers and had lost only three blacks. Now, instead of proceeding to the planned rendezvous further north, they'd cut in towards us.

By 1500hrs they'd arrived. They looked like shit; we looked worse. Half an hour later we heard the rumble of an AC130. Kruger popped green smoke and out came our supplies. We moved en masse to get them. We weren't taking any chances.

That evening was quiet. Not only from the Simba, who must have been full, but also from us. Some of the more rattled from first squad sought counselling from the third. I didn't bother; it was too much like one cancer patient seeking sympathy from another. We were all fucked. As the sun came down again, Kruger gathered all the whites together. He told us he'd been tasked by the Colonel. Seemed that the Simbas who'd hit second squad this morning were now in a village to the north-east. It also seemed that some of the rebels actually lived in that area, making the whole village hostile. The Colonel had also given Kruger a list of names we were to lift. They were supposedly stationed there. It all seemed like a load of shite to me. How they'd come by this, I don't know. It's not like we had pathfinder units spying from the fucking trees, so all they could have gone on were Simbas defecting for cash – hardly the best. As he spoke, I soon began to see that his hands were tied. Reluctantly, he was delivering orders he didn't agree with. I could tell, not by what he was saying, but by what he wasn't. We'd set off in an hour, in total darkness, and make a few miles before holing up for the night and hitting the village first thing.

The mission was to engage the Simba and destroy their village. I'll refrain from giving its name. We were to explode any mud-brick homes, set fire to the thatched ones, shoot livestock, poison wells and destroy the enemy. The assault plan called for a newly formed second and third squad to sweep into the village, while first squad, mine, would be held in reserve to regain any momentum lost after the initial onslaught. The village had about 600 residents. An irrigation channel marked its western boundary while directly north of the residential area was an open square used for holding village meetings. To the south and east of the village was dense jungle. We'd hit from there. In total we were about 200-strong. We'd be outnumbered, but we hoped that with our surprise and their indiscipline they could be routed before having a chance to put their boots on.

I went back and explained this to the ANC boys. They seemed to like it. Like me, they wanted to move from this forsaken place. They might have fought for us, but they were superstitious jungle bunnies at heart, and while we knew that second squad had fallen victim to an ambush, they preferred to mix that with other, less worldly explanations. As well as that, they were fed up with all the false peaks we'd been hitting. Attacking and occupying a village would get us out of the fucking jungle, even if it was just for a few days.

By midnight we had walked as far as we could. It was completely dark. Kruger was still unhappy about our task, not because of its nature, but because he was marching our entire force into the lion's den on orders from a voice through a radio, sitting at a desk, x amount of miles away. If 60 or so men couldn't hold a defensive position the night before, what the fuck were we doing pushing an assault with little understanding of what we were up against? While the bulk formed an NDP, he instructed thirty or so ANC boys led by two Belgians from third squad to push the extra hour towards the village and set up as close to it as possible. He wanted them in position as the sun came up. I slept reasonably well that night. Most of the others didn't.

The next morning we sat and gave our weapons a good clean. Like a team polishing their boots before the big match, so we sat, butterflies in our stomach, thinking about the event to come. Once again, the lull let my mind wander home, to Susan, to what she'd be doing right now, and to how if she had any idea of what I was up to, she'd kill me herself. I looked up, and once again saw a low cloud canopy above. I knew this would make air support impossible. We'd never relied on it before, but this assault was one of the few times it would have been handy. 'Time, gentlemen,' Kruger announced with a smile on his face. He'd had word back from the recce team. No movement.

The slow snake towards the front couldn't go quickly enough. I just wanted it over with. I'd accepted my fate, and all this fucking about, to me, was like rearranging the deckchairs on the *Titanic*. By 0800hrs we were in position, but saw no Simbas. Kids had begun to play on the paths. Mothers, their infants wrapped over their backs, began grinding the Milimeal. The younger lads attended to the animals while the old men sat out, sparking their first smoke of the day. In fact, everything was so picturesque that had the tourist board wanted to bus us in for a 'genuine and authentic' village experience they couldn't have done much better. We paused. Then, after a while, we paused some more. I knew Kruger was looking for something, even just one gunman would have been enough, but nothing, and by this time, I hoped nothing would appear. I was a killer and, by my own definition, I was evil. But I was a warrior, not a murderer. And in those times, it was the small differences I clung onto for sanity. But then it came, someone on the far flank said they'd seen them, a load of men moving from one hut to another. Like me, those beside me saw nothing, but that didn't matter. It was now a case of the Grand Old Duke of York, who had 200 men, who marched them up to the top of the hill – but wouldn't march them down again. This, after all, was the fucking Congo. We were in.

We fired like fuck, peppering the southern area with small-arms fire and backing it up with several thumps. As the mud huts disintegrated in clouds of dirt, we saw the masses fleeing. Then, like *Dad's Army*, second and third went in, charging across the 100 yards of no man's land before disappearing. As the smoke got thicker, the shooting got louder and, 'thankfully', we began to hear that distinctive 'popping' sound of AK47s. Without waiting to see what gap to plug, Kruger gave us the word. I stood up to run, but felt a thud. I looked down and expected to drop as the boys around me dived for cover. I wasn't shot. I looked again and saw that one of my grenades, pinned to my chest, had been hit by a bullet. I thought that was it. Blown to fuck by my own grenade! But instead, it just fizzled violently, then stopped. They looked at me, I looked at them, and made a note to change my pants.

Within a minute we were in, but within another, the fighting was over. The so-called Simba stronghold had been routed. Soon, though, the reason for this was clear: only a handful of fighters had ever been here. As the smoke cleared, I stood next to Kruger. He was shouting orders to the section commanders to sweep the area. At once, the men began their usual search-and-destroy task of pulling people from homes and interrogating them. The village population were obviously traumatised. As is usual with skirmish conflicts in Africa, villages are pawns. One week the rebels come. They murder, rape and steal their way through a population. The next week the government comes in and does the same in revenge for the villagers collaborating with the enemy. We didn't know it yet, but we were only doing the done thing. It was never a Simba village; there were no Simba villages.

As they started to separate the men from the women and children, I could see that the atmosphere was deteriorating. The ANC boys had revenge in their eyes. We'd told them that everyone here was a Simba; that's what we'd been told ourselves. And to the ANC, we were the word. As the search carried on, the fumes began to rise; all it needed was a spark. And it came from nowhere. I saw it before I heard it. Kruger's head disappeared. His lifeless body dropped. The man mountain, a warrior beyond all others, had disappeared in a heartbeat. I heard a second shot and looked to my right. I saw a boy of 14 sprawled in the dirt. He'd shot Kruger; one of us had shot him. An ANC lad went over and, like a penalty kick, booted the boy so hard that it vocalised the air left in his lungs. Startled, he emptied the rest of his clip into the corpse. It disintegrated before our eyes.

Soon the killing began. The first victim was a man stabbed in the back with a bayonet. Then a middle-aged man was picked up, thrown down a well, and a grenade lobbed in after him. A group of 15 to 20 mostly older women who had gathered around a communal hut to kneel and pray were all executed with shots to the back of their heads. In the square the separations intensified. To begin with, it was the men of fighting age from the rest, but now they were seemingly choosing at random. From the western side, they rounded up a large group of about 50. They were of mixed age and sex. One of the South African mercenaries, Robby Van Heusen, who had tried to assert some form of overall command as leader of third squad, shouted me over. As I got there, he gestured me and four ANC boys over to the ditch with his gun, before he was called back by another white. We stood there staring at the condemned. We did nothing. Five minutes later he was back: 'Haven't you got rid of them yet? I want them dead. Fucking waste them!'

The ANC boys began to fire into the group from a distance of 10 ft. People were all messed up as pieces of heads and flesh flew off their bodies. A woman, I remember, stood up and tried to leg it with a kid in her arms. She didn't run two steps. The few that survived did so because they were covered by the bodies of those who didn't. At one point, a two-year-old child who'd somehow survived the gunfire began running towards the square. Robby grabbed her, threw her back in the ditch, then shot her. May he burn in fucking hell.

I strapped my weapon over my back and tried to shut everything out. I walked one way, then another, but in every direction lay systematic sadism. Everywhere women were being raped, raped in their huts as their husbands and fathers were made to watch, then the women, battered and bruised and shaking in terror, were bound and gagged while their menfolk were tortured. I can't describe what they did to the children, but no one was spared. In the square, the assembled group, probably around 50, mostly children and teenagers, were made to stand to attention as the ANC soldiers and a handful of whites got drunk. As the hours went on, the kids began to drop. The ANC had told them that if they fell over, they'd be brought to the front and beaten to death. They were.

I spent four hours wandering the village, and, wearing blinkers, I searched for the radio. We were supposed to be an army, but I wasn't even sure if anyone had bothered to contact HQ to tell 'Colonel Fucking Arsehole' what was going on. What were our orders? They certainly weren't this. I'd tried till I was blue in the face to stop this, to get through to the others, but when I spoke, they wouldn't listen, and if they listened they couldn't understand. Until this day, I've never felt so powerless to act.

At around 1800hrs it became clear that the massacre had now become an orgy of evil. The units had broken down into barbarism with no one in command. Every ANC man was either drunk or on drugs, while the whites either aided and abetted or encouraged it as a spoil of war. Soon I felt it was 'drink and be merry for tomorrow you die', so I got drunk. I found some whites and sat with them drinking the villagers' drink, a brewed jungle juice that looked like vomit. I drank a lot. I was trying to put out the flames, but it only fuelled the fire. I hated this place and everyone in it, but most of all, I hated Robby Van Heusen.

I left the hut. It was starting to get dark. All I could hear were shouts and laughter sandwiched between screeches and cries so high-pitched that my blood began to boil. I longed for a Simba attack. I'd probably have helped them. I'd taken a few steps but stopped. I'd no idea where I was going or what I was doing, when I saw it. Cast within a shadow of the setting sun lay a bundle of rags. It moved. I walked over – and saw a baby still clinging to her dead mother. The mother, battered and bruised, lay dead outside her home, and her child, her wee girl, sat snuggling against her as if her mum was sleeping. I snapped. I turned and walked towards the square. I was looking for Robby – he'd started it. He wasn't there so I went to the hut where I'd just been drinking. Nothing. I went towards the irrigation ditch, passing a wood-cutting area where I picked up a hand axe. Nothing at the ditch, so I turned and headed back over the bodies, which littered the ground. In another direction I passed a dimly lit hut. From behind the thatch I heard shouting. I walked in. To my right was Ivan; the sick fuck was raping a girl. He'd pinned her down on the ground, legs wide apart. He was in her – but wasn't fucking her. In a sight that only comes back to me in my nightmares, he'd slit open her navel with a blade, had reached in to grab his own dick, and was wanking himself off. He looked round, but didn't stop. His cold, lifeless stare, devoid of emotion and humanity, simply looked right through me. Beyond him lay a pile of disembowelled women; he'd been at it all day. It didn't register; the shock box in my head was too full. There was only one thing on my mind: Robby Van Heusen.

As I continued, each step energised me. In my mind, I'd appointed myself his judge and executioner. He was on my side as a white, but he'd taken me to a place from which I'd never return. And for that, I fucking hated him. I walked back to where I'd started; I entered the hut, and there he was, sitting at the table with two men. From the far side of the room, through the dim orange glow, they saw my eyes and they knew. But for me, it didn't matter. I had my ace and it was guiding me. At pace I walked forward, head down and axe in hand. He watched me all the way, but said nothing. Within three steps my walk had become a run, and two steps later I was there. He stood to raise his pistol, but before he could fire, I'd sunk my axe right into his skull, taking half his head away, the downward motion crashing it into the table, where it stuck. A second later his half-headed body dropped.

A second after that, Fowler, the man on his left, drew his bayonet and tried to stick me. He slashed the back of my neck, but I grabbed his arm and pulled him over the table. Stirling, the man on his right, did nothing. I tumbled about with Fowler in a fight to the death. I punched. I kneed. I bit his face. I bit his neck. I bit his ear off. Then on his back, I head-butted him over and over and over again, before trying to stick my fingers through his eyes to feel the mush of his brain. But just before I managed it, I was hit by what felt like a wave. And as I flew into the corner, I realised I was under Stirling and some other guy. They'd both charged me off. I tried to get up, but they fought me down, and as they did I felt a pop in my knee and a pain shooting up my spine. I lay there under their weight and gasped for air. After a minute they cautiously stood up but said nothing. So I dragged myself to my feet then stopped. I paused. I looked at them. I looked at Fowler. I ran my bloodied hands across my head and wiped my brow. Then I hobbled over to the table and took my axe. I didn't cry. I didn't yell. My work was done.

In pain, I stumbled out and back towards the tree line. If I couldn't stop the murder, I wanted fuck all to do with it. In fact, if it hadn't been so shit, I'd have slept in the jungle. After a few attempts I found some shelter where I wouldn't be bothered – a hut with half a roof and a large chunk blown from its rear. As I lay down in a corner, I took the safety off my weapon and pointed it towards the entrance. Anyone coming in would get it. But within seconds I was asleep.

The next morning I woke up to a wind that shot through the roof and pinned me down. As I scrambled about, like a man slammed under a pressure hose, I realised it was a helicopter's downdraft – the Colonel had arrived. I readied myself, and poked my head out the door, but not too quickly – a large, hovering chunk of metal provides a tempting target for the enemy. He got out, dusted off his pristine khaki bush suit, and walked towards the assemblage, saluting as he went.

'Some fight!' he said, as he shook hands with Stirling – the South African now assuming control. I looked at my watch: it was 0900hrs, the longest I'd slept in a week. Around me, like a bunch of hung-over revellers, the ANC boys crept from their bedlam-like bedrooms, rubbing their eyes and fixing their clothes. As the rotor blades stopped, the smoke returned to reveal parts of the village being torched. The narrow paths, now reclaimed from death, almost looked scenic again. Not bad, I thought, as I staggered along. Seemed like the cabin crew had cleaned up well before landing. As the Colonel mingled, I walked up to the square. Still standing to attention was the horde of tiny, silent, hate-filled faces. From there I looked west towards the ditch – the operation was in progress. Several of the large adjacent wooden huts had become the designated crematoriums, and the dead, stacked from floor to ceiling, were being tended to by the ANC, who were now sending them off with a couple of AN-M14 incendiary grenades – another fine invention of ours.

I walked back over to the Colonel's walkabout. He'd set up a temporary HQ and was taking a roster while our dead were laid out. Problem was, we only had two dead and I'd killed one of them. As Kruger's headless body was tagged and covered, the Colonel stopped over Van Heusen's and asked what had happened. Seemed nobody knew. I looked at Stirling but he wouldn't look over. Now there was a thing. When the count was done, the Colonel stood in the middle and told us what a great job we'd done – no mention of the dead villagers or kids in the square. He spoke like we'd just thrashed a rugby team. Fucking mad! Then he played us into the bigger picture.

Seemed by now the Simba were on the run, and while we'd been fighting our battle, the rest of the 1,000-strong mercenary force had been winning the war by retaking the towns of Boande and Kindu. By that time, the Simba leadership, cooped up in Stanleyville – a major city by Congolese standards – had decided to hold a thousand white hostages, including a load of Belgian nuns. The Belgian and American Paras were planning a rescue once we'd made it into the area. This meant we were off with no time to lose. I, however, knew my war was over. Soon my knee would swell like a football, and there was nothing I could do about it. It could have been worse. So, helping where I could, we spent the rest of the day fucking about doing bits and pieces, cleaning weapons, packing ammunition, disposing of massacred villagers, the usual sort of thing, while another AC130 flew over and kicked out more supplies. Nobody really said much; I think the shock of what had happened was beginning to set in. It was one thing to rape and pillage and then fuck off. It takes a special type of Nazi, though, to rape, pillage, then occupy. As the day went on, the powers that be decided that the village was now a military base, so the remaining locals who weren't already dead were basically told to fuck off – which they did.

An hour later it was my turn to go. Only I fucked off by helicopter. The only two people I wanted to say goodbye to were dead, so I saved the fanfare and slipped out the back door. As we began to lift, I looked down at all the poor bastards I was leaving behind. All they had was hope and I knew what that felt like – like shit: not because of what it is, but when you feel it. They say that where there's life, there's hope. But really it's where there's hope, there's life – something I'd realised as I'd stared down the wrong end of a .50-cal. machine gun. It only comes when there's fuck all you can do. That's why we hope. And in the jungle I'd hoped a lot. 'Thank fuck for that,' I said to myself as the nose dipped forward and we headed for base. Then I closed my eyes, took a deep breath and hoped never to hope again.

CHAPTER II

COMING HOME TO CHANGE

The trip back was a bastard. It took ages. I'd wanted home so badly I'd have swum, but luckily a banana boat saved me the bother. After three weeks at sea I saw Portsmouth, just a dot in the distance, sandwiched between grey sea and an overcast sky. It's funny how somewhere so shit can make you feel so good. As I stood for an hour, watching the dot get bigger, the cold air blasted my face and the smell of Britain became like music to my nose. Whilst away, I'd spent ages making a list of things to do when I got back. Like a Cambodian fantasising about food, even the blandest things seemed fun, but now, just being back was enough.

I'd been away for months and was well short of the money I'd wanted – but while trying to get home, none of these things mattered. Of course, now I was back, they did. Being a mercenary in those days was nothing like now: no companies as such, no down time or rotations, and certainly no insurance. I'd been taken on for a job and I hadn't seen it through. Thanks to my knee, I was given a back-paid salary and a few quid for my trouble. That's just the way it was back then. As soon as I hit land, I made for London.

Arriving at Waterloo was a shock. I was just one of the millions of faces and for the first time in a long time, I didn't stand out. Even though it was fucking freezing, just walking around was great, as everything seemed new again. Strange as it is, you can get used to a shithole. I phoned Susan's mum in Edinburgh to tell her I was back, and that I'd be there the next day. I think they were pleased. Me, I couldn't wait to get back to my wife and back to my friends for a party. Being steaming on an all-black freighter with my boozing buddy 'Tripod' was one thing, getting out and about in Edinburgh with my pals was another. But before heading north, I had a message to run.

I'd been given a number to call when I got back to Britain. It was thrust into my hand by the 'quartermaster' in Leopoldville. I knew it was for the Secret Intelligence Service (SIS, more commonly known as MI6). It seemed that every Brit had got one, but as they never knew who'd make it back, they couldn't afford to be fussy. When I called, I was to ask for Dorian, which I did. I could hear the stupid cow at the end checking through a filing system to see what it was regarding and where to pass me. A man's voice came over the phone, sounding just like the Colonel – another fucking Empire-builder. I asked for Dorian and he laughed. I knew it was a code word; I was just pissing him about. I'd had enough of people like him. He gave me a time and a place to be, and that was that.

I crossed over the bridge and hit the Strand. But as I walked about, killing time, I began to lose interest. The novelty had worn off and I'd returned to my bubble – a loneliness imposed by my own sense of insignificance. At least in the Congo I'd been somebody, but here, I was just another minion competing for space. I couldn't wait to fuck off. By four in the afternoon I was standing outside the Prince of Wales pub off Tottenham Court Road having a smoke, when they drew up. They must have been used to getting fucked about, 'cause when they saw me, they looked kind of surprised. Looking back, it was probably because I was barely 20 – they wouldn't have expected that. I'd expected a couple of arrogant pricks, but they weren't. They were down-to-earth and we had a good laugh. We had a few pints and they passed me a few quid. After what was essentially a debriefing, they asked me about my plans for the future. I said I was thinking about it. I was. So were they.

It's called the sleeper but I didn't sleep. I was just too excited. Every time it stopped, I imagined myself running to the driver and breaking his jaw. I was sure they were doing it deliberately. I'd come halfway across the world on a slow-moving boat, but now, even though I was so close, I'd never felt further away. When we finally reached Waverley, I was out of the trap like a greyhound. But fuck, if London was freezing, then Edinburgh was frozen. I'd been in the jungle for too long. With my kitbag slung over my shoulder, I sprinted up the steps like Santa with a drink in him, then legged it down Leith Street where they later built that monstrosity, the St James Centre. Susan lived with her mum and dad at McDonald Road, just down Leith Walk and on the left. As I rounded the corner, I could see her face. She was sitting at the window, waiting anxiously. Even through the dark streets, our eyes met, and the look on her face was a picture I'd carry for the rest of my life. She ran outside, wrapped her arms around me and wouldn't let go. For the first time in my life I experienced unconditional love. It's a special thing that you can't describe till you have it. Then, keeping a hold of each arm, she pushed me back, looked me up and down, and laughed. 'You're just as I remember you!' God, I wished she was right.

War isn't where young men grow up, it's where they grow old before their time. I'd always fantasised about returning home to a hero's welcome from a grateful wife and a proud family. But I soon found my fantasy shattered. Although Susan had been delighted to see me, it was all about me and nothing about my actions. And when I got in at 5.30 that morning, her parents got up and said hello, but within minutes went back to sleep. At 9.30, when her dad left for work, he woke me up and said, 'Listen, now that you're back, when are you getting a job?' My parents were even worse.

Suddenly I realised that the real journey back was going to be an even longer one. It only took a few days for me to see that my descriptions of the Congo, told in the terminology I was used to – language that integrated death and destruction with banter and laughs – frightened my family, embarrassed my mates, and would often start trouble. So, in an unspoken agreement with everybody, I negotiated the price of my re-entry – silence. I rarely talked about what had happened to me in the jungle. To begin with, this silence became a welcome forgetfulness; but it soon transferred the conflict from the jungle into my mind. For me, the Simba War was still going on, because the essential ritual of 'coming home' had been denied by a city that knew nothing about it, and by a family who'd refused to hear about an aspect of my life they'd long since disowned.

When I first went to the Congo, I'd noticed that every mercenary had something in common, that those seasoned warriors all carried a self-styled insanity, and I'd wondered why. Now I knew. I knew it was the only camouflage that worked while fighting the jungle's second conflict – the moral one. I'd often tried to understand why I was the only one who'd wanted to stop what happened that night in the village. Even if some never took part, their inaction still amounted to complicity. In common they'd suffered a loss of human feeling, but couldn't take responsibility for it and instead had blamed war for changing them. But now, like them, I was going through that very same process, while the one thing that still haunted me was not the memory of killing but of the pleasure I found in doing it.

Nevertheless, life went on, and as time passed, I made myself busy with its many monotonies. We got a council house in Giles Street at the foot of the Walk, which I spent money on furnishing. It was far from great, but it was ours. We bought a wee car and made trips through to Ayrshire and over to Fife where I was born, which was great, for a while. But I soon hit my glass ceiling and once again felt restless. I was missing the highs and lows of adventure and spent my days dreaming of Africa. To me it was the Wild West where opposites collided and paradoxes shared space. It was 'paradise on the edge', and that was appealing. Still, poverty's a prison, so I left Africa in my dreams and knuckled down at home. As '66 became '67, things were steadily beginning to happen. But again, no sooner were we moving than the ground got muddy, and when it did, I lost money, even my car. Edinburgh was a funny place. It was a town which seemed like London, but acted more like Dundee. Underneath its cosmopolitan façade lay a conservative and Masonic heart. This meant that you were either legit or dodgy and it left little room for the likes of me. I was in a hurry: in a hurry for wealth, in a hurry for adventure and, most importantly, in a hurry to avoid normality. To me, a life of getting up in the morning and going to bed at night, where one day was as uneventful as the next, was second only to death through starvation. And all the time, like the sword of Damocles hanging above my head, was my ever-diminishing nest egg, now running dry like the last few grains of sand from an hourglass. When it finally went, it hit me.

It had all been for nothing, and now I was living it. Nothing here had changed, but I had. And I could feel it. I'd given so much, but gained so little, and what little I got had been taken away. It just seemed that the harder I pushed, the further backwards I went. And now, standing with nothing but the clothes I was wearing and the contents of my flat, I was back to square one. I stepped out that morning to a clear winter's day. I was a proud man, a military man; I paid attention to detail and took pride in my dress. But that morning, I'd let go. I was a penniless and frustrated man with nothing to offer. Deep in my own self-pity I staggered along the shore towards Newhaven going nowhere fast. After an hour I reached Granton Harbour. I was knackered and hungry. As I stood on the breakwater watching the boats and feeling sorry for myself, the only thing that gave me any comfort was the fact that nothing could possibly get worse. But then, just at that very moment, this fucking seagull shat right in my eye. Bastard!

It never rains but it pours. That's what they say. And right there and then, they were right. I turned round, and now half-blinded, hobbled back across the jetty to Lower Granton Road. I was tired of swimming upstream and was ready to let go. But now, just a breath away from conceding defeat, I saw it. As clear as day it was there – my very own message from God – 'Take Courage'! In big red letters, a giant billboard poster was shouting at me. I couldn't move. I stood there staring at it, oblivious to the traffic now screaming past me. My body was still, but my mind was smoking as, for the first time, my ace card came without facing an opponent. And it was then that I had my very own epiphany: that fighting your fellow man was the easiest fight of all – for that, there's hatred, just pure fucking hatred – but the hardest battle is the one with yourself. I'd survived the Congo through attrition. I'd fought best when death was beside me, and the more the jungle hurt me, the more determined I was to beat it, and I had! I had changed, but I wasn't a victim. I wasn't a survivor, either, I was a fighter, only now I was battling a new enemy – my own self-doubt. If I'd faced fear in the Congo, then it took Granton Harbour and some seagull shit before I beat doubt. I might have spent my wages but what I gained from the Congo carried no price. Fear halts men, it avoids them suffering, but the Congo had pushed me to both the extremes of humanity and myself, and now everything in between was my domain. How privileged was I? I was standing in a world with no shadows and I'd just opened my eyes. As I walked up Granton Road, my bottle came back. I had taken courage. At the top of the street, shining in the cloudless crispy air like a crystal tower, stood a mansion, which later became the Royal Forth Yacht Club. 'One day,' I said. 'One fucking day I'll own that.' And I did! (I also found out that my 'message from God' was an advert for Scottish Courage – but anyway . . .)

Soon after, life's monotonies became a means to an end, and with the drive back in me, I was training hard and keeping myself fit in case the fight of my life was just around the corner. As part of that I ran four times round Leith Links each morning. There weren't many joggers in those days, so apart from shift workers and the odd pest, I normally had the place to myself. I loved it. Often the mist would roll in off the sea and mix with the chimney smoke rising from the houses and factories. I loved a heavy atmosphere, one you could taste, a misty greyness with no wind to move it. It would cocoon you, making you the only person on earth. In my head, I'd be running with Kruger or Mark. I'd wish they were still alive; we'd have made a good team.

On one of these mornings I had set out a bit earlier, determined to get an early start to the day. As I ran my usual route through the mist, I saw a figure sitting on a bench dressed completely in black and reading a newspaper. As I passed him, he didn't look up, but somehow within the darkness I felt a familiarity. In my head I'd just seen a ghost, but I knew from experience that the living could hurt you more than the dead. So I stopped.

'How are you, Rod?' said a low, sinister and unmistakable voice.

I turned round. I even squinted to see his face, a weasel-like structure completely devoid of emotion.

'Ivan?'

'How you been, Rod?'

Surprised, anxious, cautious, suspicious, were only some of the words to describe how I felt. I thought I'd left hell in the Congo, but now, for some reason, Satan's protagonist had come calling. I walked over but didn't sit down. Ivan stood up, ruffled his trench-coat collar, folded the paper under his arm and tucked his glove-covered hands in his pockets.

'Seriously, Ivan! What the fuck are you doing here?' I said. After all, there'd been a distinct possibility that night in the village of me chopping his fucking hands off.

'I'm putting a team together. I want to do a job.'

'What, raping women and cutting them up? You don't need a team for that,' I said, now feeling aggressive.

'You're finding it tough, aren't you? What after losing your car and all that.'

I looked at him. I wasn't sure what pissed me off more, the thought of him spying on me or the fact that the patronising fuck was now treating me like a kid. I felt my fist clench.

'Come on, Rod, let's walk. Hear me out, that's the least you can do,' he said with his blank face and out-of-focus eyes.

I thought hard, but then what did I have to lose? He wouldn't have found me for nothing.

'All right,' I said.

As we walked, he began to talk freely. He told me he'd been back in the UK for six months and, apart from three weeks in London at the start, he'd been working in Newcastle. After I left the Congo, he'd gone on to fight in Stanleyville with Major 'Mad Mike' Hoare, the British commander of the mercenary battalion, on Operation Red Dragon. The capture of Stanleyville had essentially finished the Simba rebellion and resulted in their two key leaders, Gbenye and Soumialot, taking exile in Cairo. So by the end of that year, 1964, the great Simba struggle was reduced to a few pockets of resistance. Ivan had stayed with Hoare's forces until they'd reached the Sudanese border in April 1965. No doubt he'd enjoyed every minute of it, but a year later, the work had dried up. Now he was back and, like me, was restless. He said he'd been working in Newcastle for one of the big crime families, and had been knocking heads about. I knew that meant he'd been killing. He said the job he wanted to do would interest me, but that we didn't have a lot of time to do it, so I'd have to be quick.

He told me he'd met a man who worked for a big retail firm in Newcastle: I'll call them Savills. Savills ran around 20-odd outlets, all within the city centre, selling clothes and other bits and pieces. Some shops did homeware; others catered more towards the rag trade. As well as these, the owner ran some other places, including a couple of pubs. In all, it was a cash-heavy business, which meant at the end of a given day, the firm sat on a pile of takings. The takings would, of course, be banked, and for that a security van would come to each premises. Recently, though, it seemed that Savills was starting to feel the pinch, and between a downturn in their business and the fact that each shop manager was probably robbing them blind, they decided to change the system. The first thing they did was to find savings, and a big one was in the letting go of the cash-in-transit company. Instead they employed a couple of heavies to go round each shop and pick it up themselves. It was then returned to head office, where it would be counted against the sales registers. Finally it would move to the bank in the owner's van, protected by his own team of nasties, which included a dog.

After Ivan had finished, without indicating whether I'd be in or out, I asked him why the hurry. He told me that he knew somebody who'd been yapping, so it stood to reason that we had to get in quick. 'Oh, right,' I said, but I knew it was a pile of shit and had more to do with his own timetable. He said that if we hit on a Friday, they could be carrying as much as £8,000. In 1967, that was a lot of dough. His idea was to do the job then bolt back up to Edinburgh, probably changing cars halfway, and he thought the best number of bodies to do the job was four. I then found out that I was the fourth, and he'd already planned to meet the other two later that day. 'Listen, Rod,' he said. 'It's a quick and easy job. We'll go in hard, they'll shit themselves, and we'll be away in minutes. Two grand each! What do you think?' He paused. 'Listen, have a think about it. If you're up for it, be at the Tam o' Shanter for 1300hrs. That's where I'm meeting the other two.'

I didn't have to think for very long.

At the appointed time, I got to the door then stopped. I could say it was because I had doubts over life as an outlaw, but really it was because I'd battered the landlord as a favour for a favour. I already had my cut-throat in my pocket but, before going in, I had to adjust the axe now strapped to my leg. First sniff of trouble and it was out. I opened the door and stepped inside. I was met by a sea of stares from the lunch-time Leithers. To me, their faces all looked the same. Each one no oil painting, and with lines that could be read like a palm, revealing their tormented lives. Between the waif-like men with their home-drawn tattoos and the women with their collapsed jaw lines, wee mouths and pale complexions, it was like poverty had a stamp, and it had marked them all. It wouldn't mark me! I walked across the bar, the smoke so thick that it stagnated in layers beginning a foot above the floor, a floor whose red and well-worn carpet was littered with fag ends and bits of chewing gum now blackened with age. Further inside this characterless space, and through the clinical light, I could see three men sitting at one of the many identical tables. It was them. The spare seat had its back to the floor, so I picked it up and budged in at the wall. We sat like an audience.

Ivan made the introductions. Colin Patterson was the man to my left. A heavyset man from Edinburgh who chain-smoked his fags, he'd cut his teeth in the King's Own Scottish Borderers from 1962 to February 1964 while in Aden on security operations. He'd really got a taste of things, though, when they were called back in May to aid the Federal Army, which was fighting Yemeni insurgents in the Radfan Mountains – a bastard of a place to work in. The year after that he'd found himself in Borneo, patrolling the Malaysia–Indonesia border. No doubt we'd soon be sharing some jungle stories.

The guy next to him was called Derry, and enjoyed the nickname

'Londonderry'. At first glance he seemed more like a regular at the pub we were in than a regular in the Army. Ivan reckoned he was in the Paras. I reckoned he had the paras – the 'para-noias'. Anyway, he was from Glasgow and I thought maybe that would explain it, especially the sectarian nickname. Ivan bought us a round, which seemed to perk him up a bit. A few rums later, we were all having a laugh and getting to know each other. Derry had a great big 'Mars Bar' down his left cheek. He proudly told me that he'd got it off his bird, and that now they were getting married! We exchanged stories of war and woe, and while I told him of fighting the Simba, he told me about his wife-to-be – Linda. Said he'd met her in a bar after she'd stabbed a man's kidneys with her nail file. He'd helped her escape. Said it was love at first sight! Fucking hell, I thought. His stories were more frightening than mine. Colin was more my kind of guy. He was a serious soldier who seemed naturally fit, which was just as well as he chain-smoked more than anyone I've ever met. As usual, however, Ivan just sat and stared like he either wanted a fight or a fuck. I knew from experience he wanted both.

A few more rums after that and we were discussing the job. Ivan lay down a briefing like he was planning an attack. He had photographs of the head office, the owner, the heavies, the van they'd be in, even the fucking guard dog. He pulled out an OS map of the area and started pencilling off the necessary sites and locations. He said he wanted to roll this Friday, which gave us three days. I said he must be fucking mad. He was! He wanted to hit the van before it left the office yard. The yard was only ten minutes from the city centre, but it was on the north side, and that suited us. He said he wanted to hit it hard and fast, like an ambush. As the van got between the neck-high gates, we'd block it off with the motor, then pop the windscreen and chuck in a canister of CS. Their van didn't have a divider between the front and the back and we'd be in gas masks. Then, when they spilled out, we'd give them a quick bashing, take the money and fuck off. The money itself would be in a large sports holdall, which was often hidden under the driver's seat.

Then he added that we'd all be armed, and that he had four Browning P35s, the pistol adopted by the British Army to replace its

53

Webley and Enfield .38 revolvers. I put my hand up. 'Wait a minute,' I said. 'Just to clarify – is this a robbery or a fucking hit?'

They all stopped and looked at me. Then I leant in and whispered. 'Listen, I'm no going duck shooting with a carbine. A P35's for killing, a sawn-off is for robbing. It's big, it's bad – people can look down its barrel and shit themselves. You can pull the trigger and pepper their legs or blast away from a distance. You canny do that with a P35!'

They looked blankly at me.

'What are they anyway, Model 1946s or High Powers?' I asked.

'1946s,' replied Ivan, meaning the ones purpose-built for the military.

'Fuck that,' I said. 'You guys do what you want. I'll get my own.' Unbelievable, I thought. Fucking P35s. I got some more drinks in.

For the next hour, we sat and talked through the various scenarios for hitting the van. Ivan wanted the van to be stopped so the front doors would open on one side of the gates, while the back would open into the yard. This meant that when the gas went in and each man bolted out the nearest door, their team would be split. But in reality, this would be tricky to time, and in the end, all that mattered was that the van should be trapped at the gates, so we decided to ram it. Then we talked about who was best for what. This really came down to who should go after the money and who should drive the car. Sorting the driver is an important part of robbery. To begin with, you need to keep the car running; having it stall or break down is of no fucking use. But second and most important is the fact that when you're doing a job, there's such extreme violence that the adrenalin makes you shake; the last thing you want to do is drive. The driver, then, needs to be calm and able to make decisions. Derry, as the smallest, would drive, while Ivan would go in after the money.

Finally we talked about fuck-ups. What if there were more bodies inside? What if the police passed by? What if one of us gets hurt? To all these questions, we gave different ideas, some of which we negotiated on, and others on which we had to agree to disagree. But at the end of the day, the one thing that we did all agree on was that we were coming back to Edinburgh with a bundle of money, and if anyone got in the way we'd slap them about, or shoot the bastards if we had to. We were a serious team and we weren't there to fuck about. As the end of the meeting came, Ivan held up a cold bony finger and said, 'Remember. It's all about removing choices. When we hit, we need to hit hard. We need to instil so much terror and so much fear that they're only capable of what we're demanding. Right? We've got to paralyse them.' Then he looked at each of us and waited on a nod. I nodded. I'd just made a pact with the Devil.

Our next meeting was to be on the Thursday, the day before the job. By then we were to have fixed our own ends. I was to get the car, which I knew I could get, as a mate of mine had a MkI 1962 Cortina he'd nicked for a job he'd never done and, better still, he'd done a bit of custom work on it by reinforcing its body. Colin was getting the van; this would be our second motor, to be stashed somewhere along the A1. Ivan was going back down to Newcastle to do another recce and sort out his shooters, while Derry, well, fuck knows what Derry was doing, probably drinking and getting slashed off his bird.

As I left the pub, I fought my doubts. Looking back, I was fighting against common sense. It was a risky job and we were doing it on a whim. Our captain was a maniac and our driver a weirdo. But I was in a poverty trap and struggling for sanity; it had to be worth it. I had hit rock bottom so many times that I needed to move up, and now, at last, I was about to. I knew that robbers were divided into two groups, the 'planners' and the 'amateurs'. The planners are the professionals while the amateurs rob on impulse. Now, at least, I could consider myself an 'amateur planner' – a step in the right direction.

Later that evening I stopped by my father-in-law's at McDonald Road. I told him I wanted a shotgun. Shotguns were commonplace in those days if you ran a second-hand shop. He asked me what it was for. I didn't want to lie so I didn't answer. Archie knew the score. He told me to come back the next day. So I did. When I arrived, he took me down into the basement, which was the self-contained flat where I'd once lived with Susan. As I nervously followed him, the familiar smell of dampness and paraffin began to fill the air. It reminded me of less desperate times. In the extra sanctity of the living room, now only furnished with memories, he unsheathed a shiny, single-barrelled 12-bore shotgun and held it out. I put my hands on it, but he wouldn't let go. He just looked at me. He was a man of few words, and was nobody's fool.

'You be fucking careful!'

I just nodded. What could I say? I was about to do a robbery! But he just kept staring, almost like he was figuring something out. Then he let go and left. I stood for a moment, and for the first time, it became real – then the greed kicked in and I made for the hall. At the bottom of the stair was a small, darkened workshop; it's where he stashed his knocked gear until time had laundered it. Running along one of the walls was a wooden workbench with a large metal vice bolted on the end. I knew what I had to do. I found a hacksaw and began to remove the barrel. It seemed surreal, standing under the single bare light bulb, surrounded by stolen debris stacked so high it acted like Ali Baba's wallpaper covering the untreated brickwork, which crumbled like the black metallic shavings now falling with each stroke of the saw. No sooner had I broken sweat than it was off. Then, with the care of a craftsman, I sat for an hour and filed the edges. If I was to fire, I at least wanted the shot to go straight. I uncocked the gun, looked down the barrel, blew, then repeated the ritual over and over again till I felt confident enough to put my name to it.

The next day, I met the boys in the Regal Arms pub in Morrison Street. I didn't want to hang about this time so I took a lager shandy. Having the ability to stay focused for business was something that did me well in the years to come. I told them about the car. Ivan said there was no change from Newcastle and Colin told us that he was picking the van up that night. Ivan said he'd been giving the route some more thought, and decided on leaving the van as close to the job as possible. This meant less time in the job car. He took out a map and pointed to a place 13 miles north of Newcastle and just to the east of the A1: a place called Morpeth. He said it was both rural and quiet, and he'd already been, so he knew a few places to leave it. It was all one to us, so we agreed. Colin said he'd get the petrol in the morning for burning out the Cortina and keep it in the van during the job. With that, we four vicious bastards raised our glasses and toasted our success.

'What's wrong with you, Rod?' said Susan the next morning. She'd made a cooked breakfast, but with all the butterflies, I couldn't eat.

'Nothing, doll,' I said, with little sincerity, before I swigged my tea and sought refuge in the bathroom. As I stood there brushing my teeth, I began to daydream. I was right back in the Congo, the morning of the village attack, but somehow this seemed worse. There were just too many things to factor in. In the Congo you either fucked them or they fucked you. But here, hitting them was just the beginning. I had no control and I hated it. I had a son now, I had responsibilities, what fucking good was I dead or inside? I bent over and rinsed my face. Too late now, I thought, too late to back out – if I do, I'll have to kill Ivan, 'cause there's no way he'll forgive me. I straightened myself up, imagined my billboard, then went out to kiss Susan and cuddle young Roderick. The next time I see them, I thought, I'll be loaded. And I left.

'What the fuck is that?' I said, as I pulled up at the foot of the Walk. There, parked up with Colin and Derry inside, was an Austin 35 van – a right piece of shit.

'Na, man,' said Colin. 'It just looks shit 'cause the guy's never cleaned it, but it's the MkIII version. It's got a 1098cc A-series engine.'

Fucking hell, I thought, my first fucking robbery, four soldiers assaulting a guard dog with machine guns and making a getaway in a bucket. But just as I looked to heaven in disbelief, someone from hell jumped into my car – Ivan. 'Right! Let's do it,' he said. 'I'm with you.' And with that, our convoy was off. We'd hardly crossed Princes Street when it suddenly dawned on me; I was to spend close to three hours alone with Ivan. Bastard! And that was three fucking hours longer than I'd ever planned on doing. Then he piped up.

'To me, there are three types of hooker.'

'What?' I said. 'What you on about hookers for? We're about to . . .'
He cut me off.

'The happy hooker, who's genuinely into servicing the boys; the unhappy hooker, who despises her work and makes it pretty obvious;

and thirdly, the professional, who may or may not be fucking miserable, but is at least decent enough to pretend that she's into it. That was until I got to this brothel last night, where I first met the fourth type, the aggressive hooker!'

This guy was fucking mad. He put on a Glaswegian accent:

'"Right. I'll dae you, I'll dae you, then I'll dae you," says Big Mags fae Glasgow, as she belted through the door grappling the knickers out her fanny. So I sat there and patiently waited my turn.'

He said it proudly, like it had been an achievement.

'I might have been number two out of three, but as I waited numbers four and five turned up. "She'll be sitting on an ice bucket the night, Ivan," I said to myself.'

I started to laugh. I never knew he had it in him – not that he was laughing himself; he was deadly serious.

'Five minutes later, the dirty bastard before me came out, lit a smoke and wandered down the stair. So I boldly walked in. She hadn't even bothered to get dressed for me to undress her again. "Right!" she said. "C'mon and get stuck into me." I wanted to cut her up. But we had this job on, so I didn't. As I approached the beached whale, I readied my 'harpoon'. "Oh, aye," she says. "You're goin' ti get it!" Then she grabbed a hold of it with two hands, like she was wielding a broadsword, and tried to rip the fucking thing off. I wasn't having it. So I grabbed it back, flipped her over and did her arse, saying, "No, hen, you're goin' ti get it!" And she did. She wasn't happy. So when I'd finished taming the mighty beast, I legged it, kegs in hand and left numbers three, four and five to reap her wrath.'

'That's an interesting story, Ivan,' I said, now laughing away.

'I tell you, Roddy. There's good money in whoring. That's what you want to do with your share, open yourself a brothel. Think about it; that bird last night was stinking, but she must have shagged at least 15 punters. Imagine getting a place where you're working a team of five or more. That's a load of money. I'm telling you, doing hookers is my thing; it's big money nowadays.'

I looked at him. He had a point. 'But I'm a family man,' I said. 'I don't think the wife would be too happy.'

COMING HOME TO CHANGE

'It's just a business, Roddy. That's all it is, just a business.'

If I was expecting any conversations during that journey that weren't about prostitutes, I was going to be disappointed. Ivan talked about hookers for the length of the A1. Looking back on it, it could have been worse.

As we approached Morpeth, he directed me off the slip and into the open fields. He knew exactly where he was going, and stopped us with the town a couple of miles off in the distance. To our right ran a long leylandii hedge and, behind it, a small semi-derelict cottage that was just out of view from the road. Colin backed up the van, while Derry took the wheel of the Cortina and I jumped in the back. Once we'd sorted out our gear, we set off, and for the first time, I really felt the tension rise. I drew comfort from the fact that, although we weren't professional robbers, we were professional killers, and this gave us an edge. We spent the rest of the journey thoroughly checking our gear and running through the drill, military-style. When we hit the leafy suburbs, the adrenalin began to flow. At Ivan's command, Derry turned one way, and then another, and within two minutes we silently pulled onto the road where Savills was based. We stopped, had a look around, then drove past it a couple of times before coming to a rest about 100 yards from the gate. The roads were quite narrow, while the yard itself was the size of a couple of tennis courts and was surrounded by a red brick wall, probably about 9 ft high. The building was all Savills and amounted to three storeys, again all in red brick. The best way to describe the street plan is like a big T, with the gate facing directly down where the T-junction met. From our position, we had an uninterrupted view into the yard through the iron-railing gates. By now it was approaching half-three.

The only notion of timing that we had to go on was the time the banks shut. We figured they'd be out by four, but we couldn't be sure. Sitting waiting was murder and we looked well dodgy: four shaven heads sitting in a Cortina and looking nervous. I could see the van – it was backed up to the main door – but nothing else. 'Move, for fuck sake,' I kept saying to myself. But it didn't. Between the cramped conditions, the tension and Colin's constant smoking, I could feel myself getting angrier and angrier, which I knew wasn't good, as soon I'd have someone's life in my hands.

Just then we saw a dog, a black German shepherd, and then a man – a big man. He laughed over to someone before opening the driver door for the dog to jump in, then he disappeared and returned a moment later before going in after it and starting the engine. We started ours.

'Make sure your belts are on, boys!' said Ivan, again taking command.

Colin took a last drag on his fag and flicked it out of his inch-opened window. He turned to me and smiled. I grinned nervously back, then he shoved on his mask and drew his head straps like a kamikaze tightening his headband. 'Let's fucking do it!' came a muffled battle cry from behind his carbon filter.

My heart was racing and my hands were sweating. I loaded my gun, my hands fumbling over the cold steel as I kept my eyes glued to the target. I clicked it shut and placed it by my side. I took a deep breath, pulled over my mask and wiped the lenses. Now I was ready. We saw another man, not so big, but still tough-looking. He stood right in front of the van for a minute and finished his smoke. He was laughing with someone else we couldn't see. He shouted to someone in the office, then he jumped in the passenger seat and turned to the back of the van and gestured. They began to roll.

'Ready now. Ready,' says Ivan to Derry as Derry slowly eases out to a steady crawl. The van begins to move some more, but the gates are still closed. Have they seen something? What the fuck are they doing?

Derry begins to simmer, now revving the engine. 'Come on, what's happening? Fuck sake!'

'It's all right,' says Ivan, like the officer from *Zulu* waiting till the warriors made range. 'Steady now, hold it, hold it. Steady.' From nowhere a woman runs out and opens the gate. 'Go! Go! Fucking go!' screams Ivan.

Instantly I'm stuck to the back seat as Derry floors the pedal and tears down the street like a drag racer. We approach so fast that they only see us when we're upon them and, for that moment, time stops.

Like a flash photo, I see their faces. Then, bang! Never mind ram it, we fucked it! We hit the bastard so hard that we smashed it back through the gates with their passenger's face bursting against their own windscreen. We halt, we see their driver's limp body splayed against the steering wheel. Then we're out. The CS goes bang; there's smoke and chaos everywhere. Derry throws the Cortina into reverse; the sound of crumpled metal resonates as it separates itself from the mangled van. I run through the smoke, all the time screaming, and grab a hold of a body; he's choking in the smoke and crawling about blind. I pull his hair and smash his face into the ground. I kick his ribs over and over again, before placing the barrel of my gun against his lower back. 'I'm goanna shoot you in the fucking spine! Where's the fucking money? Now!' I kick him again and again. He's trying to speak but he's too busy choking to even cry. I look to my left and into the van. I see Ivan crawling about inside.

He jumps out and signals with open hands. It's not there. He runs round to Colin's side and grabs the man he's holding. In a headlock he calmly walks him back and puts the gun to his head. 'Where is it, you cunt?'

At his feet is the German shepherd, now struggling for life. Ivan points his gun down and, bang! He shoots it. Bastard. But worse, he only shoots its leg off and now it's screeching in agony as its blood pisses out. The man's unable to say anything. He's a big man, but he's terrified to his soul and is shaking all over. Ivan looks up to the office – there are a few terrified faces, now watching the unfolding matinée in disbelief from a window. Ivan leans forward and kicks down on the man's knee joint, shattering it with a crack that even the audience can hear. The man flops down and rolls about in dog blood, and as he does, Ivan cocks his P35 and sticks it to the man's crotch. 'Last time! Where is it?' He's about to shoot his cock off when the main office door flies open and a sports bag's hurled out. It's our bag. Ivan checks; it's full of money. 'Let's fucking go!' he screams.

Within a heartbeat we're back in the car. 'Go! Go! Go!' we shout to Derry, as he screeches away with our doors barely closed. We tear off our masks and look back to see the ruined yard. It's still smoking and it looks like a bomb's hit it. It had. We're all gasping for air and shaking our heads. 'Fucking hell,' we're saying. 'What a fucking rush!' As Derry speeds like fuck, the front of the Cortina is smoking. It's shredded after the impact and is sparking along the road. We need out of this fucking thing. The half-hour to Morpeth seems like a lifetime – and it could be, but luckily there's not a single panda in sight 'cause, by now, they must be swarming the Savills yard. Still, we're all busy, we're trying to bag our evidence so we can torch it with the car. I'm looking for anything and everything: my gloves, my mask, my sweatshirt – fucking anything.

Finally, we hit the country lanes and, like a rally driver, Derry negotiates the windy roads while I'm praying for no oncoming traffic. At the last minute, the bastard sees the opening to the cottage and swerves violently, almost making us flip. He comes to an abrupt halt about 30 yards from the van. He jumps out and runs over to start it, followed by Ivan who jumps in the front. Me and Colin grab the petrol from the back and set about torching the Cortina. 'Come on! Be quick!' Ivan screams. 'It's not like nobody saw us!' As I frantically empty the jerrycan, Colin sticks our bags under the seats, then starts popping the windows so the fire can breathe. 'Come on!' shouts Ivan again. Derry's now revving the van like Stirling Moss. We're ready, and I'm just about to throw in my Zippo when I hear Ivan shouting to wait a minute.

I turn round, but we can't hear what he's saying. 'What?' I shout. I look at Colin. He shakes his head. I look back at Ivan. He looks up and tuts then jumps out, and as he runs over I can see that he's telling me to grab Derry's gun 'cause he's left it under his seat. Prick! So I turn to do so but, to our total fucking horror, Derry puts his foot down and belts off – leaving the three of us standing. He's fucked off on his own and he's taken the money. Bastard! We were stunned. We were so fucking stunned that for a minute we just stood there in silence and stared at each other.

Nobody said a word . . . then, 'Did that just happen?' said Colin, looking around. Ivan nodded his head. Again, we were quiet. And as we were, the full extent of our trouble began to hit us. We were standing in the middle of a field, in England, with a petrol-saturated car, four used firearms and two canisters of CS, after committing a robbery with such violence that it had reduced four grown men to tears. And what's worse, we'd just lost the money. If you've ever felt a second that lasted an hour, this was it. I was distraught. I was so distraught that had I not been so angry I'd have shot myself. I'd survived the jungle. I'd beaten the Simba. I'd buried my ghosts and done the crime of the century – but now, I'd just lost the lot to a sneaky weasel-faced bastard who'd left us to rot. That was tough to take.

'Right!' shouted Ivan. 'We need to get the fuck out of here. Torch it anyway – the police won't know what's happened.'

We took several steps back and I threw in my light. It went up like a spark to gas. 'What now?' I said to Ivan. It was getting dark, and with just a T-shirt on, I didn't fancy a night under the stars. He gestured towards Morpeth. So the three of us legged it across the fields, only pausing to bury our guns in a ditch. Half an hour later we were there. It was pitch black. We scoured around looking for a car to steal, but there was literally nothing. We were in a race against time and could feel it. The police would have found the car by now and, although they would never have imagined that we were strolling through Morpeth, the likes of us would definitely get a pull. Five minutes later we heard a car, so we scrambled over to a crossing and hid behind a verge, where we'd jump it. But when it slowed down, I saw a young woman with three kids in the back. Fuck that. I jumped up and told Ivan to fuck off. It wouldn't have mattered to him, but it did to me.

'What the fuck's your problem?' he barked.

I just looked at him and shook my head. 'Na, mate. No fucking way.'

Just then we heard a rumble, and then the grinding of metal on metal. It took a moment for us to click, but when it did, we bolted; we bolted along the street and up the stairs and hit the platform just as the guard was blowing his whistle. Then, with a leap of faith, like three teenagers running for a bus, we jumped on at the last second and collapsed in a heap on the carriage floor. We'd made it!

We picked ourselves up and sauntered into the nearest compartment. It was empty. We each lit a smoke – fuck, we were gasping − and then sat back, looked at each other and pissed ourselves laughing. Well, me and Colin did anyway. I don't know if it was the release of stress or what, but we laughed so hard the tears were flowing, as the three amigos − the big, bad war veterans and heavy-duty robbers − were now making their getaway on public transport. What a bunch of pricks!

Two minutes later, the hysteria bubble burst as Ivan reined us in. 'If we don't find him tonight, we've lost the money.'

'I know,' I said. 'But where the fuck is he?'

We both looked at Colin. He shrugged his shoulders. 'Well, I don't fucking know.'

'What about his family?' said Ivan.

'Oh, man, no, we can't.'

But Ivan looked straight through him. 'What about his family?' He raised his voice. 'That stupid slut that he keeps going on about. Where does she live? You know, don't you?'

Colin thought about it, then nodded. 'Yes, I know where her flat is. It's in Glasgow. But I don't know her. I've never even met her.'

'Even better,' snarled Ivan. 'Glasgow it is. Tonight! Right, Roddy?'

'Right,' I said. I was well up for it.

When we got into Waverley, it was just after nine. Colin phoned his brother, who turned up and gave us his car − another fucking Cortina. He stayed out drinking while we drove to mine for a change of clothes, and then down to my pal Pete Stanfield's lock-up, where I kept my tools. With the hammers in the back and our blades in our pockets, we set off for Costa del Glasgow − the 'badlands'.

By the time we got through, it was raining heavily and the streets were becoming deserted; there was no M8 in those days.

'That's it there,' said Colin, leaning into the steering wheel and looking up through the windscreen. 'That's it there with the light on.'

Ivan looked round. He was checking for the van, but it was nowhere to be seen. 'Right, we'll have to go up.' Then he turned to me and said, 'No sense in three of us going up. You stay in the car and keep your eyes on the window. Any problems and I'll chuck something through it.'

I looked at him; it kind of made sense, but I knew he was up to something. 'All right,' I said. 'But don't you be going over the fucking top. Colin, fucking watch him.' Colin didn't really say anything. Why should he have? He'd never seen him do the things I had. I jumped in the driver seat and watched them disappear up the stair.

It was Colin who later told me what happened. He said that when they got to the flat, Ivan rang the bell.

'Yes?' said Linda from behind the closed door.

'I'm a friend of Derry's,' said Ivan. 'Is he in?'

'No, I've no seen him since Thursday morning.'

'It's just that I owe him £20 and I'm away first thing. I'm back off with the Paras at 0600hrs. I don't want to let him down, but it's not like I'm going to post the money, is it?'

'Stick it through the letterbox.'

'No offence, darling, but how do I know you're Linda? I mean, you could be anybody. I've seen you in a photo. Goan open the door so I can see it's you.'

Colin said there was a pause. Then the door swung open and, without a thought, Ivan grabbed hold of her throat and pushed her in. Colin closed the door behind them.

'Where the fuck is he?' he shouted. She spat in his face, so he slapped her. She went mad, as she was prone to doing, and bit Ivan on the face, so he punched her stomach, hard, and knocked the wind right out of her. 'Right, you fucking slut. You're going to tell me where that cunt is.' And with that he went through to her kitchen and grabbed her electric kettle. As he came back, he stuck it under his feet and smashed it, then tore out the element, still attached to the flex. 'You are going to tell me. Understand?' he said, before slapping her again and ripping off her skirt and knickers. Then, by the throat, he bundled her against the wall, plugged in the flex and rammed the element right up her fanny. 'You've got 20 seconds, slut!' The minute she felt the heat, she literally shat herself and blabbed out an address. Then, when Ivan let go, she dropped to the ground and pointed to a mirror hanging above the fire. Behind it, sitting on its hook, was a door key. Ivan took it, then slowly walked back over, grabbed her face in his hands and licked it. 'You're lucky we got company,' he whispered. 'If you ever open your mouth, I'll come back alone.'

Fifteen minutes later I saw two figures emerge from the tenement door. Ivan was flicking a key up and down in his hand. 'Let's go,' he said as he jumped in the front. 'We got an address.' I looked back over my shoulder to Colin. He just shook his head.

After fucking about for half an hour we finally got to Govan from the east side of the Paisley Road. 'That's the address here,' said Ivan, reaching into his trench-coat pocket before putting on his gloves. 'And look – over there,' he gestured with his head. It was our van, its nose jutting out from behind an old Morris. I felt my adrenalin surge. He was here. We parked up a few feet from the van and I got out to have a nose – stupid bastard hadn't even ditched it. I went back to the motor and grabbed my axe. I was ready for trouble. With its head in my coat pocket and the neck running up my sleeve, I walked through the rain and over to Ivan and Colin now standing in the darkened doorway. You had to be careful in Glasgow. You'd go to do one and a hundred of the fucks would pile out of the woodwork – all cousins and uncles with their razors and coshes. We jarred the door and took a few steps in. The stair met us with a blanket of darkness and an overwhelming stench of piss.

'Christ!' said Colin, wincing. 'How can people live like this? It's fucking disgusting.'

It was. He sparked his lighter, and with the naked flame we crept past the doors and up two flights till we hit number eight.

'That's the bastard there,' said Ivan, now kneeling down and gently peering through the letterbox. 'The telly's on. So someone's home.'

He took the key from his pocket and quietly slotted it into the keyhole, then with the least amount of pressure began turning the lock. The rusty mechanics began to grind before it gave with a click. We were in! 'Ready?' whispered Ivan, and then, turning round, began to mouth – one, two, three. Then bash! The door flew open and we bundled down the hall. A startled Derry jumped off his armchair and – bang! Ivan hooked him, breaking his jaw instantly while sending him careering onto a table.

'Forget about us, did you, cunt?!' snarls Ivan while he grabs his balls, squeezes them tight and pulls him off the table, slamming him onto the ground. Now, with sheer venom, he stamps all over him, again and again and again, before falling down and biting him in a frenzy as Derry screeches in terror. Then Ivan leans back, spits in his face, takes out his blade and holds it to his eye. 'Where's the money? What've you done with it? Don't tell me a weegie fuck like you knows how to spend eight grand.' With his palm pressing down on his face and his thumb in his mouth, he scoops out his eye like a boiled egg. Derry lets out a gargled scream, while the blood now flooding his lungs begins to bubble. 'Turn the fucking rooms over!' Ivan shouts to us. 'I'll check in here.'

I went into the bedroom and ransacked it – nothing. Then I joined Colin in the living room and took it apart with my axe – still fuck all! Pissed off, we went back to the kitchen, where Derry was now convulsing on a blood-soaked carpet. 'Take a seat, boys,' said Ivan calmly, pointing to a busted old sofa lying against the wall. So we did. But as Colin lit a smoke and passed one to me, I suddenly realised that we'd just sat down to the Ivan torture show.

'Now, Derry!' said Ivan, leaning down and scooping up the wee felly like a loving parent and propping him in an armchair. 'Derry! Listen, we're not going to hurt you any more. OK? You made a bad choice. You fucked up. Right?' He was now caressing his head. 'But that's it. You've had your punishment. Just show us where the money is, and we'll fix you up, we'll fix you up good. I promise. Right?' He paused, but nothing. 'Derry, Derry!' he barked again and again, trying to break through the hysterics. But Derry, his eye socket a mash and his jaw just hanging by a thin piece of sinew, was clearly fucked. So Ivan reached into his pocket and pulled out a roll of gaffer tape. He took an end in his teeth and pulled out a length. Then, with both hands, he elevated the shattered jaw and, with all the care of a medic, taped it shut. He paused for a moment, as if waiting on a thank you, then taped down each of Derry's arms like in an electric chair.

'What the fuck's he doing?' said Colin quietly in my ear.

I just looked at him. I had little pity for the bastard; his move in Morpeth could have killed us all. Fuck him, I thought. 'Where's the fucking money?' I shouted in a burst of rage. But Ivan looked at me as if I'd spoken out of turn.

'Children, please,' he said as he removed his gloves to reveal a knuckle-duster. That's why Derry's jaw was so fucked! After taking it off, he began caressing Derry's head, before running his face across his hair and breathing it in. The fucking weirdo was in a world of his own. And all the time, he was whispering in his ear. I couldn't make it out, but Derry didn't like it. After ten minutes of this perverse ritual, Ivan asked Colin for a smoke – which he gave him. Ivan lit it, but then he walked back over and took mine. Now with a lit fag in each hand, he leant right into Derry's face, kissed him gently on his taped-up lips, then rammed a butt up each nostril and held them tight. Fucking hell, did that boy suffer. His hands contorted and his skin turned red, while the muscle cords in his neck stood out like steel bands as he fought the tapes with a strength from nowhere. But the more he struggled the deeper he breathed, and the deeper he breathed the more he fried, until finally he stopped and was quiet. When he did, Ivan let go of his nose, and the spent butts dropped like cartridges from his smoking-barrel nostrils.

'Oh, that's great,' I said. 'That's just fucking ace. He's fucked! You've killed him. How the fuck can he tell us where the money is if he's fucking dead?'

Ivan just ignored me. He was still in his trip.

'So?' shouted Colin. 'What's the fucking deal? What now? You've got serious fucking issues, mate!' He stood up and started pacing around, trying to figure out, like me, just what the fuck we were up to.

Then Ivan took a hanky from his pocket, wiped his forehead and hands and neatly folded it back. He cleared his throat. 'Don't worry, boys, everything's just perfect.' And with that, he strolled over to the vertical-drum washing machine and pulled out a holdall.

'What the fuck?' I said, bending down to unzip it. It was full of money. 'How long have you known it was there?' Ivan just looked right through me. 'You're one sick bastard.' But as I said that, a huge smile came over my face. 'Yes. You are a sick bastard. And we've done it. We've fucking done it!' I turned to Colin and he bear-hugged me. And so, while Ivan stood showing more interest in the body, Colin and I jumped about like loons.

As soon as we got our bearings, we sat and counted our takings. It came to £7,530, which, between three instead of four, came to £2,510 each, which we divvied up there and then. The only thing now was to get the fuck out of Glasgow – minus the stiff. By this time it was approaching four in the morning, so we had to think fast. Just then, Ivan took out his wad and threw fifty quid over to Colin. 'That's for your brother's car – I'm buying it. And this is what we're going to do.' Surprised, we looked over. 'We'll roll him up in this carpet, throw him in the boot, come back and give this place a scrub, then I'll drive you to Glasgow Queen Street for the first train through. The body, as I killed him, becomes my problem. Deal?'

Me and Colin looked at each other – that was as good a deal as we were likely to get. 'Fucking deal!' we said. So, under the cover of darkness, and with the rain still driving down, we bound up Derry, the double-crossing fuck, in his own soiled carpet and bundled him into the boot. We gave the place the once over and locked the door behind us, before heading off with Ivan at the wheel.

'I hate it when they talk to you,' said Ivan.

'What?' I said from the passenger's side.

'Hookers. I hate it when they talk. I mean, when I go in, I'm all randy and shit – but to them it's just a job. I'm just another punter, just another few quid before they knock off. But to me, it's an event. I don't want to talk about my business – or where I'm going for my fucking holidays, you know? I just want them to shut the fuck up and take what's coming.'

'Yeah, mate, that must be murder,' I said sarcastically. 'Fancy wanting to talk. Fucking hookers. They should just shut the fuck up like the come-buckets they are. Isn't that right, Colin?'

'Eh? Oh, that's right. Fucking come-buckets!' he said as he woke up. We started to laugh – it felt good. We'd both had too much of Ivan for one day and were dying to get home; and while he ranted on about hookers, I began to dream about my money and where it would take me. I'd been given a second chance, and this time I knew exactly what to do with it. Just then, we were there.

'Out, quick,' said Ivan as he pulled in. 'This isn't where we want to be hanging about.' So we did. But then, with the door still open, I put my head back in and leant over to shake his hand.

'I'll be in touch, Roddy,' he said.

'I look forward to it. Oh, and thanks for . . .' I gestured towards the boot. 'You know.'

'No problems, Roddy, it's my pleasure.'

'Pleasure?'

'Oh, yeah,' he smiled. 'Pleasure!' And off he went.

CHAPTER III

EMPIRE!

The journey back from Glasgow seemed no different than that of the Congo. So when Susan's reaction to me stumbling in at eight in the morning was less like Rome's citizens at Victory Arch, and more like a sour-faced lemon-sucker, I reacted by throwing the telly through the window. It was the kind of thing I did when there were a thousand tomorrows. Now, in my prison cell, I've only got today and it's filled with regret.

Women are a funny lot. And men are hysterical. But together we become a love–hate tragedy. It's always been that way and I could never see why. Now, in prison, I can. Like the Buddhists have said for years, it's only when you strip away life's illusions that the reality appears. Being in a cell is no illusion. Love is perfect, but it ticks. Like the rapture when your team scores a goal or the rush of your horse winning a race, it's only a spike, and it always crashes. Back then Susan and I argued: not a lot but, like so many others, we could withdraw affection like the flick of a switch. My mum had always said, 'Son, you'll know a girl loves you when she won't get angry, in case it makes you upset!' In her own way she was right – but about the wrong thing. Real love isn't based on anger and conflict – that's addiction. And where an 'alkie' hits the bottle to block out the pain, so I used Susan to alleviate mine. And for as long as it worked, I had my salvation – but even salvation ticks. It ticked until she failed to meet the needs of my own insecurities. So when my pain returned, it came back stronger than ever; but, like blaming vodka for being an alcoholic, I saw Susan as the cause. What an arse! Me blaming her meant that she blamed me, and as we both attempted to manipulate and punish the other for not matching up to our expectations, our competition for victimhood became an endgame in itself. Now, looking back over a long life of blaming, I'm like a man who sat in the middle of a frozen lake and lit a fire for heat – my pain is as strong as it ever was; only now I'm alone. Bastard!

It took me about a week to get it together. I'd come down with a flu that knocked me flat, and so in my sweat-soaked bed I was treated to my very own delirium cinema as my temperature soared. It was hell. Susan never left my side – she was a window to heaven. As soon as I was able, I did what I should have done right away. I split the money into three, and stashed it away. When someone else knows about a job, you've got to assume you'll get a tug from the police. That's how most folk get done, either by getting picked up 'on the spend', or by getting grassed on for their own clemency. So an oily tick like me, 'suaving' it up 'doon Leith' with a wad of English, was asking for trouble. As soon as I could, I got a job. I took a job as a doorman at the Cavendish nightclub and sat it out for six months until I had a falling out with 'Dave the Knave', one of the other bouncers. His bird fancied me – something made pretty clear one night when she shoved her knickers in my trench-coat pocket on the way in. What probably pissed Dave off the most was that, at the end of the night when the staff were all sitting about having a free pint, I calmly walked over and said, 'Dave, do us a favour and hand these back to yer missus for me.' He never forgave me, and for the harmony of the door team one of us had to leave. Being the only one with a life, and on account of my small fortune under the mattress, it was me.

About four months later, I was up the town and had been drinking all day with my pal Steve Thompson. We ended up in the Cavendish quite early on; in reality it was because we were too steaming to get in anywhere else, and I don't know if it was something in the water or a change in the wind, but Steve, the ugliest bastard in Edinburgh, scored a bird. That left me on my own, so I sought solace at the bar. A half-bottle of rum later, I stood up to take a piss, and did the usual – I knocked into someone and spilt his pint. Straight away I apologised, and like a true 'gent' the guy just laughed and told me not to worry. But two steps later I felt someone trying to wrench my head off like they were killing a chicken. I took an arm, and in my drunken stupor kicked the feet away from underneath him. A large body clattered to the ground and I found myself standing over Dave the Knave. Dave had seen what had happened and had decided that this was his chance. The problem now was that, as the crowd parted like the Red Sea, all that the other doorman could see was me towering over a startled Dave, now flat on his arse. That was it – I took a leathering. Five doormen set about me, and as five doormen could, gave me a scalping from hell. Within minutes I was lying slumped against a wall on Lothian Road.

Battered and bruised, I picked myself up and took a cab home. By this time I was living in Brunswick Street, just off Leith Walk, in a main-door flat we'd just bought with a helping hand from Susan's folks. Luckily, albeit for all the wrong reasons, Susan and the kids were along at her mum's, so, unchallenged, I lay in the bath and sobered up, before calmly patting myself dry, trying not to irritate my cuts. Once talced and cologned, I went through to my wardrobe and put on a smart shirt, a nice tie and my best suit. At the mirror I gave myself a 'Sunday best' parting, while at its foot, I sat and carefully laced up my old 'Tackety' Army boots, polished so clean they reflected the light. Finally, trench coat on and hand axe in pocket, I took a step out into a cold and misty Edinburgh evening and lit a smoke. I looked one way, then the other, then I upturned my collar and began to walk along the deserted streets, each step keeping time like an advancing army on a night out, only this time, like the old bother boys from the Glasgow dancehalls, I was wearing 'Tackety boots for dancing'.

It takes half an hour to walk from Elm Row to Tollcross, but when each step sends waves of pain shooting about your body, it might as well have been half a day. By the time I reached Goldbergs department store in Tollcross, I was fucking raging. I stopped, finished my smoke and looked up at the clock – only two and a half hours since they'd last seen me. That will do. My heart was racing but my ace was with me, and now, gripping my axe so tight that my fingers could have left imprints, I put my head down and walked straight for the door. Now, any doorman with half a brain does one of two things: throws trouble from the inside out, or keeps it out by shutting the doors and staying in. So a smartly dressed man approaching from the outside is unlikely to be recognised until it's too late. And for Dave, it was. Bang! I smashed the blunt side of my axe right into his fat fucking face, before reeling up and trying to sink the sharp end into the advancing Billy Turner's shoulder. He jumped back and knocked two females out of the way as he bottled it and slammed the door shut, leaving Dave a twitching mess at my feet. 'Come on!' I shouted at Turner, as I slammed the axe into the wooden door. 'Let's fucking have you!' But the door stayed firm. So I leant down and took a hold of Dave and dragged him 30 yards along the pavement until we reached the public toilets. 'Right, tough cunt,' I said as I sat him up against the wall and proceeded to smash his shins to bits. As Dave passed out, his legs nothing but pulp below the knee, I caught the flicker of a panda light screeching round Lochrin Terrace. Cunts! Live by the sword, die by the sword. That's how it should be. But not for this bunch of fucks, so I stood in the shadows while it shot round the front, then I bolted back the way it had come, then over Tollcross and down the back of Heriot's School via a lane called The Vennel, where I found a phone box and got a hold of Pete Stanfield. Within minutes he was there and we were off.

For the next few days I sat about expecting a pull. A hundred witnesses saw my tussle with the bouncers, then a handful saw me attack Dave with an axe, but for some reason I never heard a peep. It took me a week to forget about it. It took Dave a year to walk again.

I remember sitting one morning not so long before I went to jail, watching the news, and it was about Richard Branson trying to cross the Atlantic in a hot-air balloon. The stupid bastard was half-killing himself, and for what? I sat there trying to figure it out – why a man with so much to lose would risk it all for so little to gain? Now I smile. Just accumulating wealth seems pointless after a while. What can you do with two million that you can't do with one? And you might have ten cars but you've only got one body to drive them. And like I said, en route back from the Congo, all my problems seemed irrelevant till I stepped off at Portsmouth, and now, looking back over a long life, the pursuit of money was everything till I got it, then with it, I was bored. So why do the hot-air thing? Was it Branson's love of flight that made him dangle in a basket, or something else? Like me, I think it was something else, and that something was a double-edged sword.

About a month after smashing Davy to bits, I got word – I won't say from where – that Colin Patterson had been found dead in his Drylaw flat. Seemed that he'd got reekin and choked on his own vomit, then lay there for a week till the neighbours had noticed the bluebottles. That in itself was a shame, but what was really fucked was that when the police moved him they found a roll of English twenties stashed in his tail. So they took the fucking place apart and found the best part of a grand rammed up a frozen chicken's arse. Well, it wasn't exactly Tom Thumb's trail of breadcrumbs, but the game was on. So with Derry and Colin dead, and Ivan probably back shredding his ethnic villagers, that left me. So what did I do? Like Branson, I needed an escape and something to give my life meaning. Did I fly a hot-air balloon? No, I became a prison officer.

An ex-Army man like me, and someone with no previous criminal convictions, found it pretty easy to get in. In some ways it seemed like the right thing to do. Who'd think a 'screw' would be a seasoned crook? Besides, if I did have all that dough, what the fuck would I be doing dealing with 'bams' for nothing but wages? When I was given the choice – well, when I was asked to spell out a preference – I opted for Polmont YOI; that's the Young Offenders Institution in Falkirk. I thought that, of all the jails, a YOI would be the least complicated as it only had boys under the age of 21, and most of them, I thought, would be in for 'yobbing', and I'd have little trouble in giving them a good foot up the arse. I was wrong.

The thing about Polmont was that under the same roof you had both the convicted and those on remand, those having a 'lie down' and those serving life. Even in segregation, the 'beasts' were lumped in with non-beasts. But most of all, what got to me was that, while some 21 year olds were really mature, some of the 16 year olds were nothing short of kids. I don't think I need to spell out what that meant, suffice to say that most rape went unreported.

I was given an officer's house on the grounds, and for a while we played at happy families. But even though it was just a stopgap, I started to feel alienated. I couldn't relate to the job and felt too sorry for the boys to be of any credible use. Indeed, I'd often show more affinity with them than with my colleagues, who marched about like little Hitlers. Having said that, that's not to say I was a pushover. I was no fucking social worker – something that became pretty apparent towards the end of my stay when some of the boys, either in Argyll or Spey Hall – I can't remember now – started their dirty protests. They'd smear themselves and their cells in shite, and whoever had the job of taking in their trays or hosing them down was usually met with a barrage of it. This went on for weeks, until it was my turn. There's an expression in jail: 'If you don't shite, you'll die.' It relates to not eating, so I took it literally. Instead of taking in their trays, I'd open the door and throw it at them; then instead of a hose down, I turned up the heating. I'd put it up so high that within 24 hours they were crying for a wash – the shite had solidified and was cracking their skin, while their cell stank so bad that they lost the will to live, let alone to fight. Did I turn it down? Did I fuck. I gave it another day for punishment, and that was that – problem sorted. That was Polmont's last ever dirty protest. It was also my last week.

I left Polmont in 1971. It had served its purpose, so I moved on. Archie, my father-in-law who owned a second-hand shop at St Leonard's, suggested I get into the game. You could set your own hours, there was no tax to pay on buying second-hand goods, and not everything had to go through the books. Besides that, there were plenty of opportunities to 'make the most' of the trade, especially for a people person like me. So there it was, my first ever shop, Bostons, opened at 104 Leith Walk, just below a railway bridge now long since removed. It didn't take long for a roaring trade to whip up, but with that came trouble. There are few other professions that attract the attention of both the police and the crooks alike. The wise man, then, is the one who realises that it's best to stay on the good side of both. The police have an interest because they know you'll handle 'knocked gear' and they want to recover it. You can't fall out with them, 'cause they'll close you down. The crooks, on the other hand, make you money. So being all things to all men is the key to the game. For years, I held the key.

I liked the police. I thought the bulk of cops, even to this day, were good guys. But just like those who commit war crimes, there are those who follow orders and those who go beyond them. I saw it in the Army, I saw it in Polmont YOI, I saw it with the police, I saw it with SIS and, of course, I'm now living it with the National Investigation Service (or NIS, a special branch of Customs). Back then, the police were all detectives. Now they're academics. Old-school cops would cut you some slack if they could and, as I found out on the odd occasion, they weren't scared to take off their jackets and have a shot at the title. I certainly won't say his name, but that ginger-haired bastard, PC 'rhymes with cunt', from Leith police station, took second prize – although he tells the story like it was the 'rumble in the jungle'. Anyway, beyond that I soon negotiated myself a system and began to enjoy life. Besides, I found it a great way to clean money, both from my robbery stash and from the other bits and pieces I was getting up to.

But I soon realised that Edinburgh is a small city, and although I never bought gear from the surrounding area, primarily out of a sense of loyalty, but also 'cause every cunt was skint and I couldn't sell carpets, I couldn't display half my stock. The solution came by chance when one of the older kids that I knew from Polmont walked into the shop one morning with his dad. They were from Glasgow and had come in early one Saturday morning before going to see Celtic play Hibs at Easter Road. I'd always got on with Ryan; he was a good wee guy that had just fallen in with the wrong crowd, and I'd even jumped in the way of an oncoming pool ball for him. Well, either I got a bruised back, or he got a fractured skull. Anyway, turned out his dad, Bill Baxter, was doing exactly the same thing as me through the west, so it didn't take long to see how we could help each other. Less than a week later my van was loaded like a mobile Aladdin's cave, and off I went. In those days there weren't the tradable commodities that there are today. There were no stereos, DVDs, VCRs, mini this or personal that, and a computer was what powered Apollo. So instead we traded musical instruments, brass ornaments, paintings and pictures, and pretty much anything else that wasn't considered a fixture or fitting – although there are probably a few country houses which would argue that point.

Anyway, going through to Glasgow was a funny thing, especially if you're from Edinburgh. I know everyone who's done it will probably have felt it: the two cities might only be 30 miles apart, but could easily be different countries. Glasgow's a hard place – no doubt! But for me, the first cultural difference I had to overcome was to qualify what was meant by 'quality knocked gear'. On arriving in the Gorbals I opened the back of my van and saw he was in awe. He then lifted the door of his lock-up and I said, 'Oh, naw!' My gear stayed in the van and came back with me, but two weeks later he came to Edinburgh, and this time he had what I was looking for. Business really took off.

The profit margins on knocked gear are immense. Half the time, the wee shit that does the stealing doesn't know the value of what he's got, and the rest of the time he's so desperate that he'd wrestle his own granny for a bag of chips and a bus fare home. And for as much as I was generating money I was also generating stock. You see, Argos think they were first with their catalogues and counters, but they're wrong, it was me. Soon people were coming in and asking for something, and if I didn't have it down at Pete's lock-up, I'd phone Glasgow and 'order' it in. Soon, one van every two weeks became two vans once a week. And for a while it worked. But like anything, the bigger you are the harder you fall, and although I was still far away from falling, I could feel trouble brewing. When it came, it came from an unlikely source.

EMPIRE!

It was just another Saturday morning and I was in the shop looking over the paperwork for 363 Leith Walk. My empire had grown too big too quickly for the humble confines of 104, so I was moving on and up, albeit 200 yards up the road, to a new shop opposite Pilrig Church. From behind my counter I looked up to see two men standing outside, both big guys, but made to seem far bigger by their ill-fitting trench coats. As the wind gusted down the Walk, their scruffy hair lashed about to reveal their poor complexions and rodent-like features. The taller of the two had a tattoo on his neck which said 'cut here', then a line like you'd find along a juice carton – fuck, that looked tempting – while the smaller of the two showed them up as the vermin they were, as, like a yob in court, he stood dressed for the day in his out-of-place suit. What a prick! Still, they looked like they could handle themselves, so I removed my watch. They looked about then headed off. Two minutes later, they came back and walked in.

'There's been a lot of problems round here, you know? What with those windows getting smashed up the road, and that shop getting fire-bombed at the foot of the Walk,' said the smaller of the two with a hoarse Glasgow twang, as they stood side by side at the edge of the counter. I just looked at him. Then he stood up on his toes, leant forward, put his hands on the counter and whispered, 'We can help you, you know.'

But before he'd even finished his breath, I took a heavy steam iron, which rested an inch away from my hand, and smashed it right across his pal's head. Bang! He dropped. Then, with the back-swing, I lashed it right across the wee man's disgusting potholed face, while keeping a hold of his lapel and thrashing him frantically time and time again before he fell to the ground. As he did, and with all the hatred and contempt I felt, I threw the iron directly down onto his balls, and it burst one, the blood soaking his pants like ink on blotting paper. Upon this, I turned round to his pal, now getting up, and began punching and punching until I'd punched myself out to where I was practically lying on top of him. As I gulped for air, I pulled myself back onto my knees and leant up to the counter, where I'd hung a large Nepalese kukri. 'Right, cunt, what's going on?' I said as I held the curved blade along the 'cut here' line of his neck. He wasn't responding but I could see he was alive. With a quick flick of the wrist, I gave it enough pressure to slice the skin. The blood now began to flow.

'We're sent by the Fat Man!' gargled a voice behind me.

I slowly stood up, and with the bloody knife in hand, towered above the wee man, now convulsing on the floor in all kinds of pain. 'The Fat Man, eh?' The Fat Man was one of Glasgow's players. He'd obviously got word of what I was up to with Bill Baxter, and fancied his chances at getting a few quid out of me. 'Right,' I said, leaning down and cutting off their shoes with my kukri. 'You tell that fat cunt that, since he's tried to take from me, I'm going to take from him. Starting with your shoes!' I picked the bloody men up and slung them out the door. 'You can buy these back when you've got the money,' I howled, waving their footwear. Just then I looked to my left. It was PC 'rhymes with cunt', of all the fucking plods to be first on the scene. Time for a 'lie down', I thought. I thought wrong. He looked at me, then looked at them, and just seemed to get it. When the ambulance came, he just smiled and went with them, so I put their shoes in the window, but they never came back.

Two weeks later I thought about having the Fat Man done in, but there's times to fight and there's times to talk, and this was a battle I didn't need to wage. So, with shuttle diplomacy at its most primitive, my envoy, a scrawny jailbird from Saughton, spent the next two weeks ferrying back and forth to hammer out a deal. And the deal was simple: leave me alone or else! So he did.

I took all that as an omen. My scam with Bill had worked because Bill knew to keep his mouth shut and cover his tracks, but the two vans had meant two drivers, and I'd always known it would only be a matter of time. To make matters worse, Bill was ill, and Ryan was still a wee yob, so that was that. I cashed in my chips and ran.

Opening 363 came with a bit of luck. The Old Chain Pier Bar down in Newhaven was a landmark for many a year. It's where the Edinburgh and London Steamship Company berthed their boats the *London Merchant*, *Edinburgh Merchant*, *Belravock* and *Belhaven* while running a weekly schedule between Leith and London in the years before shuttle flights and intercity rail. Bamboo Betty, so named on account of her bamboo specs, was as permanent a fixture as the bar was itself and, as such, the sailors would bring her stuff back from all over the world – in 1970s Edinburgh, that was about as exotic as you could get. Anyway, she died, and I caught word that whoever had taken over the bar wanted shot of all the 'junk'. Well, that arse might not have seen the value in what he had, but I did. So I slung him a few quid and went to take it, and when I did, I could have filled the van 20 times over. Along with the various curio imports came three huge dust-covered tea chests, and inside I found a mass of amazing Japanese stuff. As we raked through the pristine kit down at Pete's lock-up, still packaged and never before opened, we found all sorts: shoji screens, tatami mats, kimonos, yukatas, happi coats, Peking faux marble foo dogs and countless bamboo wall scrolls. It was great!

A few days later, Graham Reynolds, who owned the Ship pub, and before that Fairlys – where many a hooker had serviced a sailor and which had sported a caged puma in the corner – walked in and asked if I could get my hands on any Chinese furniture. He said he knew it would probably be tricky to get a hold of, but was prepared to pay top dollar. 'Well,' I said, 'I might be able to help you out there! I know a Chinese man who's moving back to China.' And with that, Graham took possession of his new 'Chinese furniture', and I took possession of his money. About three weeks later Graham walked into the shop and stood right in front of me, snarling away. For a minute we just stared at each other, then Susan came through from the back with two mugs of tea. 'All right, Tojo,' she said, calm as ever. We all fell about laughing – good guy, Graham.

The first six months of 363 were good times. There was a shift in staff down at Leith police station, so I decided to ease back on the banditry until I got a feel for who was pulling the strings. I had plenty of money and enjoyed having less pressure. Soon I found that that decision was to pay off. The new 'honcho' was a prick, and had made it his life's ambition to break me. I knew that from time to time he'd watch me, and for the most part, I could live with it. But some weeks before, some bastard had done a 'tie up' off Trinity Park. He'd broken in during the night, tied up a couple and robbed them blind. Inspector Dixon, I'll call him, was determined to link me into it as fence for the gear. Cunt! So, I thought, you want to piss me about, I'll do the same to you. The next day the detectives were there as ever. I couldn't see them, but I could sure feel the eyes, something I'd polished up in the Congo. And my mate Davy Cowen walked in.

'All right, Roddy?'

'I'm going to stab you, right?' I yell at the top of my voice.

'Wow, what?' shouts a startled Davy.

'Stand still while I run this fucking bayonet through your chest, then I'm going to push you down the stairs,' I growled, pointing to the open trap door.

'Now, Rod! C'mon, we're friends,' he pleaded, now quaking from his bad choice of lunch-time visit.

'No, you arse,' I grinned. 'Not for real, the cops have been outside all morning and it's time I flushed them.'

So while Davy breathed a big sigh of relief, I jumped round the counter, and with the biggest theatrical swing, thrust the First World War bayonet right between Davy's chest and arm, then once again for good measure, before shoving him down the basement. Like greyhounds out of the traps, they were in and on me, grappling me to the ground, while the Inspector stood tall and proud over me. 'We've got you now, McLean! Pearson, down the stairs.' So PC Pearson, on the Inspector's orders, timidly crept down the stairs to find the bloody mess. Instead, he found Davy, fag in mouth and brush in hand, sweeping the floor. 'Morning, officer, everything all right?'

Fucking golden. Fuck you, Inspector Dixon!

For some time after that, and probably because I'd genuinely taken a back seat, the police eased off. Edinburgh's always been a village. I decided then that this was probably a good time to move on up in the housing market, and so we sold Brunswick Street and bought 31 Inverleith Row for eight and a half grand. It was a great house. With three floors and a back that looked out onto the Botanic Gardens, it sat at the gable end of a row of town houses. It needed a bit of work done to it, which I set about in no time, and I decorated it with the finest furniture money could buy, including the odd bit of staccato. It was the start of the good life. But, as always, the good life needs to be funded, so my brief lull was over.

By the late '70s a few of the young cops who I'd been mates with when they were on the beat had risen to the dizzy heights of CID. And I can't remember exactly how it first started, but I think I'd bought in four sets of brand new golf clubs, which turned out to be stolen. Well, DC Black, one of my CID pals, was in for a visit and he saw them. I was pissed off because I'd only just got them and they'd cost me a fortune. So when he went to grab them I suggested that he let me keep one, just to get my money back. He paused and thought about it long and hard. Essentially I was asking him to be an accessory to 'reset': the crime of reselling stolen property. Then, to my total fucking amazement, he said, 'Sure.' And off he went. When he did, my next plan of action suddenly came to me.

Meeting the cops felt a lot like seeing Ivan and the gang for the first time. Contrary to popular belief, I've never been a police informer. I've never taken money nor have I ever been a witness – that's a matter of record; but sure, I'd befriended them. I'd made a point of it. I mean, they're the biggest gang in town. Who wouldn't? But doing it wasn't easy. I remember walking into Kushi's Curry House on Lothian Street, one of the first Indian restaurants in Edinburgh. This was a taste of the real India, not the sanitised crap you get now. With a deep breath, and a fixing of my coat, I slowly opened the door and took a step in. It was one room, more like some bastard's lounge than a diner, where round formica-topped tables and 'hip for the time' chrome seats were spread randomly across the floor. Like before, I knew this meeting would change my life for ever, but as I stood there staring at the far away table, time seemed to stop. I was about to cross another line, and this was taboo. I could feel a cold sweat break as the hairs on the back of my neck began to rise. My mind scrambled from thought to thought like the tuning of a radio, whose white noise was interrupted by a window of dialogue with no beginning or end. I'd already made my peace for being so bad, so long as I was doing it for the right reasons. Now, as I stood there needing to justify what I was doing to myself, the weight of the whole world seemed to sit on my shoulders. Within a heartbeat I began to pat my pockets like I'd forgotten something, then I stepped back outside and briskly walked along to Nicholson Square, where I sat on a park bench and tried to focus.

Now in jail, I've had time to define my thoughts, but back then they were only feelings that I couldn't label. Heraclitus, a Greek philosopher who lived before Socrates and Plato, stated that 'all things are flowing'. And by that, he meant that we live in a constant succession of moments where we go from hot to cold, from happy to sad and from being at peace to readying for war. And while we take decisions based on how we feel at the time, all moments pass, leaving us with the consequences of our choices. As I sat in my temporary lunacy, I found myself staring at a blackbird pecking for worms before flying off to its nest. Ashamedly, I envied that bird. All it had to do was to live in the moment. It had no past, no conscience, and in its blissful ignorance it carried out each task like there was no tomorrow. But me, I was in a constant struggle to define my own self. I knew more about what I didn't want than of what I did. No matter what I achieved, I soon became bored, and always found myself pushing the envelope, not for the outcome but for the thrill of doing it. I was never about to bed down with the cops, but I was cutting a deal with them. Was it always going to be like this? Like a dog chasing its tail, was it all in pursuit of something that I already had? On the other side of the park I saw an old alkie. He opened his half-bottle of Bell's and took a long swig. Fuck, that tasted good, as he saluted the bottle like an old friend. But a moment later, the second mouthful only seemed to sustain him, while the third became the norm. A few minutes later the bottle ran dry and he sank into a world of hunger as he craved for more. But as he sat and rummaged through his empty pockets, so anger filled his soul, and he soon became a hollow man, no different from an animal. Then, within a heartbeat, I watched him sink back to hell, where he stayed. He was home. He'd gone full circle and had achieved nothing. That's when it hit me. The dial in my mind stopped and the white noise became dialogue. The bird was no different to the old wino: they both performed one simple task and it became them; but me, I was in a state of flux like my thoughts. And that was an asset. I was a risk-taker who played for keeps and everything in between was just a means to an end. I steadied myself and jogged back round to the curry house. This time, I opened the door with confidence and made straight for the table where the unsuspecting troika awaited. I smiled as I sat down. After all, I thought, you've got to break a few eggs to make an omelette.

To my right was my mate DC Black. He was one of those cops who were always in a hurry for promotion but, unlike some, was a fair man who led from the front. I liked him and we'd helped each other out over the years. Beyond that, you'll have to excuse the brevity of detail, as he's still on the force and Edinburgh's a village. Sitting on the right of him and on the left of me were two officers who I later referred to as Dumb and Dumber. Officially they were still in uniform, but were at least five years the senior of DC Black. They both looked like they'd stepped out of the C&A catalogue. Thankfully, they didn't say much. I'm not going to attempt to reason why, but whether these cops were chasing crime targets or just in it for themselves, they'd decided that what I had to offer made sense. There's no doubt that, by now, I was a major fence, and that was of interest to the Musketeers. Basically, for every four bits of stolen gear I got my hands on, I'd keep one to sell for a small profit, and they'd get three back to record as recovered. In it for me was that I'd have the protection I needed and plenty of warning if necessary – and in it for them was a set of great recovery figures and a few quid at the end of each week to keep Dumb and Dumber off the streets. DC Black, I should iterate, never took nor wanted a penny, a testament to the character of the man. After we'd agreed on the details I got up and left. I was never really there for the socialising. I had it all worked out and I was feeling good. I had a load of stuff down at Pete's lock-up that I couldn't touch anyway. They'd get that first, but that would suit them 'cause it was high-profile gear, stolen from a High Court judge's house, which would be a feather in their cap and would cement their trust in me. How they'd come about it without a body to go with it was their problem. Like I said, I was never a grass.

Anyway, life was good. Some weeks before that I'd just bought my first yacht, the *Io Vado*. And now, filled with the thrill of conniving, I was walking back down to the house in a happy daydream, while figuring out how to turn my pleasure-seeker into a money-maker and open a whole new world of opportunity. But that, however, would have to wait, 'cause when I got home, Susan was raging.

One of the biggest injustices from all the press coverage I've had was the portrayal that somehow Susan was a kept woman. In fact, she'd worked every day of her life, and had run her own business, totally independent of anything I was doing. So, that morning, when she was down in Leith doing her banking, I'd asked her to check on a flat I was letting out at the foot of the Walk, just behind the Kirkgate Shopping Centre. Anyway, she now wanted my tenant, Steve Gilmore, out because when she'd gone round, she'd seen the guy had made a right cunt of the place and had found a load of comics that sexualised kids: drawings of five year olds touching old men's cocks. Obviously that wasn't on, but when he'd come back he'd told her to fuck off, so she went mad. Now, had he been alone, she'd probably have stabbed him herself, but he'd been the big man in front of his pals. So cut a long story short, within an hour, the Reverend 'Sparry' Harrison and me were en route. Now Sparry, or 'Sparrow' said with a Scottish accent, was so-named on account of his size, but Christ he was a demon of a man and not one to be crossed. He had a fascination with knives and a fixation on using them. And, unlike many loyal team members I've had over the years, his reputation went well beyond the remits of Royston. It was near the end of another long day and, to be honest, my head was so full of plots and plans that the last thing I wanted to do was to deal with some fucking halfwit. So when I got to the door, I stuck the head right in him, punched fuck out of his pal, then threw all his furniture down the stair. When he came to his senses, he started mouthing off about who he knew and what he was going to do. The usual. So I just gave him another foot up the arse, took twenty quid off him for repairs, which I'd found in the kitchen, and locked the door behind me, leaving him battered, bruised and homeless. In the scale of things, though, Gilmore was pretty well off, considering what he'd said to my wife and his attitude towards me. As I got into the van, I'd already forgotten about it and was soon back to my plotting. That was until the next morning.

It was Susan who found it when she opened the door to get the boys off to school. Sitting on our front step was a milk bottle filled with petrol and an unlit match. Now that changed things! They talk of a red mist, like when your blood boils and your vision closes in. It's like a tunnel of rage and nothing can break it. Looking back, I've had bigger threats from far worse people, but, for some reason, the actions of one bastard and a petrol-filled milk bottle took me to a place which was all-consuming. I called the 'Reverend', and within half an hour we were tearing about the place trying to find him. We searched everywhere: flats, pubs and fucking doss houses – the lot – but nothing. And all the time I was getting more and more worked up, thinking about him, thinking about how he felt doing it, how he thought it would scare me, how he thought he was the big man by threatening to burn down my house, my family, my kids, the dirty paedophile bastard. When you live on the dark side, there are few rules. Honour amongst thieves is a pack of shit. But there is one – and it's simple – don't fuck with people's kids. And Gilmore had fucked with mine.

By four in the afternoon I put a call in to a mate of mine at Fettes, the Lothian and Borders police HQ. He was a civilian but had access to their files. He said I should call back at six, which I did, then he said I should pick him up in half an hour in Stockbridge. When I met him, I slipped him a few quid and he passed me an address. It was in Newport Street off Lothian Road; it was the scumbag's pal's flat, and he'd given the address when he'd been lifted the year before for touching kids up at the baths. So an hour later I was sitting with the Reverend in the van. We sat in silence. Then, after three hours of sitting, we sat some more, until finally I called it a day. Bastard!

As the weeks went by, I'd like to say that I calmed down, but I didn't. I think the only way to describe it is like when you're totally in love with some bird and she's being all cold, and so you go to sleep thinking about her and wake up dreaming about her and, even though you go about your business, she's always there, even if it's just as a feeling more than a thought. And the phone, how I stared at the phone, hoping for news. I'd became like a man possessed, like a drug addict who needed his revenge for a fix. Years later, at HMP Shotts, I took one of those self-improvement classes. It was a load of touchy-feely piss but it got us out of the chokey for an hour. They talked about neurotic stimulus generalisation (NSG), a condition that sends messages to your brain on a near constant basis, so anything you associate with the person you're fixating on sends your heart racing. So if they drive a red Ford Escort, then every red Escort you see gets you going. In my case it was a long-haired, 'soon to be dead' cunt. And let me tell you, in the very late '70s that narrowed it down to most of the male population.

It was about half-eight one Monday morning when my luck changed. I got a call saying that Gilmore had been lifted in Oxgangs after having battered his bird senseless. But even though she was black and blue and he'd thumped her so hard that she'd miscarried, she was adamant that she'd fallen down the stairs: unlikely in a ground-floor flat, but anyway. If I wanted him, I'd have to follow him from the jail 'cause they couldn't press charges. I called the Reverend but he was otherwise engaged, probably with Arthur Guinness. So I phoned around and threw a team together.

I was firing down Greenbank Crescent heading for the jail when to my surprise I clocked the bastard standing at the bus stop on Oxgangs Avenue. For a second I was goanna swerve in and hit him, but instead I took a left into Oxgangs Gardens and burled round. I jumped in the back with Gary while Phil took the wheel. That's not their real names but, as you'll soon see why, I can't say anything about them. Phil pulled out and drew alongside the bus stop. It wasn't yet half-ten, and between the lull from the rush hour and the women doing their shopping, the place was totally deserted. 'Sorry, pal,' he said. 'I'm looking for Comiston View.' Steve Gilmore squinted a bit, then cautiously approached the open window and put his head in to answer.

'It's up there,' he said like a dismissive imbecile.

'Where?' said Phil, but before he could answer, I threw open the side door of the Transit and coshed him a fucker with an iron bar, before Gary grabbed his feet and we wrestled him in like we were pulling a body out of the water. Phil put his foot down, and we were off, the diesel engine revving and smoking as the side door slid open with me struggling to shut it. When I did – he was mine! We taped his hands and feet and I stuck a rag in his mouth soaked in petrol from a can I'd kept in the back. He couldn't speak but his eyes were defiant. Good, I thought. I wasn't an Ivan and this made it easier. As we moved, I just sat there staring at him. We said nothing; there was nothing to say. We went straight down to Leith and backed the van up into Pete Stanfield's lock-up. Pete used to give me a couple of rooms for my own ends, while he worked through the front as a welder. Luckily he had some heavy work that day with the grinder, and that's a noisy business. So Gary and myself carried Steve through dark and damp industrial space and strapped him into a rusty old office chair. We removed the rag. When I did, he began to plead. He knew he was fucked. To be honest I can't really remember what he said. I saw his lips moving but I couldn't understand what he was saying. Like I said, 'all life is flowing', only now it had dramatically changed its course.

Ponytails are only good for one thing: grabbing a hold of. So Gary took a hold of his hair and held his head back, while I took my pliers and tried to open his mouth. He kept it tight, so I broke his nose with my fist then took a door wedge and jammed it in. Then, still in total silence, I watched myself, slowly and with much care, remove every fucking tooth from his mouth – apart from the front two: I snapped them off so he could feel the cold metal constantly rubbing against his jagged stumps. It took half an hour, but he stopped yelling after 15 minutes, and with each pull, Gary would force him forward, just enough so the blood wouldn't drown him. When I'd finished with his teeth, I stood over him breathing heavily, and as I did I snapped back to reality where I found myself about to pour a bottle of drain cleaner over his head. I stopped short. Like I said, I wasn't an Ivan. We stood him up and tied him face down on a plank of wood, which we angled up so he couldn't choke, and we left him to get some breakfast. In my mind, the release of tension from catching him was worth more than the stress of ripping his face apart. The bacon and eggs tasted great!

When we came back, I already knew what I was going to do with him. He was still alive – just – although he was probably more unconscious than conscious. I took one of the tea chests which I'd got from the Old Chain Pier Bar and we stuffed him in. Then we stripped off and burnt everything, only then realising that the boiler suits which I'd wrongly assumed Pete had kept for us to change into had been used the day before to mop up the insides of a rusty oil drum which had burst in his yard. Bastard! I rummaged around in my gear, but could only find a couple of kimonos left over from my curio import coup.

'You've got to be fucking joking,' said a head-shaking Gary, now standing in his Y-fronts.

'What? They're boiler suits. I didn't say anything about them being British.' And, with a serious face, I threw one over.

'Come on, man.'

'So what?' I said. 'It's a Japanese suit, big fucking deal. It's what the samurai wore.'

But when we stuck them on, he looked at mine, then he looked at his.

'They're not the fucking same!'

I started pissing myself laughing.

'Sorry, did I say samurai? I'm the samurai; you're a geisha!'

'A what?'

'Geisha. You know, a Japanese hooker!'

What a laugh!

So, while Pete ground his metal out the front, a barefooted Shogun and his staccato slag, Gary, stuffed the semi-dead 'paedo' bastard, with teeth, into a tea chest, and made ready to move. After manoeuvring the chest into the back of the van, I grabbed a couple of bags of quick-drying cement and a couple of buckets. I called the Reverend and told him to go to the house and get me a change of clothes, then to pick up my other van and go to the cash and carry and get sea stores for a couple of days, which he did. When he arrived, it was hitting just after five, so we stuck everything in the Sherpa and left the Transit where it stood. If we had been seen grabbing Steve at the bus stop, the chances are the police would have been looking for it. I dropped the Reverend off, before heading on to Granton Harbour where the *Io Vado* was moored. I had no intention of sailing off for more than a few hours, but two men loading a single tea chest onto a boat at night was one thing; if they were loading a whole load of supplies as well, then that was another. By the time the clock struck seven, we'd cleared the breakwater and were heading out of the Firth of Forth towards the North Sea. But soon, like the fog, my red mist was clearing, and I stopped. I had intended to toss Steve Gilmore, the dirty, petrol-bomb-threatening, 'paedo', woman-bashing scum, to the dishonourable watery grave he deserved, but sense got the better of me and I didn't. Instead, at a specific location near Fife, which shall remain nameless, I opened the chest and booted his sorrowful arse onto the beach, where I knew he'd be found. He was.

When we got back to Granton, it was fast approaching three in the morning. I slung Gary the van keys and told him to take off – I'd square him up the next day when I'd go round for the van. I was going to kip the rest of the night on the boat – it had been a long day. I removed my oils, scrubbed myself down and poured myself a stiff drink. My body was shattered but my mind was far from at peace. I lit a smoke, put on some Simon and Garfunkel and began to dream to the 'Sound of Silence'. As the boat gently bobbed up and down in the stillness of the night, I could feel something inside me had changed for ever. Sure, I'd used all sorts of violence before, but never for pride. If he was really going to burn my house down, he'd have done it. But he didn't. He was just a wee guy in big man's boots, and I'd taken it to the extreme. In myself I knew why. Deep under the layers of excuses I'd readily constructed to justify my own aggression lay the truth. The lion may be the 'king of all beasts' but there's no way in which he knows it; he kills when hungry or under threat, not to prove a point. I was now in a world of anger – not simply being angry, but rather a state where I believed I was fundamentally better than anyone else, and worse, had taken delight in displaying it. For that, I was sorry. I knew from experience that this was the downfall of many a man.

A few days later, when the dust had settled, I set about making good on the plans I'd made before my Stevey Gilmore sabbatical. My deal with DC Black was really taking off, so much so that at times I wasn't only 'Argos' to the punters, but to the police as well. If they needed to recover something, the chances were I'd be able to dig it up. They appreciated that. It didn't take me long to realise I could sustain the business with far fewer hours, so I went from working normal shop hours to just five afternoons a week and a full day off on a Wednesday. This shift gave me all the time I needed for my boat. And within a short period of time my day excursions were becoming overnight trips, until finally, like a modern-day Viking, I set off to cross the North Sea.

After three days I sighted the lighthouse on the island of Stangholmen. From there it was just a short hop to Risør on Norway's curving southern coast, south of Oslo. Risør's a stunning place, with its cluster of historic white houses all built around a small picturesque fishing harbour. In the summer it's popular with artists and tourists, and is a favourite with Norway's yacht owners. I liked that. As soon as I arrived, it felt like another glass ceiling had shattered – I felt alive. Norwegian summers are marked by the midnight sun, especially north of the Arctic Circle. At Nordkapp, in the far north, the sun stays out from May to July, but nowhere in the country, even as far south as I was, experiences true darkness in that time.

Risør was like any transient port. It was as close as I'd get to being like that blackbird I'd once envied. No one knew who I was, or where I'd come from, and, like being on a long-haul flight sitting next to a stranger, you could be anyone you wanted to be and no one was there to say otherwise. I found it easy to meet people, and even easier to gain their trust. I quickly fell in love with the place, with the people and soon with a girl. When I first saw Karla, I almost fell over. I can't say it was love at first sight, but by Christ it was lust. She was every bit the caricature of a Scandinavian goddess; a tall, blonde, blue-eyed bombshell with legs so long I'd need a footy to fuck her. And when she spoke, her Abba-like accent gave me the raging horn. I had the smitt.

EMPIRE!

That summer I made frequent trips back and forward, while wrestling with my conscience. I hated having to lie to Susan, it really tore me apart – but when the heart takes over, your head seems to stay up your arse.

It didn't take long for Karla to see my true colours, and, as luck would have it, she wasn't exactly training for a life in the convent herself. On one of our trips around the country, we spent a couple of days in Oslo. Now, Oslo's a funny town: it's a beautiful place but, unlike most European cities, it isn't full of architectural wonders. The closest thing they have to an old town is the district of Frogner, and it was while taking a walk through there that we bumped into a friend of hers, Andor. Straight away I got a good feeling about him. He seemed a genuine guy who always looked you in the eye and really seemed to give a fuck about what you had to say. When we met, he was just finishing work and was on his way to pick up his wife, but said we should meet later and have a few drinks. As we then walked about before seeing them, Karla told me a bit about him. She said he was a jeweller, but straight away I knew she meant jewel thief and, once again, I liked that.

While the two birds got pissed and nattered a load of shite in Norwegian, I set about testing the water with Andor. You see, in those days, there was no global village like there is now. I mean, to give you an example, if you'd wanted to go out in Edinburgh and eat a pizza, you'd have been hard pressed. So the thought of a trade in illicit jewellery seemed too good to miss. A pal of mine, Polio Eddie, so-named on account of his debilitating affliction, was a major fence for jewellery and the likes, so I had an endless supply. But the problem, of course, is that anything worth a fuck is bound to be missed and, by the same token, recognised. Not the case, I thought, if it came from another country. So cut a long story short, when I returned two weeks later to Risør, I brought a few samples to show Andor, which he liked, and when I got back to Edinburgh, I went round Polio Eddie's to show him my swag from Norway. He bought the lot in a heartbeat. Soon each trip to Norway became worth two to three weeks in the shop, and as the money rolled in so did my ambition. The seafarer was reborn.

The turn of the decade meant a few changes for the better. I sold 363 Leith Walk for £6,000 and with a mortgage I bought 21 Albert Place for £12,000, which became the most infamous of the three Bostons. Then, a few months later, I bought next door, number 20, for £9,000 off my brother-in-law Robert Thallon, who was already playing out his own epic life. I opened it as a jewellers, and Susan began to work it. Next door again was a sweetie shop, number 19, which I bought for £5,000 and converted into a main door which accessed the flats above, which I already owned. Then, when the building at the end of the small alley between number 19 and the Old Salt pub, which was owned by British Rail, mysteriously went on fire, I bought that too.

They say all roads lead to Rome, and as I sat amongst the smoking timbers of number 18 Albert Place, my good friend and soon-to-be business partner made a suggestion. A brothel. I'd like to say that I wrestled with the idea for days before setting my morals aside in the name of hard currency, but if Davy hadn't suggested it, I would have. I'd often thought back to Ivan's words on the subject, and he was right, there was a fortune to be made in 'riding'. But it was more than that; you'd never know who'd come in for a service, and sometimes discretion carried a price. Like the phoenix from the flames, we built the club from scratch. It took us a year. And while the workmen toiled through the day, the materials and supplies would miraculously appear during the night like the elves and the shoemaker. At the back of Albert Place lay the old railway, and on that, like an army of ants, the 'borrowed' bricks and mortar that built Barkleys Sauna were marched along by a coalition of the willing and the terminally short of cash.

By the time the sauna opened, I was making a fortune from Norway, I'd started to run a system to London like I'd done through in Glasgow, and had bought some land where I was building a load of houses. On top of that, I still had my flats, plus the odd bit of loan sharking and various other bits and pieces which I'll come to in due course. At first, I thought that running a brothel would make me feel like a kid who owned a sweetie shop. And to be honest, before I opened it, I did think I'd be eating a lot of 'dolly mixtures'. But you don't – not if you want to stay in business. Again, the key to any success is self-discipline – no more so than when you're working with vice. For those that don't know, and for those that do, but would rather pretend that they didn't, an Edinburgh sauna's a simple operation. On walking in, you're presented with a desk, usually stationed by a dolly bird who takes your entrance fee and gives you a towel. That fee belongs to the house. Once inside, there's a lounge, where all the girls sit – a good number of staff is about six. You go and take your shower, come back, sit down and have a drink, perhaps browse some gentlemen's literature, and then select the young maiden of your choice, who will then take you down the stairs and shag the shit out of you. Each sauna can differ, but again the house normally takes a cut of whatever she charges you. So, really, she's self-employed and rents the room from the house. That way you make your money twice, with no wages to pay.

Saunas in Edinburgh are tolerated; I've always respected the city for having a relaxed approach to the business. And it makes sense. You see, with a sauna, the birds are safe, as are the punters; and whereas any fucking thing could be getting in your car, at least there's some sort of quality control when you're paying an entrance fee. And with that, I don't just mean less mingers, but far less junkies. The downside for me, of course, was having to deal with the birds. After being in the business, I can tell you that the myth of the 'happy hooker' is exactly that, a myth. I'm no physiologist, but it can't be easy, getting it tight ten times a day every day. So, soon, like at Polmont YOI, I found myself getting caught up in their individual lives, probably the biggest cardinal sin for a pimp. I decided to take a sure step back from all that. But then trouble paid us a visit.

One of the birds, Angie, was into her bondage. She'd string the bastards up and batter fuck out of them for a score. Personally I never got it, and I'd always said that if she was too busy, she should send them through and I'd knock fuck out of them for a fiver. She always laughed – I was serious! Anyway, she was a great bird, but like a lot of them, she'd have a good drink before starting her shift. That didn't bother us; it's not like they were driving buses, so long as they weren't falling about the fucking place. Anyway, the second shift started at four, which meant Angie and a couple of the others were in the Old Salt from just after lunch, when, for some reason, one of the regulars decided he'd had enough of them being there. He called them for everything, and sent them packing. I'd had a word with Davy about it, but we decided not to shite on our own doorstep, so we left it. The next day, though, his son was at the bar with him, and when Connie, this wee Glasgow bird who'd nipped in to buy some fags, got the same treatment in front of all the other punters, we decided to take action.

It was about half-two on a Friday when Davy arrived and parked up in front of the shop. A builder by trade, he wasn't the biggest of guys, but what a fucking temper he had, and he certainly wasn't one to shy away from a problem. I turned to Phil, who was in seeing me at the time, and asked him to watch the shop, then I reached behind the counter and picked up the McLean weapon of choice – a hand axe. Then, with my head down in the usual manner, I marched through to the Old Salt with Davy in tow brandishing his favourite, a baseball bat. Being a Friday, and as the workies all finish at half-one, the pub was heaving, but we just burst in and ran right up to the bar. I took my axe and sunk it right into the fucking wood, sending splinters and shards flying as Davy took a swing at the punter, clipping the top of his head and sending him tumbling. 'Come on, tough cunt!' I shouted. 'Let's fucking have you!' I ripped out the axe from the gouge, which still survives to this day, and jumped over a fallen stool to smash his legs to bits like I'd done to Dave the Knave. 'You want to hassle my staff, cunt?' I kept yelling, but no sooner had my feet touched the ground than the pair were up and away, scampering out the door as they both shat it like the bullying fucks that they were. We'd made our point, so I gathered myself, jumped back over, then turned to the sea of gobsmacked stares and, with my axe held high, shouted, 'Did any cunt see anything?' There was a long pause with no answer. 'Eh, anyone see what the fuck just happened?' This time the odd anonymous 'no' came back, while the rest of them stared at the floor. 'Right!' I said. 'Just as fucking well!' And with that, I left.

Back in the shop, I shelved my axe and lit a smoke; I'd always found it easy to get angry but difficult to calm down. We'd nipped the problem in the bud and, as far as I was concerned, the matter was closed. About ten minutes later, I heard shouting outside, and as soon as the bus which had stopped outside the door had pulled off, I could make out Davy, so I jumped round the counter and ran outside. Basically, when Davy had parked up, he'd blocked in some guy's motorbike, and when the guy had gone to move it, he'd burst his tyre. Now he was blaming Davy and Davy was telling him to get to fuck. After about two minutes the guy punched Davy a fucker and sent him flying, so of course I was now wrestling with the cunt, rolling about on the pavement. It didn't take me long to see that, although he was a fit guy, he had little fight in him, and after a few digs he'd essentially taken a step back to make an exit. But just then, from fucking nowhere, Davy cracked a baseball bat right across his head, splitting it like a watermelon.

I don't know whether it's a sixth sense or just a good nose for aggro, but as soon as his limp body hit the slabs, I knew there'd be comeback. After the Steve Gilmore escapade I'd promised myself that I'd only pick up the war-hammer through need and not through choice. The Old Salt was a threat to my business, so sorting it out was a necessity, but sorting out this prick, now a wilted pulp on my doorstep, wasn't. As the ambulance men scooped him up and carried him away, the police seemed more determined than ever to make it an issue – probably on account of it happening in broad daylight and in full view of anyone who cared to look. Still, in the eyes of the law, I was just breaking it up, so I wasn't lifted. Davy was. The next morning I got a call from a mate of mine at Leith police. I won't say who, but he was calling to say that the cunt Davy had clobbered was from a family of tinkers – well, Masons, but they had a tinker mentality – and he was one of four brothers. When I heard that, I felt my adrenalin surge.

When Susan gave birth to Steven, I was over the moon, not only because I was having another kid, but because he'd be a brother to Rod, and I knew that having a brother in life is an asset. Friends come and friends go, but a brother will fight to the death for ever, and in my world that's hard to come by. I sat for a moment with my cup of tea and lit a smoke. I'd have to play this one right – I'd have to use my head. If I went chasing after them, I'd get grabbed. Everyone knew about it and, like I said, if brothers are prepared to fight to the death, then I'd have to kill them all – and that meant doing life for a bunch of tinkers. Fuck that! No, the only way to deal with it was let them hit me. That way I'd have a fighting chance of avoiding jail when I cut their fucking throats out. Like the morning of the attack on the village and like the morning of the robbery, I stood in front of the mirror and stared without seeing. Today I was a warrior; today I was alive! I took a deep breath, covered my face with water and steadied myself. Once again, like I'd done ten years before, I kissed goodbye to family like there was no tomorrow, and left for work.

The drive took ages, only a couple of miles on the road but a hundred in my head. For some reason I felt anxious, like I had too much to lose, and now, just as things were really taking off, I'd been shoved back to square one. Bastard! As I sat in traffic at the foot of Canonmills staring at the grey road, the grey sky, the taxis pulling in and out from amongst the vans making their deliveries, the fear which had engulfed me like it does all men began to wilt, only to be replaced by a deep, envious loathing of the faceless people around me. All they had to do was perform their automated tasks. My fear had made me jealous. They didn't have to deal with what I had to. I felt alone. But as I sat, I began looking inside. I remembered the simple journeys that I'd made, so heedless of other people. Was the guy who pulled up next to me at the lights having the worst day of his life? Was the Indian who sold me my fags at the counter on autopilot, his head embroiled in his own personal tragedy? All through my life I'd made countless trips with a heavy heart, and, deep within my own introspection, had always planted myself at the centre of the universe. I'd envied the happy: the couple standing laughing at a bus stop, the whistling bastard jumping into his flash motor, the average Jim, suited up and unaware of his own blandness. But only now, looking at the insignificant dots of people at a distance, did I realise the relativity of suffering. The dots stood alone, but not in isolation. Regardless of what was happening, it had happened to a million dots before, and would happen to a million dots to come. And now, for some reason, my own insignificance, the very thing which had until now been a foe, was a friend. As I pulled open the shutters, like the raising of a portcullis, I knew that today it would be sorted. I'd let go of mortality and now stood at the ready.

I'd thought about putting a team together and hiding them in a van along the road, but I'd just have them sitting there all day, so instead I opted for a gas gun, a bayonet and, of course, my hand axe. By lunch-time nothing had happened, and soon, being a Saturday, I got caught up in the pace of trading. It was only when a young friend of mine, who knew about the problem, said he'd seen two of the brothers standing outside the Army and Navy store a few doors up, that I knew it was game on. By half-three, the three brothers and two other fucks were all drinking pints of 'Dutch courage' in the Red Lion. They'd need it. Half an hour later I was standing talking to my wee pal Gavin Castle, when from nowhere all five of them came steaming into the shop, bulldozing my punters out of the way and knocking them down like skittles. I dived behind my counter and clenched my gun, just as the lead brother raised his blade to slash me. Bang! I discharged the gun right in his fucking face, blowing out his eyes as he crumpled to the ground like the wet bag of piss that he was. No sooner had he dropped than I grabbed my hand axe with my right hand, and with my bayonet in my left began swinging like a freestyle swimmer, hack-hacking away and cutting anything I could. As the four powered down on me, I fought like fuck and for tomorrow as I tried to push the chaos out the door and onto the street. And all the time I was saying to myself, 'Stay on your feet. Stay on your feet,' 'cause I knew if I went down I'd be dead. Finally the whirlwind began to move, as we all flew out the door in a total frenzy, and when we did the man to my left dropped.

I didn't know it then, but my mate Gavin, who'd legged it at first, had run back and stabbed one of them in the back, puncturing his kidney and lacerating an artery. Just then I lost my axe as it stuck in some cunt's femur, leaving me half-shredded and seconds away from dropping to my knees. When I did, I lost my bayonet as the two that were left kept kicking and punching me like the rabid dogs that they were. Then I felt a thud on the back of my head, which jolted me forward, but as I reeled back up, I looked skyward through my mashed-up eyes and saw a raised hand brandishing my bayonet, ready to strike. As I closed my lids and prepared to die a winner, I threw up my hand as a reaction, whereby the cold steel embedded in my palm and severed my fingers. For that, and that alone, I'd lived.

Now, had it been downtown New York or lunch-time Mogadishu, few eyebrows would have been raised; but it wasn't, it was Costa del Edinburgh and I was in trouble. They wanted to throw the book at me, and in part they did, but not in the usual way. I had to pull strings and call in favours to avoid prosecution and, even though it was self-defence, the bottom line was that I'd gone too far. My time had come to move on. So, while my hand healed up, we bought next door to the house, number 30 Inverleith Row, and knocked it through to make an old folk's home, while I buried an old ghost and bought 1 Boswall Road, the old Yacht Club, for two hundred grand in cash. That felt good. Edinburgh had served me well and for a while I enjoyed my retirement, but I soon found my wanderlust was all-consuming. I needed a goal, I needed an adventure, and like it always did, opportunity came from nowhere.

'Hello, Rod,' said a voice from behind the railings. I didn't turn but shuddered. I turned the key to lock my Bentley, which was parked beside my Jag under the towering presence of the Boswall Road residence – the symbols of my triumphs. 'What's wrong – you forgotten me?' I took a deep breath and glanced down to see a distorted reflection staring up from my royal blue paintwork. It was him. I stopped and, still unable to face him, I cursed his timing like a cleaned-up junkie facing a dealer. Like 20 years before, I'd been looking for something and found it in him. Now rich with cars, and a swimming-pooled home with more rooms than I knew what to do with, I should have been happy, but I wasn't – it all seemed so hollow. And it was. I paused. Then, within that pocket of indecision, I paused some more. The smell of the salty Firth came drifting across my drive, bringing with it a scattering of autumn leaves, which danced around my pristine shoes and onto my well-worked flowerbeds. I had got it all – but was it me? I glanced again and began to smile. No – never!

'All right, Ivan. It's fucking good to see you!'

'And you, Roddy, and you. God,' he said, standing back and looking about. 'You've done well for yourself, I must say. You really are the man who's got everything, aren't you?'

I said nothing.

'Really, I mean it. Nice cars, a big house, plenty of money – absolutely everything.' He paused. 'You must be bored shitless!'

I was taken aback; that wasn't the compliment I'd been expecting. But I shrugged my shoulders; it was the truth.

'Why don't you come and work for us? We're looking for shipping contractors. You know, ones we can trust.'

'Ones you can trust, eh? Well, who's "us"?' I asked him. 'And where would I be working?'

'South Africa. I'm serving my country again.'

'Oh, God.' I knew what that meant: trouble.

'Interested in hearing about it?'

I thought for a second, but no sooner had I thought about releasing the hounds than I began to get a feeling I'd long since forgotten: excitement! I'd missed that. Then, after another minute of soul searching, I walked to the gates.

'All right, fuck it! Susan's going to kill me for this one, though,' I moaned. 'Right, you mad bastard, you want a pint?'

He knew me too well.

Two weeks later I bought two sister ships from Glenlight Shipping in Greenock, and named them the *Boston Trader* and the *Boston Belle*. Then, a week after that, we sailed them through the Caledonian Canal and on to Leith Docks, where I began their refit; a bastard of a job, which resulted in the scrapping of the *Belle* as she lost her integrity. But who cared? I didn't. Within weeks I would be back where I belonged: on the edge and pushing the envelope. And whereas before, I was lamenting an end, now, I was celebrating a beginning. I couldn't wait.

CHAPTER IV

LARGE FISH 'N' SHIPS

The locals call it Mosi-oa-Tunya: 'the smoke that thunders'. And while I sat there sipping my Mainstay and Coke, it did. There's a magic here: the towering column of spray so thick it becomes a mist, the roar of the water so powerful it's felt in your chest as it plummets into a terrifying abyss where, somewhere at the bottom, snaking away in the distance, Victoria Falls becomes the Zambezi River. This was Africa as I remembered it; the land where paradise beds down with bedlam. I was home. I'd left my diesel-soaked rags in Durban and now sat in my blazer and flannels on an opulent chair on a colonial veranda harking back to a bygone era. I was at the Victoria Falls Hotel, awaiting my host – the Fern.

The Fern was an old friend of mine. We'd been in the Guards together, but while I went off fighting someone else's war, he'd stayed in and fought our own. Now, long after the Army, he'd risen through the ranks of SIS and found himself stationed on the seventh floor of Corner House, so-named because it sat on the corner of Samora Machel Avenue and Leopold Takawira Street, Harare, at the British High Commission. As part of his brief, he oversaw Mozambique and, as fate would have it, he now oversaw me; the result of a chance encounter in the unlikeliest of places and under the worst ever circumstances as, once again, I'd managed to stumble into someone else's conflict in the name of money and mayhem.

In the late '80s, Mozambique was still in a war, which had been shafting the country since 1975. After independence from Portugal, democracy fell flat on its arse. Frelimo, the governing party, established a one-party Marxist state and outlawed its rivals. Renamo, the rebels, were formed in 1976 by the then Rhodesian government (Zimbabwe before its independence) to fight its own rebels: the Rhodesian liberation movement operating from Mozambique. With Zimbabwean independence in 1980 (the blacks taking back their country), Renamo was taken over by the South Africans, who used it to destabilise Mozambique. Supporting them was a way to frustrate the feared 'black communists' in the neighbouring countries. At its military peak from the mid to late 1980s, Renamo comprised well over 20,000 fighters and received financial support from anti-communist movements in the USA, West Germany and Portugal.

On the other side was the FAM, the armed wing of Frelimo. The FAM was a conscription-based army, which, during the 1980s, comprised as many as 80,000. While some units were well trained, the FAM depended on Zimbabwean support and Tanzanian soldiers. Otherwise, they were pretty shit.

After much fucking about, the then governments of South Africa and Mozambique signed the Nkomati Accord in 1984. The treaty was a promise not to support hostile acts against each other. Mozambique kept their promise and closed the ANC bases, so hated by the apartheid government, but South Africa unofficially continued their support for Renamo, in part, due to a fracturing in the South African state when rogue elements in the military began conducting their own war in Mozambique. And one of the ways in which they did this was by using people like me: civilian contractors whose ships ran under flags of convenience. So in amongst legitimate cargo, I'd run weapons to Renamo – a highly dangerous but lucrative pastime.

For the security services, both British and foreign, the nation's strategic importance went well beyond its geopolitical position. To begin with, Mozambique had enormous mineral potential. The world's largest reserves of colombo-tantalite, which is used to make nuclear reactors, aircraft and missile parts, are located in the central Zambezia province. Mozambique is also the second most important producer of beryllium, another highly desired strategic mineral. But beyond that, the country, located on the Indian Ocean, has a 2,000-mile coastline with three major ports: Maputo, Beira and Nacala, which were all well suited for naval bases during the Cold War.

Now, here's the twist. Because Mozambique supported Britain during the Lancaster House negotiations leading to Zimbabwean independence, Mozambique, a Marxist country during the Cold War, enjoyed surprisingly good relations with the British government, who even handed them masses of aid and military assistance, particularly between 1984–7. It's also thought that Margaret Thatcher played a role in dissuading Ronald Reagan from supporting Renamo – something of a coup, considering they supported every other bloody thing that attempted to fuck the Soviets. What did this all mean? Well, in lay terms, although the Fern and me were allies in the war, technically we were 'enemies' for the battle. But then that was only technically – I was no fucking 'Morse tapper'! As I said, I was in it for the cash and the adventure, but if I could help out Queen and country, then all the better.

Since 1986, South Africa had declared a state of emergency. Thousands of activists were detained while hit squads eliminated scores more at will. The leading element in this repression for the military was an offshoot of the Special Forces known as the Civil Cooperation Bureau (CCB). These guys were bastards. And as Ivan was a leading member, that made them my employers. As usual I did nothing in halves, so instead of making a few quid by taking a load of small arms and flogging it to the highest bidder, I was attempting to stash boxes of light weaponry – donated by the CCB – and ferry it up the coast in a gauntlet of death. I hoped it wouldn't be mine.

My first ever meeting with the CCB took place in the Sheraton International, Pretoria, less than an hour's drive north of Johannesburg. At the time, Pretoria was a staunch bastion of hard-line Afrikanerdom, with its historic buildings and jacaranda trees, whose purple blossoms blanketed the city like a covering of sugar over rotten meat. To me, Pretoria was every bit the picture postcard and, like nature itself, cared little for politics, unlike Ivan however, who did. Although I was meant to meet him, he got pulled away at the last minute, leaving me to face them alone. But fuck it, I thought, what difference would it make? With at least another two weeks before my boat was ready, and another month's sail-time down, it was still important to touch base with them. Anyway, I'd heard a lot about the characters I'd be dealing with, and although I'd already met a few of them at an earlier stage, this was to be the first time we'd do business. I was nervous. Having said that, I was also here for another reason.

Johannesburg owes its existence to a precious yellow metal called gold, and is surrounded by mines that descend for miles into the earth. After spending a load of money on property and the buying of my boats, I still had a lump of cash that I needed to secure. These were the days before Proceeds of Crime legislation, but the law could still take your dough, and I wasn't having that. I'd always had a policy at home that the passports never left the mantelpiece. And now, by that same logic, I was looking for somewhere to go in a hurry. So, to me, buying gold bars at source and stashing them in a safety deposit box seemed like an obvious thing to do. Besides, I knew that Ivan and the CCB would help me.

Ivan had put me in touch with Eugène De Jong, a former member of 32 Battalion – the famed Special Forces unit of the South African Army that was in the midst of working with insurgent leader Jonas Savimbi in Angola to hold the Cubans at bay. He was also someone who'd play a leading role with Executive Outcomes, the South African mercenary outfit who'd soon service Africa's mining cartels, and with whom I'd later do business. I'd already met with him in a smoky room in London, but that's one of those things I can't go into. To be honest, I was out on a limb. Looking back I'd have done it differently, but then having the bottle to be 'limbless' was one of my assets. I was alone, in a land where life felt cheap, trying to set up a deal with the most unfavourable section of the world's most unfavourable government! Potentially, I couldn't have pissed off more people if I'd tried.

From start to finish, the whole meeting could have come straight from a film. At the airport, the evening before, I was met by a white driver in a black suit, unusual for the country, who seemed to know everything but gave away nothing, while my only contact with my hosts was a note left in the hotel lobby, insisting I spare no expense and enjoy the full fruits of CCB hospitality. I politely declined when the hooker arrived at my door; they obviously didn't know I'd owned a brothel, and so knew every trick in the book. Half an hour later a man arrived, said his name was Stefano and was here to please. I couldn't believe it. I'd obviously been the only punter to knock back a shag, so they'd thought I was a 'shirt lifter'! I just laughed.

The next morning I woke up early to run a few laps of the surrounding area before breakfast. In reality I was scouting for the British Embassy; the first sign of trouble and I'd be over the fence. My meeting wasn't until the early evening so I spent most of the day watching videos and smoking fags. As the time approached, I started to feel the nerves. Once again I was about to have a meeting that could change my life for ever, only this time it wasn't my own doubt that gave me the fear, but my inability to control those around me. I'd spent years being a big fish in a small pond and, within that pond, I'd built myself security as I sat on the inside looking out. Now, my wanderlust and search for adventure had brought me here, and here was the real badlands. As a kid on the trawlers, I'd lie alone in my bunk, all damp and cold in the ship's deep bowels, picturing it capsizing, and saying to myself, 'Down is up and left is right!' That was Africa: a world devoid of logic, which changed like the wind. Still, each change was duly noted.

Surveillance is an art. Cops watching you are usually pretty easy to spot. They're mid-30s, clean-cut with uniform sideburns. And although they'll moan about it, special cops, like the drug squad, aren't much better. You see, they can dress the part and talk it up – fuck, they can even stop washing for a month – but unless you live the life you're trying to portray, there's always the giveaways, like teeth, nails and a healthy skin. Besides, most of them are in their prime and male, in case it kicks off. And it often does. Now security services are good, but

Customs are better. Customs and Excise, albeit a shower of bastards, are the magicians. They could be anybody – and when I say anybody, I mean anybody! Old fat bastards who couldn't catch a bus or wee skinny women who couldn't fight sleep: nothing was beyond them. Anyway, I knew someone might be onto me, I just didn't know whom, for what, and, more importantly, what they were going to do about it.

As the time approached half-six, I made my way down the stair to where I'd meet Eugène. On entering the bar area, I felt the familiar feeling of an upmarket hotel-chain lounge. In the corner sat a failed concert pianist, playing to an audience who didn't listen, his efforts reduced to audible wallpaper, especially to the bar staff, whose stifling courtesy leaped out from behind their kitsch golden-embroidered waistcoats. Although still early evening, the mix of people was as unique to the chain as the uniform interiors themselves. At one end of the bar sat a heavy and suntanned man, his big calloused hands protruding from a poorly fitting jacket. His obvious discomfort in a tie was only upstaged by his jeans and the white socks he revealed when he leant forward from his bar stool to sip on his cold Lyon beer.

A few spaces along sat a suited man, reading a book and enjoying his drink. His relaxed manner suggested familiarity with a life of international solitude, a salesman of some kind, or something that kept him on the move. He was the sort of person who'd have the same ritual each evening, of having a drink then heading off to a table for one, before getting his 'arse skelped' by the likes of Angie, in whatever currency his host country used. Behind him, sitting at a table, was a big-hatted Japanese lady in her early 50s. Her large-framed sunglasses, Hermes scarf and safari-suit outfit complemented the small chihuahua dog she was feeding peanuts to and treating like a child – fucking mad! Not too far away from her sat two mutton-dressed-as-lamb types – the only fucking thing missing from these gold-diggers was a prospector's pan. So I decided to steer clear and, after giving it some thought, I opted for a seat by the window. At least that way I could keep an eye on the door. After about five minutes, two men arrived and made their way over.

'I'm Joost De Vries and this is Eugène De Jong, who you've already met,' said a large figure with some effort as he took a deep breath to lean over and extend his shovel-like hand. Then, falling back into his chair and loosening his tie to reveal a button line about to burst, he opened a file, which he made no attempt to conceal, and began to browse by licking his fat fingers and flicking from one page to another. After a minute of awkward silence, he continued in his rough Afrikaner accent, 'Thanks for coming to see us,' but with a pace and monotone that suggested he was thinking aloud. I instantly began to hate him.

At that point, I stopped him. I was no fucking kid and this was no fucking interview. 'Wait a minute, pal,' I said firmly. 'Put your file away. If you need to browse your notes at this stage, then I don't want to do business with you, right?' I leant in. 'Let's cut the shit. I've got a boat, and I'm going to be running the east coast. I want $20,000 off you per trip, and I get to carry my own cargo as well. Beyond that, I'll run as much as you want to where you want it.' The fat fuck almost choked on his own tongue, while Eugène smirked. 'Oh, and by the way,' I added, 'do you know anyone who's selling gold?' The beefy bastard took an already sweat-soaked hanky and began to mop his porous brow.

'All right,' he said, and with that he slammed shut his file before rocking back and forward like an Olympian on a luge, in an attempt to hoist himself up. Christ, I thought, as he finally made it, it's like a fucking eclipse. Then he smiled. 'Nice meeting you, Rod. Eugène will take care of the rest.' And with that he was off.

Eugène, on the other hand, was more my kind of guy. In some ways he reminded me of Colin Patterson. He was a big lad, and serious about his work. But you could tell he'd been to hell and back, and when he had, he'd felt out of place. He explained to me how things were done, who else was doing it, and the type of gear I'd be carrying, before detailing the various risks. Of the half-hour we spoke, he spent 25 minutes on the risks. I couldn't wait! With that, we made a gentlemen's agreement before heading off in his Mazda pick-up to a favoured gold trader, where I parted with a hundred grand. I then stashed the gold in a Pretorian bank sympathetic to CCB. That would be my equivalent to a Liechtenstein bank account.

My contacts had soon placed me right at the centre of their dirty war. From the outside, their world seemed like a warren of secrecy, so complex that even the rabbits didn't know what was what. But from the inside, it was a lot simpler, and it didn't take me long to map out who was who. My contract was to be with Free State Shipping. They were a front company for CCB and their actions over the border. To add an air of authenticity, they'd also supply civilian products, so anything from shampoo to beer fetched a price, and, like anything in a war zone, that price was handsome. Having their front companies trade wasn't all that unique. In fact, another CCB agent I'd met, Slang van Zyl, a cop of ten years, was forced to quit after ten months because the private detective agency he was fronting became too bloody successful. In time, Free State would make good money, and even though I'd do my best to rip them off, they'd still get a few quid for their troubles, which kept everyone happy.

After a month's preparation back in Edinburgh, we were off. I'd always planned to make the most of my long journey down south, so I stopped off in Freetown, Sierra Leone, to do a bit of shopping. Apart from being the capital, Freetown's the principal port of Sierra Leone, and is one of the best natural harbours on the west coast of Africa. I already had a ship full of knocked generators, which I'd sourced in England and had a buyer for in Namibia, a country still under South African administration, but Freetown was a buyer's market, and I couldn't resist it. You never knew what the specials would be: diamonds, gold or even arms. What I was to find was even better. Forged money in those days was literally only as good as the paper it was printed on. Even now, with today's digital colour printers, making quality fakes costs nothing, but what gives them away is their waxy feel. A friend of mine, 'Mad Irish Willy', a true swashbuckler and major drug haulier, put me on to an English guy, Matt, who then came to see me. As soon as I saw him, I could tell he was no bandit. Apart from the stubble and the yellow teeth from coffee, he was every bit the spook. I didn't like it. But when he pulled out his dollars, I swear I couldn't tell the difference. He said the paper had been stolen in the US en route from the mill. Technically, then, what he was offering was real dough! And all he wanted was ten to one. That's one dollar for every ten fakes. In the end I gave him ten grand in sterling for just short of two hundred grand in dollars. If I couldn't tell the difference, then there's no way some Somali fuck, in poor light and with a good foot up his arse, was going to.

After two days in Freetown we were getting set to leave. I'd just made my last all-important purchase: a Type 77, 12.7 mm belt-fed, anti-aircraft machine gun. It was a fucking belter straight from Chairman Mao himself. As we manhandled it up to the bridge, where I could make the most of its 800 m surface range, I saw a man standing on the dockside. He was an old friend of mine, an SAS man who'd started in the Guards with me. I can't say his real name, so I'll call him Ian, but soon he'd also become part of the Executive Outcomes outfit and was someone I've had recent contact with over a job in West Africa. Although I was surprised to see him, Freetown was a former British colony, and was still friendly to the Crown. So much so that parts of the British task force had stopped off to resupply en route to the Falklands, so I figured they'd have teams there from time to time. I jumped down from the bridge and gestured him over, but he was reluctant to jump aboard. I was surprised. As I crossed the gangway, he seemed anxious, and almost hesitant to talk to me. 'Sorry, Roddy,' he said, constantly looking around. 'I can't stop, you know how it is – just need to let you know that Matt had his throat cut last night off the fuzzies. They'll be watching you. I wouldn't stick about.' And with that, he was off. As I stood there trying to figure it out, part of it came to me: Matt and Ian must have been working together, possibly for the British services, and I'd just been given a warning to get out of Freetown, and a helping hand in getting to South Africa. You might even say a $200,000 one. Somebody really wanted me there. Still, I wonder how they knew?

So, with little thought, I decided to take his advice and shift. Africa gives few warnings and no second chances. If they were watching me, and they really had cut Matt's throat, then the chances were they'd know I was sitting on a pile of cash – which I was. In port, it's a risk you take, something you have to factor in when you're picking your crew. For the *Trader* I employed a team of five: three locals hired as skeleton crew, and two whom I'd brought with me from Edinburgh. The first was Brian Daily: a great guy. A total fucking madman who was probably the best grafter I've ever known. In all the years I'd used him, I never once saw him standing about clawing his arse. His whole family was Polish – 'Daily' coming from his mum marrying an Englishman. And standing at over 6 ft 4 in., with biceps the size of Bristol, Daily could fight for fun. Like the rest of them, he was an Army man, but had got a dishonourable discharge after a fight one night while stationed in Osnabrück, Germany. Five locals had jumped him and his pal after a night out as they crossed a bridge back to barracks. Daily had pulled his blade and set about cutting them to shreds, while his pal, an Army boxer, gave them a bit of the old 'Mills magic'. During the fight, Daily had lost his knife, and so grabbed a hold of whatever he could and bit some bastard's nose so hard that he snapped off his own tooth – and left it embedded in his face. Now that, taking into account five burly farmers attacking two drunken squaddies, and the fact that he'd 'taken the knife off them', should have been self-defence. And it would have been, but Daily, the mad bastard, then proceeded to pick each of them up and hurl them over the bridge! So instead of tea and medals, it was bread and water, and a four-year stretch in a German chokey. Still, at least it taught him the language.

The second of the two was a Welshman called Taffy. Another wee man with a big spirit, he was a Falklands War veteran who'd fought at Mt Longdon with 3rd Para, but had spent the next three years suffering from post-traumatic stress, so he'd joined the Merchant Navy as he liked the space and, believe me, the sea's a great healer. And it worked. But soon, 'Taffy the Cured' got bored, so he joined me. I was glad to have him. He was an easygoing guy who never moaned, and as long as he had plenty of fags and three square meals a day, he'd soldier on under most conditions. Apart from that, though, another thing which kept Taffy going was the fact that the further south we went, the cheaper the hookers became. Come to think of it, by the time we reached the Cape, I'm sure there were a few tins of Spam missing!

LARGE FISH 'N' SHIPS

As for the locals, I'd picked them up in Freetown. They were 'Mad Irish Willy's' boys, local Mendes men from the south of the country, and they came with a recommendation. Time would tell whether that was to be justified, but little did I know that that time was soon. Anyway, as the *Trader* eased herself out of Freetown, the sun began to set while a blanket of stars appeared before the darkness fell. Freetown's a humid place, so a cool sea breeze which ventilates both your body and soul is like sunshine on a rainy day. Next stop, Namibia.

The *Trader* itself was a well-worked supply ship. The bridge and berthing space sat at the stern overlooking a long deck, ideally built for all kinds of freight. It was never the fucking QE2, but the living quarters weren't all that bad – especially compared to other work ships. The crew berthed aft in one large compartment that spanned the full width of the hull. Rows of portholes on both sides kept it bright and well ventilated, while I enjoyed my own office space and quarters, which sat just behind the galley. The galley itself was surprisingly spacious, with a long rectangular table and two rows of seats welded to the deck. Above hung a large TV set, which I'd linked to the latest VCR money could buy, specially stolen for the job. To the untrained eye, this kind of ship can seem like a death trap. As seasoned travellers, we're all used to glossy paint jobs and the fine finishings which make living rooms of our travel space. A freighter's a more hostile environment. There's a lot of surface rust, a lot of smoke and a shit-load of noise. Sometimes it's from the engine room, sometimes it's from the waves bashing against the structure and sometimes it seems to come from nowhere. But, like the noise, Africa has a habit of generating things from nowhere – and it's usually trouble.

After a couple of hours I slowed her down to 4 knots while we had our dinner. The sea was like a plate as the stillness of the night struggled to find wind to breathe. And while the moon shone down, casting a mirage of silhouettes on the distant boats ferrying to and from the port, I sat staring at this real-life canvas while using the horizon as a frame. It was almost the end to another very long day and, as I hadn't planned on leaving till late the next morning, in our rush to exit I'd been unable to sleep. So, earlier than normal, I gave

Taff the wheel, and while the rest of the boys enjoyed *An Evening with Bernard Manning and Thirty-Three Strippers*, I headed onto the deck for a quick hatch check before putting my head down. As I walked about, I felt content. After years of struggling through Edinburgh and all the shite that went with it, I'd rewarded myself by coming back to the same fucking place I'd started. I should never have left. As I walked the length of the deck, deep in my thoughts, I was interrupted by a weird smell, almost like really potent BO. After trying to figure it out, I blamed it on the algae and left.

It felt like I'd been asleep for two seconds, but when I heard the thump on my cabin door, my watch told me it had been two hours. I jumped up and threw on my jeans, then, bare-chested, I flew out onto the deck where right at the bow, some 70 yards ahead, I saw a ball of people scrapping like fuck. 'What the fuck's going on?' I shouted, ready to lose it. The last thing I'd have on my ship was a bunch of drunken bastards brawling away!

But as I ran over, I heard Daily behind me. 'Watch out, boss!' and then the sharp crack of a .9 mm discharge. The human ball stopped moving. A second later I was there, and found my three Mendes covered in sweat and standing panting over a crumpled figure now lying flapping about like roadkill in the wind. I couldn't believe it – a fucking stowaway!

I grabbed a hold of the guy and dragged him the length of the deck, back to the bridge house. He'd been given a right good hiding. But now, even though everything was in hand, my three Mendes kept ranting away. I asked Joseph, the oldest of the three and the one with the best English, what the fuck was going on.

'Mr Rod, Mr Rod,' he flapped in his pidgin tongue. 'That one is a bad one.'

I looked about and paused. Then, unsure, I looked at Taff and Daily. We all looked back at him. 'A bad one?' I said. 'What do you mean?' I held out my hands as if to say, why?

'Is Temne!' he replied.

'Temne? What the fuck's Temne?' I said, turning to Daily. Just then the second of the three, Brown, stood forward and, signalling himself and his two colleagues, said, 'We Mende. He . . .' pointing at their pulped-up victim, 'Temne!'

'Ah, right!' I said, the penny dropping. 'He's from another tribe. Sierra Leone's got near 20 of them. I think the Mende and the Temne are the two big ones. Right?'

No one answered.

'Well, what do we do with him?' said Daily.

As I stood there thinking about it, Joseph piped up again. 'Mr Rod, we . . .' And with his hands he mimed throwing the bastard over the side with weights tied round his ankles. 'Is a bad one, Mr Rod.'

I put my hand out, but more to shut him up than to say no to his idea. No doubt it was an option.

As we stood about, now trying to decide on the condemned man's fate, I had a hundred ideas running through my mind. To be honest, I could have done with an extra body, and since the bastard was as good as dead anyway, I had plenty of shit jobs he could do for the privilege of being kept alive. On the other side of the coin, something wasn't sitting right. Part of me was sure he was tied into the whole dockside affair, but I couldn't figure it out. Anyway, whatever I was going to do would have nothing to do with whatever football team he supported. Mende, Temne – who gave a fuck? I'd left 'yobbing' in Edinburgh.

'Are we sure that's the last of the fucks?' I shouted to Daily, as I went to spark a smoke. He looked at me blankly. So while Daily gave the place a good going over, I sent Taff back up to the bridge. Ten minutes later, Daily was back.

'Nothing! But I found his bits and pieces under the bow crane.'

In his hands were a couple of maize cobs, a pack of smokes, a small torch and an ageing Colt 45 handgun.

'Some stowaway! Sure that's it?' I said, now holding the gun and checking the chamber.

'Definitely, boss.'

'And a torch? A torch? Why's he got a torch? He's a stowaway. He knows he's going to be adrift for days, yet instead of water, he brings a fucking torch. Who's he wanting to signal, eh?' I felt my anger start to surge, so I took the torch and leant right down into his face. Then, in a lowered voice which became a whisper, I spoke to a man who couldn't understand my words but knew exactly what I was saying. 'What's this for? Eh, cunt? Who're you trying to flash?' I took my cut-throat from my back pocket and held it to his neck. As I pressed it in, I saw the terror pulse through his body, while each one of his heartbeats seemed to energise me. But when it did, I sensed that for the first time ever, another man's fear was making me stronger. So as soon as I realised, I stopped, but sat there transfixed. This wasn't who I wanted to be, but by default I'd become it, and now, like so many times before, I was wrestling with my own humanity. Then, almost on impulse, I whispered, 'I'm going to let you live.' I paused. 'For now – even though my common sense has already killed you. I don't know what this is for.' I held the torch against his cheek. 'But if you've put my boat in danger – so God is my witness, you'll suffer!' Then I stood up and went back into the galley to grab a roll of gaffer tape, which I tossed at Daily. 'Tie the bastard's hands and feet and stick him in the engine room shite-house.' I laughed to mask my introspection. 'If there's no problems by morning, we'll let him out.' Humanity had won!

While Daily set about his task with the help of the Mendes, I bolted up to the bridge and found Taff glued to the radar. 'What do you see?' I said insistently.

'Nothing, boss. The usual traffic, but nothing on us.' I had a glance then took a seat and tried to figure it out. I looked around, then down at my safe. Inside was thirty grand in dollars and ten grand in sterling, but lumped in with my fake bills it reached the best part of a quarter million – a shitload of dough. Fuck! Then I had my cargo, thousands of pounds' worth of generators and satellite phones, which I'd had knocked for the occasion. I looked at my watch: only half past midnight. It was going to be a long time till morning. I lit a smoke, grabbed an OVD rum and walked out onto the upper deck: a small walkway that led around the wheelhouse. The night was so beautiful, so clear, yet filled with such uncertainty. I hated the waiting game, and on a boat it was worse. Trouble at sea is different from fighting on land, 'cause when it really kicks off, you can't just dig a hole and hide, you've got to stand your ground and take it. I thought back to Allan Patterson that day in the armoury, of how I'd have no one to call and, more importantly, of how having a heart in Africa was like a lead weight around your soul; it would kill you. In my dream-like state I saw him thump me. I saw him thumping me over and over again like a stuck record in my mind, while all the time this voice kept whispering '*Si vis pacem, para bellum! Si vis pacem, para bellum! Si vis pacem, para bellum!*' – it was a Latin saying I'd learnt in the Guards: 'If you want peace, prepare for war!'

Like a bolt from nowhere it hit me: I was sitting in a comfort pocket of hope, a hope created by my own weakness as I tried to rationalise my inaction as the right thing to do. And it wasn't! I wasn't rationalising it, I was justifying it. I was justifying my own fragility. 'Fuck that and fuck them! If it's a fight they want, they'll have it.' Within a heartbeat I felt my ace begin to bubble like a simmering pot – then bang! It blew. Within two steps I was back on the bridge, then within two more I'd raised the Type 77 machine gun's tripod to cover the deck. 'Any problems, Taff – let fucking rip!'

He smiled. 'Sure thing, boss.'

'Oh, and stick her up to 14 knots. No need to save diesel tonight.'

A breath later, I was tearing down the narrow staircase, my clammy arms sliding against the cold metallic walls as she pitched in the swell. I continued down into the galley hold, where I stopped to pick up my R4 and a bunch of 5.56 mm rounds. The R4 was a South African-made light machine gun with a folding stock, which suited both Paratroopers and sneaky bastards like me. Weapon slung over my back and cut-throat in hand, I bolted forward, through the dark and noisy oil-stenched engine room to where Daily and two of the Mendes were standing. 'Right – out the fucking way!' I blasted, pushing the Mendes aside before swinging the door open to see our prisoner slumped against the can. 'Right, cunt!' I shouted as I grabbed his head and slashed him a fucker, right across his face, before I set about his body, slash-slashing away like a man putting some flames out. 'What's your game, eh? You cunt. What's your fucking game?' Then, with a surge of anger, I took the lacerated fuck, now squealing like a pig, and hauled him up to the deck, where I threw him down in an accumulating puddle of his own blood. 'Get me his torch!' I shouted to Daily. 'Let's see what the scores are!'

A minute later Daily was back so I pulled the bastard up, but he slumped and folded like a house of cards. 'If you don't fucking stand, I'll feed you to the sharks. Got it?' But he couldn't, the blood loss had made him weak. So I reached along and grabbed a length of line, then gestured the Mendes to pick him up and shuffle him along to the bow crane, where I lashed him tight against it. As the four of us stood staring at the motionless man, I thrust the torch into his hand and held my blade tight against his throat – humanity had lost.

'Make that signal!' I snarled, but he stayed still. 'Come on. Make that fucking signal!' I screamed, now right in his face. He still didn't flinch. He had bottle, I'd have to give him that. But, by now, I'd lost patience, so I disappeared down to the engine room and came back with a jerrycan filled with paraffin. I saw Daily wince: slashing's one thing but burning's another. As I doused him, his eyes sparked back to life as the pain from the fuel flooding his wounds began to blind him. He tried to speak but he couldn't, and whatever he said was a mumble of shite. I reached into my pocket, flipped open my Zippo and, with a few seconds' pause, struck up a flame and gestured to the blanket of darkness surrounding us. 'Last chance, cunt. Fucking signal!' But once again I stood in a moment that lasted for ever, as we four, the willing executioners, now held our breath. I felt my muscles flinch, but like a child standing over a high-dive board, desperate to jump but filled with hesitation, my conscience fought my hand. It twitched forward then stopped, forward then stopped. Then finally, in a victory for barbarism which I've often come to regret, I leapt off the board and into the realisation that I'd actually done it. He went up! As the other three jumped back, in part to avoid the flames, I stood there transfixed. I felt the heat on my face, and the acrid stench of paraffin and burning flesh filling my nose, but I couldn't move. I was hypnotised by the flames and his dance within them. His body bounced on the bow like a flaming figurehead.

'How's that for a signal?' I shouted, turning to Daily. 'Well?' He looked shocked. I unstrapped my R4 and tossed it over. 'Here, better to have it and not need it, than need it and not have it.'

He forced a laugh. 'Makes sense.'

'I don't know what the deal is, but there shouldn't be a problem. Just keep your eyes open and have a Mende on the bow all night. I'll let you work it out with them.' And with that, I headed back along the deck and up to the bridge. When I got there, Taff just looked at me. He'd watched the whole thing on a gigantic television, the wheelhouse window. I suppose burning bodies were the one thing he could have done without. 'All right, Taff?'

'Aye, boss. No problems,' he said, trying to fake out a sense of normality from a stormy mind.

I scanned the radar. 'What have we got?'

'There's been a couple of boats sharing our course for the last half-hour, but now there's only this one.' He pointed to a blip on the screen at the four o'clock. It was still a good two miles off, but shadowing our course.

'I need you to get it together, Taff,' I said, standing back for a moment to interrupt his glazed reverie. He looked at me. 'C'mon, pal, this isn't the fucking time for a phone call to Andy.' (Meaning the late-night Radio Forth problem phone-in.) 'If that cunt sails within a mile, you make a noise, right?!' He nodded. With that, I took another OVD and made for my bunk, where I lay down and searched for peace.

'There's no second chances out here,' I kept saying to myself. 'There's no second chances.' But as I tossed and turned, I felt delirium encroach while I saw his eyes, full of disbelief and pain, staring right through me from within the flames. I sat up and ripped my clothes off – they stank. I bagged them up before scrubbing myself down like a surgeon in theatre. 'I had to do it. I had to do it,' I told myself over and over again, like a 'stoner' trying to fend off a 'whitey' by saying 'it's just the gear'. This was the land of piracy, and not fucking Captain Blackbeard. I mean ruthless gangs that knock fuck out of your crew and make for the nearest port, in the nearest country where the locals will protect them. And I knew the script.

The ones that only rob can turn up in their tens at a time. But the bastards after your cargo can turn up mob-handed. Fuck, I'd heard of ships getting swarmed by 70 at once. And these were prime seas and this was the prime time, between 0100hrs and 0600hrs while everyone's either asleep, on the bridge or below decks in the noisy engine spaces. And as for Joan of Arc up there, I knew he was a fucking plant, ready to signal his pals when the coast was clear. Well, fuck him!

As I lay back, the cacophony of suggestive noises did well to calm me. I could hear the distant chug of the engines and the swell against the hull, which mixed with the rhythmic tones of the propeller, twisting away ahead of its wake. From a half-open porthole, a cool breeze rolled in off the sea, scenting my digs with a salty air that I loved. So, soon at peace, I started to drift. Sometimes my mind craves sleep; it shuts me down and I welcome it. As I slipped deeper and deeper, I escaped into dreams. But soon, like the first drink to remember before the second one to forget, so my dreamscape turned from relief to retribution. In my unconscious world I was trying to run, not away, but to something I loved, someone in danger, but I couldn't, I was shackled, and around my foot lay a ball and chain, which scraped along the ground like nails along a blackboard; my blood ran cold. And the more I tried, the heavier it became, and the heavier it became, the more the noise deafened me, until finally I looked down, and to my horror saw that what I was dragging was Mark's head; Mark, my mate who'd died in my arms while fighting the Simba. I jumped up wide awake and covered in sweat, and fought to regain my senses. But the noise continued. What the fuck? In the dark I fumbled for the light, then slung on my pants and tried to source the grinding noise, now punctuated by thuds. 'Taff!' I screamed, as I frantically slung on my boots and bent down to grab my kukri, before swinging open my door and bolting out. But fuck, I'd barely taken a step when bang! I ran right into him – some black bastard in overalls. I don't know who was more shocked, him or me, but before he had a chance to raise his arm, I stuck my blade right through his neck, hitting his jugular and erupting it like a geyser. He screamed, and with both hands round his gaping wound, dropped to his knees and panicked himself to death. It was then I realised – they'd used fucking grappling hooks. It was on!

As I clambered up the stairs, I heard a scramble on the bridge. Then, as I sighted the top, I saw a pair of legs standing on the third step but facing away from me. With all my strength I swung my curved blade, slicing it through an ankle and embedding it into a left shin. Then, letting go, I leaned in and pulled the helpless cunt all the way down the stairs to the galley, where I punched him time and time again till my fist had smashed right through his face and into his brain. I wrestled my blade out of his limp body and flew back up to the bridge to see Taff in a fight to the death over an AK47. The wee Welsh madman was rolling about with a coon twice his size and foaming at the mouth like a rabid dog. He was right back on Longdon. So I ran forward and toed the coon right in the throat, fracturing his windpipe. Taff finished the job by taking the rifle butt to his head like he was digging a hole, while I jumped to the wheel and jammed it hard right, making her pitch violently as she cut into the waves. 'Where's Daily – and where the fuck are they coming from?' I screamed.

'Fuck knows!' he shouted back, still laying into the well-dead coon.

'It's got to be the stern.' But as I made to look, I heard a cracking to my left followed by the muzzle flash of my Type 77; some cunt had opened up and was peppering my deck. Bastard! As I tried to make for the door to take him out, the whole place erupted like the Wild fucking West. I hit the ground to avoid the ricochets and flying glass, and fought like fuck to get to my senses. 'Taff! Taff!' I screamed. But as I looked around, the crazy bastard was already up and out, taking the fight to them, the AK47 pop-popping away while he screamed like a madman consumed by the Devil. Still low, I crawled my way back along the floor towards the left-side door, and to the Type 77, where, with a deep breath, I clenched my knife and busted out with an aim to ripping some cunt's head off. But to my total surprise, I saw it was Elson, one of my Mendes. He was fighting like fuck with blood gushing out of his head. I laughed to myself. Here's me chewing carpet, and my boys are up and at them! I'd have to pay them more.

'Elson!' I screamed, as I darted behind him and into a hail of scalding casings.

'Is down, boss. Is down,' he yelled, gesturing forward.

So I jumped alongside him to see the whole fucking deck moving as white-hot chards of metal danced up and about while the rounds pelted down and across. 'Give it to them,' I screamed, as I slapped his back and made for the stern. When I got there, I couldn't believe it: some cunt was at the wheel of a large inflatable with four ropes hooked to the lower deck. Bastards! I raced back into the bridge and down to a darkened galley, but no sooner had my feet touched the ground than I fell on my arse. As the ship began to pitch and roll even more, I flapped about like a man on ice, trying to regain my feet. But it wasn't frozen water, it was blood – eight pints of it – and all from the legless cunt I'd done just minutes before. A second later, the deck door burst open and a figure launched himself in. Like me, he hit the deck with a thud.

'Fuck me!' he screamed, as he started rolling about. It was Daily. And he was floundering in the blood while slapping his leg. So I looked down to see it smoking; it smelt like bacon. I took my cut-throat, pushed him face down on the soiled floor and ripped away at his jeans to see a two-inch chard of steel embedded in his calf and cooking his leg. So, burning my fingers, I yanked it out.

'There's three on the deck aft of the hold hatches, and another two down below who we got,' he mumbled in between the pain.

'Where are the Mendes?'

'One's on the bridge and one was down with me. I don't know about the third.'

At that I grabbed the R4 and bolted down a level to pick up more shells. Two seconds later I was right at the stern, where I leant over the rail to the see the whites of the wheelman's eyes looking up, hoping to see his pals. Instead, he saw me. I opened up with a full clip of 5.56 mm rounds from only a few feet away. I saw him and his entire boat burst before me like a hammer to a watermelon. I unhooked the ropes and tossed them over before legging it along the thin sidewalks connected to the deck. At the corner of the galley house I took a knee and tried to catch my breath. I looked up and shouted to Elson.

'Is OK, boss!' he yelled back, standing over his smoking barrel.

So I stood up and glanced along the deck to see four bodies stretched out in a line while Taff walked along kicking them, and then, on the third, he lowered his weapon and bang, shot right through the back of his head. As I ran out from the shadows, Taff turned and pointed his AK at me. 'It's me, you daft cunt,' I shouted, trying to sound as Scottish as possible.

'Christ almighty!' he said. 'I thought you were black. What the fuck's over you – oil?'

I didn't answer, and instead turned back to the galley. 'Daily!' I yelled.

'He's back down with Brown,' shouted Taff, but no sooner had he finished than two bodies came flying out on the end of Daily's boot. Then, as each of them tried to get to his feet, Daily hobbled up and booted both down again like he was kicking two footballs along the ground; close behind him came Brown.

As soon as it had started, it seemed to be over. I couldn't believe it.

'Right!' I said, taking stock. 'Taff, back up to the wheel. Take her down to 5 knots and put her back on course.'

'Elson!' I shouted at the top of my voice. 'You watch.' And with that, I gestured towards the sea. Then, in my own pidgin English, 'Anyone, come you. Fucking open up. Right.' And, turning to Daily, 'Have you seen Joseph?'

'Na, boss.'

'Brown – seen Joseph?' He shook his head. 'Are we sure that's them?'

'I've swept down below. I found this one,' he said, stamping down on the man's head, 'in the cargo hold amongst the generators and this one,' he said, kicking the other one in the ribs, 'in amongst the phones! But, na, no sign of Joseph!'

I paused to think. My adrenalin was pumping so hard that it made me sick. I'd already thrown up twice, but this time I was sick into my mouth and had to swallow it. Puking in front of the boys was never an option. 'Right! Here's what we'll do. We'll tape these cunts up and get the rest of them out. I need to know that we've got them all. There's one in the galley, one outside my cabin and one on the bridge. Any others? Oh, and we'll cut down Joan of Arc!' I said, pointing up to the bow crane. So I slung Brown my R4 and nodded below. While he went off to look about, I bound the men at my feet, then grabbed the three from inside the galley house and dragged them out. What a fucking mess. Then, with slight trepidation, I eased myself towards the bow. From a distance I could see a row of pure white teeth on a charcoaled face, bobbing up and down as the bow bounced and dipped between the waves. 'He's going right in the sea!' I said to Daily, and with that, I cut the ties and the crisp corpse fell to the ground.

'Boss!' I heard a faint scream from the distance, and then an echo, which came closer. 'Boss!' It was Elson, who'd run down to get me for Taff. 'Boss – Taff. He – you.'

So, with my mind already on the next hassle, I picked up the bit of toast to which I'd just attached significance, and hurled it into the deep. As I ran back up to the bridge I saw Brown re-emerge carrying the last of the three from below – still no Joseph! So I left him standing guard over the dead and dying while I took Daily up to the war council.

'There, boss,' said Taff, pointing to a blip on the screen.

As I leant in I saw it was the same vessel from before. It had been sitting at our four o'clock but had decided on now to start closing. 'Fuck that!' I said, shaking my head in disbelief. I jumped over to the window to see if I could see anything – nothing, all their lights were off. With nothing else around for miles, this had to be where the inflatable had come from. Christ. For all I knew there could have been swarms of the fucks on board – their launch numbers only limited to the size of the inflatable. Again I stopped dead and lit a smoke. What was I going to do? They wouldn't have had a signal back – but they couldn't know that we'd just given their party a hiding. This was it – do or die.

'Right. Daily, on the Type 77 – get it turned. Elson!' I screamed, leaning out of a broken window. 'See me in the galley.' I ran down the stairs to see the youngster on the bloodied floor sporting a bandage round his head like a woman out of the shower. 'With me,' I said. Even though I couldn't see them, they could still see me. Down in the galley-hold I frantically emptied two wooden fruit crates and passed them to Elson, while one store cupboard along I grabbed a chair and shoved it under his arm. As I ushered him back up to the deck, I ran to the engine room and took a second jerrycan of paraffin, which I manhandled up the mid-deck stairs to where Elson and Brown now stood over the bodies. 'Ready, boys,' I said to the bemused pair now wondering what the fuck I was up to. 'You're going to like this.' And with that I propped one crate on top of the other and taped them together. Then I dragged the bodies along the deck to a point 10 yards from the galley entrance where the side railing was the lowest and sat them side by side, facing out. 'Grab them!' I said, pointing to the prisoners. My two men looked at me. 'Fucking grab them!' I shouted again, with a rage they'd only seen directed at others. Within a heartbeat they brought them over and tied them down, one on the crate and one on a seat. 'Tie them up well. I don't want them moving about.' Then, still to their bemusement, I ran the length of the deck to where I kept some spare tyres for berthing. When I grabbed two, they realised exactly what was going on. They smiled – it's another fucking world out here.

As I threw each tyre around their heads, like I was winning a goldfish at the fair, they finished their tying before Elson took a hold of the paraffin. Then, with no prompting, he filled up the empty tyre insides with the stealth of a stagehand, before standing back in anticipation of the stage show. It's called the necklace – and there's nothing beyond it. I ran back up to the bridge to check the screen.

'Still coming at us, boss,' shouted Taff, with a mass of aggression.

'Right. Bring her to port and up to 10 knots. Then, when I say so, turn on every fucking light.'

Then I sped out to Daily.

'Any minute I'm going to hit the lights full beam. When I do, you let fucking go with this, right? An arc, if you still can't see them. Set an arc and fucking lose it.'

He grinned. He may have been a brawler but this was his first action with firearms, and he'd just found a new drug. On the way back down I grabbed Taff's AK47 and, back on deck, threw it to Elson. I gestured to them where to fire when the lights went on. I think they got it. I had to take a gamble. That had to be the 'pirate ship' and this had to work. While the two captives screamed and pleaded for their lives, I waited. I waited until I could hear their engine, a ghostly rumble that drifted out from the blanket of darkness while my heart thumped and my pupils exploded as I searched for shapes in a shapeless landscape. 'Come on, come on, you bastard,' I mumbled, like Police Chief Brody enticing Jaws to bite on the cable. 'Come and fucking get it!'

Now, as I stood there, aggression at the ready, about to staple another memory into my scrapbook of insanity, I felt the warrior inside me. I took a deep breath, then struck my Zippo. Three – two – one – then, 'Now, Taff – fucking now!'

I throw down my light and whoosh! The two captives go up in a flash as the paraffin fumes explode, sending flames towering high into the night sky, cooking their heads while coating their bodies with molten tyre. Then crack! Daily opens up with a burst from hell, the Type 77 thrashing out at 750 rounds a minute, arching towards the target at 820 yards a second, while both Elson and Brown, now standing either side of the human beacons, pepper away like men possessed. I run like fuck, back up to the bridge. 'Where they at?' I shout, as I stand panting, one hand either side of the screen and leaning into it like a hyperventilating kid. 'Do you see them? Do you?' But fuck! The blip stayed with us. So I run out to Daily, who's still firing like fuck, and aim it up, doubling its range. I grit my teeth and empty the belt.

'Boss! Boss!' shouts Taff. 'Quick!' So, sweating like a whore in chapel, I run to the screen. 'They've changed course! They've bottled it! Fucking dancer!' he yells.

I stop everything and hold my breath. I hold it for the length of time it takes for the blip to hit the screen; seconds that seem like hours. Then, 'Yes,' I whisper, as, when it does, I see the blip has moved off. So straight away I whack up the throttle to 15 knots, the diesel engines billowing out under the pressure, while I jam the wheel hard over and back to our course in an effort to put as much distance between us as possible. Then, within the same breath, I kill the lights, plunging the entire *Trader* into darkness like a curtain down on our macabre performance.

For over half an hour no one moved or said a word. And hanging on like it was the last chopper out of Saigon, we trusted to hope. Hoping worked. With a clear radar screen I eased back on the pace and turned to an introspective Taff. He just looked straight through me. With a tap on the shoulder, I gave him the wheel, then reached for a well-earned smoke before taking a hold of my OVD to share it out. No doubt, they'd all earned it!

I looked at my watch: only two hours before sunrise, what a fucking night. I don't know why, but I felt that if I could just get my boat tidied before daybreak, then it would be like it had never happened; just a thought. So, as soon as they'd polished off a bottle, I got them back to work, Taff taking the wheel while Daily cleaned the shooters. I reserved the best jobs, cleaning up the blood and moving the bodies, for the Mendes and me. While Elson mopped and scrubbed, I organised the burials at sea with Brown. But by the time we'd dumped the ones from the deck and moved on to the two I'd torched, the sun had gradually begun to surface.

An African sunrise is enchanting. But an African sunrise at sea is a privilege. There was a gentle breeze with a hint of warmth, so for a moment I stood still and closed my eyes to feel the sun's rays falling on my face. A second later I opened them wide, to find the whole world drenched blood-red, where, on the distant horizon, the sun, like an all-seeing eye, bore witness to my actions. Like a guilty kid caught by his dad, I ashamedly started my clean-up while the evergreen battle between my own morality and grim necessity raged on. The necklace chars in a way that few other methods can. While the torsos resembled carbonised logs from an open fire, their heads were nothing more than collapsed scaffolds, unrecognisable but for the rows of glistening teeth, which grinned amongst the smouldering ruins. They grinned at me.

From the time I'd left victimhood on Granton Road to become a warrior, my newly constructed identity had formed a prison around me, built from the image that I carried of myself and the actions that image necessitated. And from that I now found it difficult to break out. But once again, standing in front of my actions, I began to realise that the bars weren't there to keep me in, but to keep reality out – they protected me. What did it matter – warrior or victim? All I'd done was swap resentment and grievances for anger and aggression, while instead of blaming war for changing me, I'd embraced it to justify me. And it did! I lit a smoke, and instead of kicking the two charred bodies overboard, I sat with them like we were three friends sharing a morning. I stared at them. I tried to feel ashamed; I tried to evoke an emotion; but for as much as my mind was wrestling, so my heart was silent, while what disquieted me the most was not that this act of barbarism made me feel something, but that, for the first time ever, I felt nothing. Now, like a silence that deafens, I mourned my loss of guilt. Allan Patterson had saved my life, and he was right. Once again I'd lived where others had died. I'd gone all-out without restraint and, like those mercenaries all those years before, I'd succeeded in constructing my own self-styled insanity, to be brought out like an alter ego in case of emergencies. All I had to do was smash the glass. It smashed easily.

As I finally made my peace and shoved the two human wrecks into the deep, it suddenly came to me – Joseph? I shouted for the Mendes, and they both appeared in unison, but from different hatches.

'Boss?'

'Joseph? Where's Joseph?'

They shrugged, and for the first time, I saw tears come to their eyes. It was then I realised they were brothers. I never did find out what happened to Joseph – chances are the pirates killed him and dumped him over, but I did find out about the Mendes, and about the character of those men, whom beforehand I'd simply termed as blacks. They mourned for a day, then got up and got on with it. I was astounded. Perhaps in part, it's because life was cheaper out here; but they also had a special resilience born out of their main preoccupation of just

A young Rod in Stenhouse.

First job as a 'van laddie'
for Martins the Bakers.

Life on the trawlers.

A dinner date with wife Susan.

On holiday in Athens
with Susan.

Above: Learning to kill.

Right: A proud guardsman.

The *Boston Trader* with her sister ship, the *Boston Belle*.

On the *Trader* heading south.

Moored in Granton Harbour.

The *Toto* in Leith.

The *Toto* in Porto.

Loaded up and ready to sail to
Mozambique with a UN cargo.

At sea in the Indian Ocean.

En route to Beira.

Painting the deck.

struggling to stay alive. A lot of the shit that bothers us doesn't even scratch their surface. If I'm honest, I felt humbled. Here was me soul searching, and here was them cracking on, having lost a brother for wages that only sustained their poverty. Now I was in their world, yet carrying the baggage of an Oprah Winfrey culture, where every fucking thing was analysed and justified. Like finding a cause was finding a cure. You know: Big Jim was a murderer – well, it must have been his childhood; or some fat cunt ran off with another fat cunt's wife – well, that must be because the fat husband wasn't showing his fat wife enough fat love. I mean, how about the possibility that the fat wife just wanted another bit of fat cock 'cause she was bored fatless?

In some ways, we work a lifetime to get a glimpse of what they already had – the simple life, where less really is more. Yet standing there, and watching these men work, I began to realise it was more than that. They, like most Africans, had a familiarity with death way beyond ours. For us, death is sanitised. No sooner has the body gone cold than it's taken away and, if you're lucky, or willing, is represented asleep and at peace. But to them, death is as much a part of life as is living. It seemed like they knew something we didn't. Maybe they did.

I spent the next three days making best on my war-torn freighter. R4 and AK47 rounds had left their mark, but the Type 77 12.7 mm rounds made parts of my ship resemble a cheese grater. Still, she never lost her integrity and by some stroke of luck the rounds that did penetrate the decking embedded themselves in the bags of cement that I kept for plugging holes in a hurry. When we finally did make southern Namibia, a week and a half later, I didn't have the heart to tell my boys we were back in the shit. After the storm of Freetown, both the weather and the sailing had felt a bit like a cruise, as we, the once-skeleton crew, became a body. And we did. It's often been said that there are no atheists in a trench. We soon saw there were no racists there either.

Lüderitz was a surreal place, a colonial relic resembling a Bavarian village, which clings to the coastline of the Namib Desert. And with all you'd expect from a small German town, from beer houses to Lutheran churches, it sticks out like a pest in a playground. Even the coastline is striking: home to penguins and seals cooled by the Benguela current, it boasts miles upon miles of desolate beaches, which simply fall into the ocean. Lüderitz also happened to be the northern anchor of the diamond-rich Sperrgebiet, or 'forbidden area'. Since its discovery, just east of Lüderitz, the then German authorities branded the entire area a no-go, a tradition long since continued by South Africa, who'd annexed it during the First World War. For my part, I had a hold full of 200 kw Onan diesel generator sets, each one costing a fortune, but a bargain price from me, to be exchanged for diamonds with a member of the area CCB team. I'd later learn that they trucked the generators up to Angola, and on to the mines, after a UN-sponsored deal ensured that Cuban troops left Angola if South African soldiers walked from Namibia. I also found out that my CCB purchaser was none other than the fat cunt from Pretoria, Joost De Vries. It turned out he was one of the Namibian-section heads and a long-standing member of 32 Battalion; the sneaky bastard had foreseen a settlement and was now trying to line his own pockets by being amongst the first in. He was also there for a far more sinister reason, but I'll come on to that later.

However, mooring in Lüderitz turned out to be a pleasant experience. While we berthed on one side of a long jetty, in amongst the trawlers, De Vries's men turned up, lifted each generator off and placed them 30 yards away on another boat. I knew he'd be squaring me up in Durban, so no sooner had we got there and refuelled than we left. A week after that we'd rounded the Cape, and five days later, just a month after leaving Freetown, we hit Durban: the kingdom of the Zulu known as Tekweni. We'd made it!

CHAPTER V

THE ROAD TO ATTRITION

'Oh, ya,' he said, with his rough Afrikaner accent and eyes bursting with enthusiasm. 'It's true, when you're fighting a "moont", you've got to punch low, get into their spleens and keep on digging, 'cause they've got thicker skulls than us, see.'

'Fuck off!' said Daily, having a laugh with him. 'What a load of Nazi piss.'

'No, I swear it. It's fucking gospel, man,' he snapped back, now shadow-boxing a midriff. 'I'm telling you. I've had a tonne of fights, and I've never knocked a Kaffir out yet.'

'That's 'cause you punch like a pussy,' muttered Taff from behind his tea mug. Dirk stopped and looked right at him, but Taff sat still and stared him out.

'All right, boys, all right,' I said like a chastising dad. 'Dirk – he's just having a laugh with you! Right, Taff?'

'Right,' said Taff, still holding his gaze. Dirk smiled, but Taff didn't. Realising what was happening, I tried to defuse the tension with a bottle. 'Come on, guys,' I gestured. 'Sit down and have a drink, eh?' They did.

Fucking hell, I thought to myself, these Afrikaners, they're a different breed; must be something in the water, as Dirk van der Hoff,

131

the 6 ft 5 in. colossus and latest crew member, stood before us demonstrating his skills. Officially he'd been sent by Free State to pilot us up the coast, but I knew he was here to check that the gear went to the right place; it wouldn't have been the first time a ship ended up going 'missing' to the highest bidder. Anyway, he was a good guy and well handy. Ivan had told me a bit about him as we'd shared a drink and a memory or two the night before in Durban. Dirk was in his late 30s, and had spent 5 years in one of their 'hit squads', conducting assaults into neighbouring countries, usually in pursuit of guerrillas. I knew these guys were ruthless. But more than that, I knew they were fanatics. To be honest, I'd expected a bit of friction between him and the boys, especially the Mendes, who were now part of the family; he wouldn't have been used to that. But when he walked through the door and whipped out a bible, my heart missed a beat. Then, when I showed him his bunk and he whipped out a flag, it stopped altogether.

'Dirk!' said Daily later on that evening as we sat having dinner. 'Why've you got a swastika hanging from your bunk?'

We all stopped and hung on his answer. Dirk shook his head and laughed. 'Swastika? No, it's the Three Sevens.'

'The Three Sevens?'

'Yes, it's the flag of my blood, of my people, of my Volk!' Daily looked bewildered. 'I'm a Boer, and that swastika you refer to is the flag of the AWB – the Afrikaner Weerstandsbeweging, or resistance movement.'

Daily laughed. 'What the fuck are you guys resisting against? You got a whole country!'

Dirk grinned, then, leaning into the dim light which surrounded our table, he lowered his tone. 'We're not stupid, you know. We're just like doctors in a hospital: we only delay the inevitable. Ever since the National Party came to power, we've known majority rule was coming. But for all we do to stop it, the momentum gathers, and it will until the Boer's right to exist is denied.' Then, with his voice raised and a passion within him, he sat back and took a hold of his bible to punch out his words: 'This is a battle to the death with no room for compromise! Concessions only lead to surrender! The AWB is fearless, Christian and unashamedly nationalistic. It has become the new right, antithesis to the ANC, warriors for its people and a bastion against liberalism, Marxism and Communism. The AWB demands, and will win, its ideals: a modern Christian Afrikaner Boer state – against the world.' He sat back.

'Shit!' said Daily, trying to digest his answer. 'That's pretty full on.' He paused. 'But the flag? It does kind of look like a . . .'

Dirk stopped him. 'The symbol is of three sevens joined at the base to form a wheel. The three sevens symbolise the biblical number of victory through Jesus Christ. The number 777 stands directly opposed to the number 666: the number of the anti-Christ in Revelations. The circle around the sevens symbolises the movement, and eternal life with Christ, while the red colour symbolises his blood and the blood of the Boer nation in our struggle for freedom. The white symbolises the purity of our ideal, while the black is the heraldic symbol for bravery. And we are brave!'

Brave, perhaps, but one thing our friend 'the Bible Boer' wasn't was tight-lipped. Turned out he was from a family of four brothers, and between them they pretty much covered every fucking thing that the bastards were up to. The youngest was a member of the Fifth Reconnaissance Regiment, based at Phalaborwa in the north-east, tasked with helping Renamo, while the oldest, I soon found out, was a top physicist who worked on the South African nuclear programme. It's amazing what time, a few lagers and a sense of familiarity can do for a man. And even though he dressed it up as part of the great Boer struggle, I knew it was something worth listening to. You see, since Portugal left its colonies in 1975, and the Cubans, all 50,000 of them, arrived in Southern Africa, the South Africans changed the focus of their nuclear programme from civil to military. The Soviet involvement in Africa – either direct or by proxy – pissed off the apartheid leaders and was a motivation for the making of bombs to provide a hedge against Soviet-sponsored aggression. Their strategy, said Dirk, was to use them as leverage with the Western powers, namely the Yanks and us, by demonstrating their existence and then threatening to drop one if we didn't help them out. Thank fuck they never did, but between him and Ivan, I was building up quite a picture.

Anyway, after three days of solid propaganda and the 'don't say anything, buts', I was bored to tears and dying to move. If espionage was my thing, Dirk's information would have been priceless, but it wasn't. Dirk said there'd been a hold-up with the arms we were waiting on, but I knew there was trouble at the other end; Ivan had already told me. And even though the weather was shit, with heavy fog and a stormy sea, a vessel standing still was still costing us money, and it's money we wouldn't get back. As dinner-time approached, and we were still going nowhere fast, I poured a drink and tried to phone Susan. Time on my hands always made me homesick. But as the line crackled and faded in and out, I felt the wharf shake and heard a distant rumble. Then it came to me – trucks, thank fuck! It was on.

From my bridge, some forty feet above the ground, I looked down to see four army trucks thundering to a halt. Then, like a team of ants, the locals jumped out, parted the canvas flaps and began their task. In my world of gun-running, weaponry is split into two. The first is small arms, such as revolvers, self-loading pistols, rifles, carbines, assault rifles and sub-machine guns, which are weapons designed for personal use. The second is light weapons, such as heavy machine guns, hand-held and mounted grenade launchers, portable anti-tank and anti-aircraft guns, and recoilless rifles which are designed for several men serving as a crew. I was taking 'smalls'.

I don't really know what I'd expected, but I hadn't anticipated such a brazen delivery service. Durban is South Africa's major port, and the busiest on the continent, so I knew few would pay much attention to the comings and goings of one ship – especially mine – but army trucks? I mean, what the fuck? Anyway, nothing was too heavy to be manhandled, so I stood on the gangway like a welcoming captain, while the gear was sweated over as it came aboard. About halfway through, two of the lads were struggling with a large wooden box, their legs buckling under a weight greater than the two of them put together, when the top guy slipped, and crash! The lower man took the full force of the one-by-fours in his face, which threw him over and into the berthing gap, where he disappeared under the oily water. Like a shot I was in, and, a second later, found myself fumbling with a man and unable to swim to the surface. As he began to thrash like a soluble Disprin, the panic set in and the cunt nearly drowned me. Luckily, my foot found a ledge against the wharf and, a minute later, we were pulled out to where we both sat spewing half of Durban. But as I wretched and gasped for breath, I couldn't help noticing the contempt from Dirk and his CCB pal, Mr Mysterious who never left his truck, coupled with complete bewilderment from the locals. Unbelievable, I thought, what kind of fucking country is this? Anyway, turns out that the kid I saved was some Nanga's boy – the son of a witchdoctor. So the next day, about an hour before we set sail, he turned up with this jar. I almost spewed again when I saw it. It looked like a jar of dead stuff. It was! He said it would bring me good luck, and I could pour it on cuts to avoid infection. So I thanked him and stuck it away – out of sight, out of mind.

Finally, after two hours of strapping down and taping up, we were off, slipping out during the night like an attack sub off to war. After half an hour we made the open ocean while only the silhouettes of an occasional freighter or passing fishing boat glanced our bow. After negotiating the chop, I looked back to shore and saw blackness like a curtain only interrupted by star-like lights some ten miles off. I felt alive. I gave Taff the wheel and headed for the bow, as the wind backed to the north-east and jumped from 15 to 20 knots. The view from the bow was dark and menacing as the water magnified the blackness till there was no sky and no horizon. Then, within it, I detached from reality, to where only the memories could intrude. God, I loved it!

Less than a week later, we lay a half-mile off the Mozambique coast near a place called Tofo, a remote beach on the Indian Ocean side of Inhambane. The wind was slight and the moon was full while, lit up like a layer of gold, the sand dunes ran between the mirror-like sea and a cloudless night sky. This was truly paradise on the edge, and made it all worthwhile. Dirk called Phalaborwa, his brother's place in the north-east, who got in touch with those who were waiting. An hour later came a sequenced flash of torchlight, followed by the melancholic sounds of a traditional Arab dhow drifting across the water. Like a scene out of Sinbad, the captain approached and navigated tight in before ordering his crew to stop. So I saluted and smiled and he waved back to me as Colin and my Mendes got busy. An hour later we'd finished, and were about to part when he shouted up from his boat. He told us about a bad situation further north in Beira, which meant he was under way without a second dhow. And because of that, he wondered if his men could board the *Trader* while he made the round trip with the gear. With much amusement, I looked at Daily and Taff, before looking down and with large theatrical gestures signalling, 'Nobody comes on the boat. Fucking nobody!' Then we all fell about laughing as the skipper's face dropped. Anyone trying was getting filled with lead. Sorry, Sinbad!

As his boat limped off, water washing round his ankles, I turned south and headed for Maputo. I still had a load of other goodies to drop off, and thanks to Free State and Dirk the Wonder Boy, my tonne of beer would fetch me a fortune. Maputo from a distance was like any other sprawling capital with a large harbour, and with a population of two million, I could smell the city as I rounded the island of Inhaca, one of its two landmarks that lie off the coast. Under the Portuguese, Maputo, or Lourenzo Marques, was an urban jewel with a skyline of tall buildings and an adventurers' riviera to match Havana. Places like the Polana Hotel, with its stunning view over the harbour, buzzed with intrepid socialites, as did the many nightclubs until the early hours. But then came war, and all that changed. Soon, thousands of refugees swarmed the city and crowded the buildings, rubbish lay everywhere and all major services, including water and electricity, were cut. Anyone who could, left. Anyone who couldn't, suffered.

After offloading to a government supplier, Dirk wanted to cut and run. I knew he was right, but I'd read about the place and I wanted to see it. But soon after persuading him to join me, it didn't take me long to see Dirk's point. I'd arrived on a Friday and the streets were a nightmare. Like a scene from *The Omega Man*, danger and desolation lay around every corner. In some ways, seeing war and poverty in amongst mud huts and dirt is easier to stomach than seeing it in a city, which decays alongside the poor bastards who live there. Queues of beggars stretched as far as the eye could see, all jostling for place outside the Asian businesses – a welfare state by proxy.

'Money for bread,' cried the poor bastards now reduced to suffering.

'They've come from the countryside,' said Dirk. 'Friday's the Muslim holy day, and the shopkeepers think they'll be blessed for giving "alms" to the needy. Oh, and by the way,' he said, nodding over to one of the many lines, 'take a closer look.'

I did. And fuck me! I'd never seen so many mutilated people in one place. Apart from the limbless, this was a legion of the lipless, of the earless and of the blind and disfigured.

'They're walking adverts,' Dirk said. 'Renamo started it but now Frelimo enjoys it. They cut them up so they'll walk about like mobile billboards, warning of the price for collaboration.' Then, pausing for a second, he looked at the ground and shook his head. 'You know, Rod, you've really got to stop seeing these people as individuals, 'cause they're not. They're a swarm; they don't live or think in isolation, they're a collective, like a hive. They don't feel like we do, they don't mourn like us. Life, to them, is cheap. Really, they're no different from animals. The big mistake, Rod, is ours. We're guilty of one thing: anthropomorphism – giving humanity to subhumans.'

I looked at him and started to laugh. I'd never heard such a load of shit in all my life and was about to tell him so, when, almost on cue, a stampede to our right caused us to run while the crack of gunfire peppered the streets, cutting down a mob like a scythe through grass. When the dust had settled, we saw two armed men in uniform casually walk over from a food-store entrance and begin kicking the bodies, while laughing and joking. With no signs of life, they left them lying and returned to the shop where they broke open some Cokes like nothing had happened. I looked at Dirk – he looked at me – the sightseeing was over.

If anything, that day in Maputo reminded me of my own mortality, and that I'd have to get on with it. I'd always wanted to treat this job like a 'smash and grab': roll up, tan the window, then take what I could and fuck off. And I knew that the demand in my particular market would eventually dry up. You see, gun-running is different from drugs. Because arms don't perish or get consumed, your buyer takes on a one-off basis, or at least not that often, which is good if the police intercept you somewhere in Europe, because it doesn't reveal your network, but bad because when the buyers have got them, that's it. Secondly, your bread-and-butter 'smalls', like the AK47, have an even longer existence than that, because they're simpler and easier to maintain. So for an AK47 to keep on firing, it's enough that its 16 moving parts all function; that's fuck all compared to an F5 fighter jet's 60,000, which all need to be resupplied. Unfortunately, though, planes were never my business.

So, thinking about it, I figured I'd have only another couple of runs off Free State. As the time went by, though, I began to realise just how much they operated outside their authority, almost like a bunch of state-sanctioned rogues. When it finally clicked to what extent, I saw potential. About a week later I was sitting with Ivan and Dirk in a bar near the harbour in Durban. By this time, I'd gotten to know Dirk well enough to trust him, and even though he was a blabbering bastard, I knew I could use him provided I watched what I said. Ivan, well, Ivan was Ivan, and if he thought there was a few quid in it for him, he'd fuck an elephant. So I put it to them. I had a stack of money and I wanted their help. If they could get me a load of arms, and source me a buyer, I'd front the dough and deliver it to their door. I thought, if I could just sort a big one, I could fuck off back to Edinburgh and leave the boat with Taff as the skipper. I knew he'd want it, and was more than capable. Besides, I'd had my fun and I missed my family. Two days later, Ivan turned up with Dirk. It was on.

For all Ivan's evils, I've never met a man who could plan a job better, or had a calmer head if it all went wrong. But now, sitting around the galley, committing to the unknown, I had a feeling of apprehension I'd long since forgotten. What the fuck was I doing, I thought, as I sat looking at his maps and charts. Yes, I'd been in the thick of it: the attack on the boat off Freetown, the trips up the coast, or my day in Maputo, but they'd all been by-products of necessity; and as for Freetown, well, it was how it was 'cause we'd given them a hiding! But now, back at the war council, I sat with the Devil, and I knew it! I began to wobble, but then I thought back to the Tam o' Shanter all those years before. How I'd felt unsure and nervous, but desperate for a break, and how different things might have been if I'd bottled it. Where would I be now, I thought. In the land of fucking nobody, probably!

'Roddy, you're going to love this,' Ivan said with that same emotionless stare. 'It's with one of Renamo's top boys; it's his own deal; and thanks to your man "Tiny" Rowland, he's got plenty of money.'

I said nothing. I knew I'd get a full briefing, so I kept tight. Tiny Rowland, for those that don't know, was the chief executive of Lonrho, a major industrial player for the region and a global company whose long arms reached into everything. In the early 1960s, Tiny had negotiated an oil pipeline from the port of Beira to southern Rhodesia. Opened in December 1964, it was Lonrho's primary asset in Mozambique for the next 30 years. But come the early 1980s, its security was threatened with the war, and in particular Renamo insurgents. So, in the spirit of African business, a Lonrho subsidiary contacted Renamo to arrange a deal.

In June 1982 a secret protection agreement with Renamo was reached. For $500,000 a month, Renamo would hold off till August, and then indefinitely, unless either party wanted to terminate with a month's notice, kind of like a gentleman's blackmail. The payments, made into foreign accounts, were controlled by Renamo's senior figures, who then pushed for deals covering Lonrho's tea estates in the north. In all, they ripped the best part of $5 million off Tiny. Shame!

Now, this being Africa, nothing was straightforward. The deal between Lonrho and Renamo was fucked from the start, because Renamo's main backer, South Africa, considered the destruction of the Beira pipeline a priority, an important part of shafting Frelimo. So if I said that Renamo were a bunch of weasel-faced bastards, I'd be putting it fairly. And while some only carried out symbolic acts of sabotage to keep the South Africans happy, others, despite the deal, took it upon themselves to fucking lose it. Ivan pointed out it was them we'd be dealing with. Fucking great.

While Renamo, in its thirst for war funds, tried to hassle others into protection money, including the Malawian government, Tiny and Lonrho fortified their assets with every fucking thing from triple stacks of concertina wire and a 1,400-strong militia, to watchtowers, tanks and a £6 million, three-year contract with an ex-SAS outfit called Defence Systems Limited. These were then replaced with Gurkhas from Gurkha Security Guards in an effort to ease back on the costs. Coupled with this, Zimbabwe and Malawi began to assign well-trained military units to protect both the Beira pipeline and the Nacala Corridor, another area of crucial transport infrastructure.

So what did that mean for us? Well, Ivan in his wisdom had spotted a gap in the market. No doubt South Africa would soon fill it through their usual channels, but there was an opportunity for the odd freelancer with a bit of bottle to get in early. As the stakes were upped, Renamo needed 'lights', and Ivan knew where to get them. Initially, he said he'd get them off one of his CCB mates, who'd siphon them from a larger cargo en route to Angola. I later learned that he'd got them off IMES GmbH, an East German state-owned company controlled by Schalck-Golodkowski, their then deputy foreign trade minister. This outfit, with its secret bank accounts and shell companies in Switzerland, West Germany and Liechtenstein, was at the centre of an international smuggling network, and was reportedly also used by Western intelligence agencies to ship arms to Central America, and by the US during the Iran–Contra scandal. Why he'd chosen to hide the weapons' true source would become apparent to me in due course, but for now, in my happy ignorance, I was up for it. Two weeks later, fully fuelled and kitted up, the *Boston Trader* sloped off into a starless night and tempered sea. My crew, Taff and Daily, my two Mendes, Brown and Elson, and my genetically racist Boer, Dirk, had now been joined by Ivan, Ivan the terrible – what a privilege!

On a late afternoon several days later, and a few miles off the island of Mamoudzou, part of the Comoros, I came alongside a Panamanian freighter, which shall remain nameless as it's still on the go, and took receipt of a real fucking arsenal. One of the joys of having CCB connections was the ability to use banks. I'd paid for these through my own Pretorian bank, and would receive my money, a third of which had already been paid up-front, through the same institution, but on a different account. If I'm honest, I really felt like things were moving that day. And even though the trickiest bit was yet to come, so far, it was so good. The next day, we'd land the weapons in the midst of the Muslim north of Mozambique, as arranged by Ivan, and while the whole plan sounded as mad as ever, I trusted him fully. I lit a smoke and called home, before I poured an OVD and sat dreaming as the sun sank and the sky filled with an amber glow. It was stunning, and soon that amber became golden bursts of orange, magenta and pinks mixed in with a prophetic grey, which often revealed a change in the weather. I only hoped it wasn't to be a change in luck. The weather held.

The trucks were late getting in, and problems with one of their axles meant that one vehicle angled forward, slowing the whole fucking convoy right down. Now, as the light began to fade, I knew that one of our few protections, the sun, was almost up and off, leaving us with the joys of a night-time dash through a country with more hazards than a night out in Niddrie. Taff and Daily, my two loyal grafters, sat shaking their heads with a prophetic acceptance, while from time to time throwing knowing glances. I couldn't blame them; being moored just half a mile from shore didn't exactly make them unassailable.

I strapped on my holster, readjusted my money belt, then nervously made a final check that everything I needed was on, before trying to load myself onto a truck. From the various seats on offer, I soon got the impression that the local hands, the ones sent from the mine, seemed to like the idea of putting me in harm's way. Kembo, the most antagonistic of the five drivers, offered me shotgun in the lead Bedford. I offered him a foot up the arse. Instead, I opted for the second vehicle, a decommissioned army Land-Rover, which still carried a welded front emplacement for an M60 or something long since ripped out, while behind swung a fully functional M2.50 Browning.

As the vehicles lined up, fully loaded and ready to roll, I looked around to see an audience of locals. They'd come to see us off. Great. So much for clandestine trafficking; every cunt in the jungle now knew we were coming. I took my seat on the left of the driver, an ever-smiling black man who was high as a kite and numbed by war, who sported his beret like a Charing Cross poofter and stunk like only an African man can, the result of constant sun on acrylic fibres, a stench that strips copper. As I fumbled with the double-taped clip of my AK47, he said few words except, 'Is good, boss – OK? Is good!' This was followed each time with 'a ha ha ha', his head back and mouth wide open, a laugh like a fucking madman! As I looked at my feet, I saw them resting on hard-packed sandbags, strewn across the rusty floor. I turned to my driver. 'Is for boom! A ha ha ha ha ha!' he said, now killing himself with laughter. I wished he would! I figured he meant landmines; this country was full of them – like a few feet of sand was going to save us.

I checked my watch, then looked back to a pensive Ivan now sitting like Action Jackson with a belt of SLR rounds draped across him, listening to his driver sweeping through the frequencies of his clansman-like radio, trying desperately to make it work. Fucking typical. Behind them sat another Bedford, while one back again stood the last with the dodgy axle. Fucking Africa. While each truck was loaded up to the hilt with gear, I noticed that they'd arrived with a couple of ready-armed men – Gurkhas, of all people. I figured they were moonlighting from Defence Systems Ltd, which made no sense as this shit was for Renamo. Still, having a few Gurkhas backing you up was never a bad thing.

Still waiting for Dirk to stop fannying about, I took my binoculars and looked the few hundred yards out to where the *Trader* was anchored. As well as an ocean I saw a sea of worried faces, as both Taff and Daily stood like a pair of ill kids watching their pals play football. I gave them a wave. I don't know who felt more condemned: them or me. A second later, a Gurkha dressed in full combats jumped in the back and mounted the Browning. He said nothing. A second again, Dirk appeared from nowhere in a cloud of dirt as the trucks bellowed out a black diesel smoke which whipped up a sandstorm around us. Brandishing an OS map and an ear-to-ear smile, he slung his R4 over his back and banged hard on our bonnet, shouting, 'You're goanna fucking love this, Roddy. You're goanna fucking love it!' Then, laughing away, he ran forward and jumped into the passenger side of the lead Bedford. We were off.

Still mumbling to myself about the darkness, I soon broke into a shout because, within 30 seconds of driving, my trusty chauffeur, fucking 'Laughing Larry', pulled out, put his foot down and broke forward to the front of the column.

'A ha ha ha ha. Yes, boss!' he screamed like a nutcase. I looked at him with a temper, but before I could clock him, it sank in – of course we'd be at the front, we were the fucking Land-Rover with the .50 cal. Bastard!

We were only meant to cover 35 miles of dirt road, starting on a level with Mozambique Island and finishing just to the south of Nampula. Not exactly the safest route by day, but by night, in the dark, it was pure fucking madness. I can assure you, I wasn't the only nervous adventurer that evening. When the last of the sand became dirt, Larry put the lights on 'dark out', while I took a last glance at the *Trader*, bobbing gently in the calm sea and under a half-moon. I turned back to the front and faced the void, feeling my stomach tense and the sweat beginning to roll down my back as my doubts escalated. Then, plummeting further into the darkness, headlights cutting a path like our machetes through the Congo, I suddenly realised that subtlety and stealth had become nothing more than aspirations, the sooner let go of, the better. Motors revved, gears clashed, while the rising and falling whines of engines and transmissions competed against the scrambling tyres now fighting for traction on an uneven ground. I felt like a duck in a shooting gallery.

After half an hour, even my once unperturbed driver, 'Larry', became agitated and impatient as I felt him urging, even willing, more and more speed from the straining trucks behind us. Just fucking great, I thought, the plane's captain's starting to sweat. Whether by design or by circumstance, we were stripped for combat. With no roof or windscreen, the damp, hot air of Mozambique blew over me, rippling my clothes and cooling my sweat, while fooling me into thinking I was cold. I looked up at our Gurkha, his hands gripping the Browning while, white-knuckled, he seemed ready as his eyes flicked from shadow to shadow, wishing for the best, but prepared for the worst.

I tried to relax, but was fretting. I thought about how naked I felt in the front seat, a 6-ft white man in a land of angry black men, and all with good reason to kill me. I felt powerless, unable to make decisions, unable to command, and with my very survival resting on a band with competing loyalties and no cohesion, I was back out on a limb and I knew it. In this war, a roll of the dice would play as much a part as a roll on the ground. I was back to hoping, and I hated it.

In the distance I saw a dim glow begin to appear, while Larry homed in, determined to split it in two. With each turn of our wheels, the distant light became clearer, sharper and more focused, while amorphous shades of black and grey whizzed by our sides. Soon I saw the outline of a village, seemingly peaceful but sitting slap bang in the middle of our progress. In amongst the shadows and silhouettes, I saw strands of dim yellow light bulbs, dangling in rows, forming an eerie tunnel of light in the middle of a charcoal horizon. A moment later my nose picked up the unmistakable scent of an African village: rotting garbage and human waste mixed with the fumes from their generators. Then, to my shock, Larry hit the horn, flagging our arrival and signalling our arrogant determination to plough through at full speed. The villagers dropped everything and jumped aside, before, like a tide of floodwater, we burst in. How surreal, I thought, as the bare bulbs bathed everything in yellow, turning normal people into two-dimensional cut-outs, seemingly propped up in front of their homes, now frozen in place and time. I hadn't expected them to be in bed, but I hadn't expected this either. I scanned the black aisles between the buildings, to find running kids, barking dogs and swaggering chickens. I looked at the general store in the centre and saw old men and women, their silent, tiny, hate-filled faces staring right back through me, a lifetime of war etched on their wrinkles, telling stories like tattooed prisoners, while the young girls looked away, hoping to avoid another raping. But no men – not a single young man. What the fuck? I snapped out of my reverie and into reality. This was no fucking tourist bus. And I was no fucking tourist. I forced my eyes back to work, checking out windows, rooftops and doorways, and desperate to find the bastards who were desperate for me. But no sooner had I started than we were out, roaring from the tunnel like a freight train with no time to stop. I turned around to stare, wary of showing them my back and convincing myself I'd seen hordes of angry faces vying for blood – my blood. But they weren't and, soon out of range, the threat behind me returned to the threat ahead. I removed my safety-catch.

A few more nervous miles down the road, we seemed to slow. Then the gradient rose before sharply dipping down like the top of a roller-coaster, and into a sharp S-bend where the left bank sloped up to a rocky outface, and the right sloped down some 20 ft and into the start of a shallow ravine. Great, I thought. The fucking Khyber Pass.

Then, like talk of the Devil and the Devil will come, bang! It's a blast from behind. 'Fuck me!' I shout, rolling out to the left as Larry sticks his foot through the floor, stopping us with a jolt. On a knee, I'm frantic, expecting a shower of tiny meteors to start pelting down, but nothing. 'What was that?' I shout to Larry, expecting a laugh, but he's quiet. So I look about, my eyes straining through shadows of the headlights, then up, to see our steadfast Gurkha standing tall, .50 cal. in hand, and searching for a target. Fearless bastards! 'A grenade?' I shout. 'A mine. That's it: a fucking mine!'

But no sooner had I shouted it than I realised it wasn't; it was the last truck, and the axle had finally packed in. My relief, though, was short-lived, as we went from flying ducks to sitting ducks. 'My kingdom for a mechanic!' I said to Larry, who didn't get me. Then I walked back scratching my head, trying to figure it out. We tried to fuck about with it, but after two hours we admitted defeat. Even the most ingenious solutions fall flat without a welding kit. And even though I could have blown it up a thousand times over, I had nothing for a broken axle, so that, as they say, was the ball burst! It took an hour to load the gear onto the other trucks and the same again to redistribute it when Daily's truck almost tipped as we tried to move. It took a matter of minutes to heave the fucked one over the edge and into the ravine. Finally, four and a half hours later, we continued.

I don't know if it was the pit stop itself, or whether I'd had to use my brain for something other than worrying, but as the early hours went on, I began to gain a familiarity with the road. Now, for the first time in a long time, our mad dash along Death Valley had begun to feel more like a night-time safari, where the fear of danger far outweighed the reality. I was wrong! No sooner had I begun to breathe easy, than the breeze brought with it the sound of anger. Somewhere in the distance, drifting across the bush, came the sporadic pops of AK47 fire. Somebody was getting it tight! Still, at least it wasn't us. With my mind so distracted, it took me ages to notice the sun was coming up, but when I did I became fixated. Once again, like a blood-red orange, the sun had saturated the sky and all below it in a ruby-red hue. It was like a portal to Mars from right here on Earth.

While in my trip, I scanned the distance to see another village. From the huts – part mud and part corrugated iron – I could make out smoke rising into the haze of cool air under the warm sun. I could imagine the villagers readying for another tough day in another tough life. I thought I could see people moving. I saw animals. Part of me expected us to burst through them like the night before, but instead Larry stopped short and, leaning forward with his screwed-up eyes, we took on a snail's pace as we rolled gently towards a dry river bed before stopping short. Now, to my confusion, our small column became still as the diesel engines ticked over like a stationary taxi rank.

'What's wrong?' I whisper with a lowered voice to Larry as he puts his gloved hand up to hush me. So, standing up, I turn to see Dirk now sitting on the roof of his Bedford, binoculars in hand. After a minute he jumps down and slowly makes his way over. 'What's up?' I ask him.

'I don't know, but something's not right,' he answers, keeping his eyes glued ahead. 'No fucking people. I mean there's smoke – but no folk!'

I paused, then had a look for myself. 'Do we need to go through?'

'I'm afraid so!' he said, shaking his head. 'The river cuts this place in two, and the other road takes a day. And that,' he said, looking directly at me, 'would be fucking suicide.'

I thought about it, but not for long. 'Fuck it, then,' I snapped. 'Let's do it!'

He smiled and nodded, and with that we moved; but as soon as we did, I got that feeling again. I'd been here before.

I was right. Dead bodies littered the empty streets. From some the blood still dripped from the machete slashes, spear thrusts and bullets. Others were days old, half-eaten by packs of dogs, who'd carried off limbs to chew on as bones. Women's bodies were scattered in the marketplace; a baby's body, black, bloated and crawling with maggots, lay festering across our path like an organic roadblock. To our right, the church smouldered; a priest's body lay half in, half out. While to our left, so close I could smell the salt of her blood, lay a woman, her forcibly Caesareaned foetus placed in her arms, probably while she took her last breaths. I looked back at Dirk. I saw his face contorted in utter contempt. What could I say? What could I ever say as I passed through hell carrying coal for the fire?

They say guns don't kill people, people do; and like so many times in my life, that logic sustained me. It sustains a lot of others, too, from the small to the big, like the colonialists partitioning Africa. They'd always fascinated me. There they were, standing in Berlin way back in 1885, not an African in sight, to sign an agreement which divided 10,000 tribal kingdoms into 40 states. Their only promise: to be decent to the locals and 'care for the improvement of their moral and material well-being', while 'instructing the natives and bringing home to them the blessings of civilisation'. Of course, they had to let them feel civilisation first. And thanks to Mr Maxim, they did. 'The white man came with guns,' said a Zulu warrior, 'that spat bullets as the heavens sometimes spit hail.' It hails a lot nowadays – Dirk makes sure of it.

Some miles on, we made the camp. I don't know what I'd expected, but instead of razor wire and watchtowers, we meandered along an avenue of grandiose villas, now bullet-riddled and dilapidated. Then, like a row of cypress trees leading to an Italian cemetery, they led up to a rusty old gate, half blown off and half jammed fast in the dirt. Without invitation, we negotiated our way in, but on entering I was bowled over as I left the 'now' and entered the apocalypse. All around me lay piles of scrap metal, while ruins rose up like rotten teeth as goats clambered over caved-in mining towers, long since grown over. Like a living memorial to decay and abandonment, relics of East German pride stood rusting where they'd once offered hope. W50 trucks, tractors, Barkas buses and Trabant cars, otherwise known as Trabis, lay amongst the Takraf cranes as if designed by some modern artist in a statement about the fallibility of man. I looked to my right to see a series of single-storey huts, their windows long since smashed and utilities looted, but still bearing the hallmarks of aspirations gone wrong, a hammer-and-sickle crest in a wreath of grain. Now I understood the plaque at the gatehouse: 'a gift of solidarity from the workers of the German Democratic Republic'. An attempt to export a 'model project'. The model failed.

Like a convoy of the damned we sat there, while a light breeze blew the eerie silence across our sandblasted souls like tumbleweed through Tombstone. With nothing else to do, we waited. Then finally, after ten nervous minutes, a body appeared and walked towards us. 'Por favor?' he beckoned with his hand, but stopped short. Larry went to put us into gear, but I put my hand down and stopped him short.

'No – he comes here!' I said, signalling him over. But he stayed. I looked back at Dirk, then at Larry. We were at stand-off and I didn't like it. Something wasn't right. In my mind I'd run through a hundred problems and, for each one, a hundred solutions. I'd known there was nothing to stop our intended buyers from taking us out and grabbing the gear for a third of the price. Normally, repeat business would keep you safe, but I'd brought enough to satisfy Hannibal and we weren't the South Africans, we were a bunch of chancers, and they knew it. 'All right! Enough fucking about!' I said as I raised my rifle, then in the worst Portuguese ever: 'Onde esta? Onde esta?' He just looked at me. 'Onde esta?' I shouted again, then bang! I fired a shot above his head, but after being on the road for a day, the intended miss of a few feet became an unintended few inches. He felt it. What a laugh. As the poor bastard danced like a man on fire, he ranted on like I'd shagged his bird. Not that I understood it, because it was all in Makua. Anyway, after he'd burnt himself out and we'd all had a good laugh, he came forward and gave me a look of hatred before jumping in with our Gurkha. He waved us on, but, to our surprise, we only got as far as I could have thrown him when the whole mine came alive. There's no doubt they'd have seen us coming. They must have been as unsure as we were. As Dirk jumped out, closely followed by Ivan, a large figure emerged from one of the huts, which sat in the shadow of a slagheap long since reclaimed by the grasses. Then, almost like clockwork, the various sentries appeared from every rooftop and cranny. God, I thought. If I'd hit that bastard, we'd have more holes in us than a Swiss cheese.

As we stood by the Land-Rover, still waiting for our fat host to wobble his way over, Dirk forced a fake smile, bred from contempt, and meandered halfway across to meet him. As soon as I saw him, I thought of Idi Amin – another self-styled general – and I hated him. He wasn't the friendliest either. In his late 40s, this black man with grey hair looked at us with complete derision, before reluctantly shaking our hands and inspecting his new-found arsenal. Only then did I see him smile. Then, without even walking past us, 'Idi', shaking with the obvious onset of Parkinson's, signalled to four of his men and the unload was on. Personally, I wasn't really up for sticking around. I couldn't see the point. Trading was one thing, but being entertained on a rebel base made us rebels by proxy. And that we weren't. Looking around, my first impressions of being in an industrial relic had all but gone, and were now replaced by the feeling that I'd just walked into an insurgents' camp. As I'd soon find out, though, I was wrong. Like the wind, things change fast in Africa.

To the right-hand side of Idi's office lay an old medical centre. With its faded red cross and whitewashed walls sitting amongst a camp of sandy bricks and muddy exteriors, it seemed quite the picture. But this complex, as I soon saw, was to be his designated armoury, which on entry revealed a quadrangle with rows of inward-facing windows. More for a nose than anything else, I wandered in and looked about, but was shocked to see another white face, and I seemed to know him. 'What the fuck?' I said as I stared him out, trying to place him, but as I did I saw another, then another, then, before I knew it, I was standing looking at a team of six. So I waved and, with an unusual hesitation, they smiled back, but did nothing else. Weird! Not really being the kind of place where nosy bastards are appreciated, I lit a smoke and left. When I reached the Land-Rovers, I signalled to

Ivan, and when he arrived I told him what I'd seen. He was curious but seemed more preoccupied with something else. Like fucking what, I thought. Then Dirk came over and, for the first time ever, I saw him worried.

Under his breath, he whispered, 'What you want to do about it?'

Ivan looked about then paused.

'What's wrong?' I said, my blood now starting to flow.

'We're in trouble, Roddy,' answered Ivan, still keeping his voice down. 'Look around you: the boys on the roof, at the gate, in the doorways, all around us.'

Still facing them, I began glancing about. 'What about them? Same guys as when we came in.'

'Yes, but . . .' Ivan smirked, 'what fucking way are they facing?'

I looked again. They were facing in – they were facing us!

'Fuck!' I said, still trying to keep a handle on it. 'We've been had!'

Ivan nodded.

'It gets worse, though,' said Dirk. 'You see that fat Kaffir? I've never seen him before in my life.'

'What, you think they're . . .'

He stopped me. 'Ya. Fucking government!'

My heart sank as I felt a jolt of fear shoot through my spine. Like a thousand thoughts within a heartbeat, I cursed myself for being so stupid. Fuck, I thought. Fuck! Then, as we stood in silence, just staring and waiting for our fears to be confirmed, I hoped to wake up. I yearned for that relief; the one you get when you realise your nightmare's a dream before opening your eyes to a safe dark room and a soft warm pillow. But no luck – no dream.

'Right,' said Ivan. 'They've not hit us yet 'cause they don't want to damage the trucks. So, once it's unloaded, we've had it. What do you reckon, five minutes?' He looked at each of us, then took a deep breath. Then, with one long exhale, he began describing what he saw. 'Three on the roof up there, two behind us here, four by the trucks, three walking sentry at the gate, with one at the front, and another two held up in that sandbagged bunker, and fuck!' he moaned. 'That .50 cal. could do us itself!'

'And they're just the ones we see,' added Dirk, subtly lowering his R4. 'There's bound to be Kaffirs in those houses at the gate.'

I nodded my head. They'd known we were coming, so they must have had lookouts on the villas. Even if we did make the gate, we'd never get out of the avenue. So, as we fretted for answers and a way out from our perverse position, I began to dig deep. 'Right,' I said. 'We can't make a run for it; they'll cut us down the minute we move.' I stopped to pause and lit a smoke. 'Na, there's only one way out of here, and that's to live till dark – somehow. Then do a runner – somehow.'

They nodded.

I went on. 'What about our drivers? And these fucking Gurkhas. Where the fuck did they come from anyway?'

Ivan laughed, now shaking his head. 'Lonrho.'

'What?'

'Lonrho. They came with the trucks.'

I looked at him. 'Are you fucking serious? Do they know?'

'Do they know they're delivering shooters to the other side? Of course fucking not!'

'Well?'

'It's a long story,' he said, sniggering like a kid caught in the sweetie jar.

'Well, I hope I fucking live to hear it,' I said, raising my voice, but placing a hand on my good friend's shoulder. Then, for the first time ever, I saw a spark in his eyes, as he held my gaze and with an air of peace, smiled!

'I hope so too, Roddy. I hope so too, mate.'

Like the condemned gladiators we were, we stood in our sandy arena and stared up at the audience who'd soon be our foe. It was a strange feeling, each party knowing their fate, but neither letting on – almost like having a pint with your firing squad. I could feel myself hoping. But not for long because, within a second, someone who'd been standing with Larry pulled a .9 mm and bang, shot him in the head, point-blank. Then, with no clearer a signal for their change of intention, the .50 cal. opened up from the sandbags and strafed above our heads. We hit the dirt, planning to fire like fuck, but as soon as we did, sense took over and we stopped. The firing was over and, like our hands, the game was up.

Like a dawn raid, they were down and on us like men on a mission. Then crack! I felt a rifle butt straight in my stomach, and another to my head, which stunned me cold and laid me out. With so many bastards and so many blows, a wall of pain seemed to consume me that became more of a noise than a physical feeling. After five minutes of taking a hiding, they stopped to breathe, and through my pulped-up eyes I saw their mob, 30 or so, dragging us off and lining us up. Now, like beached whales, our helpless battered bodies lay stretched in the sand. I only hoped they wouldn't burn me.

While Dirk and Ivan lay to my right, the rest of them, the Gurkhas and drivers, lay to my left. Then, like a scene from wartime Warsaw, our pistol-brandishing executioner began culling his fodder. I'd like to say I thought of my family, and, looking back, I did, but only in a sense. I'd even like to say I repented my sins, although, in part, I'm doing that now. But in reality, all I was thinking was that this cunt better well hit his mark, 'cause I felt a rage like I'd never felt before. I'd been consumed by an emotion. I'd become my ace. I knew I'd win! When the groan to my left stopped, I knew it was my turn. You'll never hear the bullet which kills you, so I took my last breath and tried to stand. But thud, I was hit again and fell to a chorus of laughter. As I started to lose consciousness, I realised that the shooting had stopped with the last man to my left. We'd been spared – for now – but for a reason.

This time, I thought I was dreaming. It was only when I felt the pain from behind my pulped-shut eyes that I realised I wasn't. Then I heard this voice, well spoken, and in English. 'Beyond all else, one must be efficient. One must cause only the damage that is strictly necessary, not a bit more. We must control our tempers and act with the stealth and precision of a surgeon, yet maintain the pride in perfection of an artist. All wars are total, and this, like any, shall be fought to the death. You are my enemy, yet I neither hate you nor personalise our quarrel, as within this war my role is as necessary as yours. Only now, your move has been made, and it's my turn, and I'm going to do it to perfection, as in this profession, my profession, I'm the best.'

Who the fuck was this? To my left, I could make out some shadows; to my right, a couple more. But this voice? Within my delirium of confusion I focused on his voice, his soft menacing tone, his hyper-articulate tongue, his obvious evil, so unemotionally clinical and devoid of humanity. He was my host. I tried to make reason of the room; I tried to make reason for being here; I remembered Ivan and Dirk; then I remembered the killings and I felt my anger again. But now it was different – so much more powerful, so much more physical! I felt a power surge to my heart, making all my blood vessels course with pressure, until finally they expanded no more. Then, a moment later, with my chest swollen as if my heart had stopped beating, I struggled to breathe. As the noise of cursing and cracking filled the room, so too did a scent of burning. To me, it smelt like bacon. Bacon? What the fuck? When they threw water on my legs, I began to stir, but it was only when they shoved a rag in my mouth that I realised I was screaming. Reality hit me. They were electrocuting me, and it was me that was burning.

'Normally one shouldn't use a gag,' said the voice archly, 'because how can one give you information when one cannot speak? Still, this is just a baton. Most people talk when we use the crank.'

I can't describe the pain – nothing has ever come close. I don't know how much time had passed before the baton's power was spent, but only when it went flat did they stop. Seeing that I had my mouth wide open and was unable to move, they threw a bucket of water over my face, which jolted me up, though it was still a while before I could breathe again. While I lay there, lashed out on a metal-framed bed, my eyes slowly opened, but stayed pretty blurred.

'Are you going to tell us where it is?' said the voice. 'Come on now. Where is the missing crate?'

I tried to think, but I didn't have a fucking clue what he was on about. Crate? What missing fucking crate? I tried to speak, but my jaw flopped. 'Please – you should try harder. Your friends have told me you know, so where is it? You were the leader. We saw you come through first – you giving the orders! Will you speak to me? No? OK!'

He disappeared from my field of view, only to return with two cups. One was full of yellow liquid and the other full of white. A pair of black shovel-like hands yanked my head back so that my face was facing upward and I couldn't move, while another pair held my nose so I could only breathe with my mouth. With a metal rod in one hand and the yellow cup in the other, 'Dr Black' opened my jaws and poured it in. It felt horrific, like my throat was on fire as I choked and spluttered, desperate for breath. Then, without rest, they poured in the white. It was really salty. Breathing became impossible, which made me cough uncontrollably as the tears and nasal mucus flowed like a torrent. 'Well, will you talk or not?'

I shook my head. I didn't understand, how the fuck could I tell them something I didn't know? Again, I tried to speak, but found it impossible.

'Very well, sir!'

The next thing I felt was the rod back in, and a set of pliers fumbling over my molars. Looking back, things do have a habit of haunting you. When he'd finally taken a grip, he asked again. 'Will you talk?' I tried to nod, but his goons had me down too tight. So he went to pull, but used too much force and the pliers lost grip, causing him to fly backwards and look like a cunt. Mr Fucking Professional! What a prick! After several attempts I heard a cracking noise and felt my mouth fill with blood as a sharp pain hit me like a knife in the head. My God! Blood gushed from my mouth and I began to puke. But then he said, 'If you vomit again, I'll make you eat it.' No need – I passed out.

When I came round again, I was pissed to be alive. It took another minute to see if I was still being shocked. I wasn't. Although blinded with a headache and struggling to breathe, I could see a bit better as I fought to get stable. Within my mind I tried to check my body, my arms, my legs, my ribs and back. I knew if I'd staved off a break, I'd be in with a chance. With a break, I was fucked. I looked around, but made little show. I felt being out of it had saved me. Then I saw him,

Dirk. They'd hung him a few feet off the ground from a horizontal metal pole running beneath his knees and hands, which they'd trussed together. This position was commonly known as the Parrot's Perch. With a paddle seemingly designed for the job, they then beat his arse black and blue, until the flesh under his skin was saturated with blood. He was screaming, no doubt, but they just kept on, and all the time were shouting at him in some language, but we got the drift. After some time, they stopped, but moments later appeared with a pot of boiling water. They threatened to pour it down his exposed anus; I think they even threatened to rape him. A minute later I saw Dr Black. He was smiling, and connecting a wire from an old electric field telephone to Dirk's little toe and another to one of his balls. Then, to my horror, he cranked it up and a charge shot up his legs, causing Dirk to convulse violently and squeal like a tortured girl. Far from content, the bastards then threw the hot water over him, making the circuit longer and the shock go further, and moved the wire up to his midriff, before moving the wire onto his throat, his mouth and into his ear. Finally, as his body smoked into the stench-filled air, they cut him down to where he flopped and convulsed like an epileptic possessed. What a fucking sight.

As my mind scrambled for reason, I tried to pass out like a kid wanting sleep so Christmas came quicker. Instead, I felt a thud, and a gun barrel pressing hard against my temple. 'I wish I could kill you right now, you fuck,' said an African voice filled with hate, as he leant down beside me. 'For six months I was tortured by your army in Heidelberg, before being dragged up to Phalaborwa for more. My treatment was so severe that my body was broken and my spirit was killed. Within days, my many bruises became one, as the blood clotted under my skin and the hair fell from my head. After breaking my fingers and toes, they pulled out my nails with pliers, then, dragging me across the floor by my balls, they nailed me to a post by my penis so I couldn't even piss. They gave me so many drugs that I lost all sense of time, while they injected ether into my scrotum, which caused a pain beyond all others. Three times they tied me up and burnt me with a crank, then each time after it, knelt me in a cage inside a darkened cell, where I lay for a month, shitting in the same place as I slept. Finally, almost a year after taking me, they put me in a padded room and turned on a siren. I nearly went mad. I will kill every one of you South African fucks – every one of you!' Then nothing. The voice disappeared and no one came back in.

I don't know how long I lay there, but I dreamt about a long cold night where the air was filled with screams and terror. But in my head I welcomed the noises, for as long as they screamed, I was all right. From time to time, I'd hallucinate as the convulsing silhouette in front of me took on an endless procession of shapes and forms. I'd even talk to them. And all the time, like a heavy fever, I was boiling hot but freezing cold, while my competing pains amalgamated into an all-encompassing blanket of agony. Soon, day broke, not that I noticed. I'd long since left my body and, like so many who'd gone before me, sat taking comfort from total detachment. My body was broken, but my spirit was strong. And within that realisation of a very small victory, I felt empowered. It felt good.

For the first time in a day, I could see around me. I was sprawled on the floor of a whitewashed room, while the dazzling sunrays belted through a glassless window, illuminating Dirk, his naked and shit-covered body still twitching in the half-light. The stench was appalling and all up and along the walls lay splatter and matter, from the infliction of atrocities as yet unfinished. To my right was the half-jarred doorway that led to somewhere else, somewhere terrible, where a gentle airflow would brush against my damp neck hairs with each person's passing. I hoped they'd keep on passing. And they did. Some hours later my inertia eased, only to be replaced with a hangover from hell. I tried to move, and found that I could, but soon saw I was bound and taped. Luckily, my sweat had loosened the bonds, so, without completely offloading my wrist restraints, I quickly undid them, and the same for my feet. I was so dehydrated that my mouth had all but stuck together, while my body felt like it was lying on nothing but bones, as it had tried to suck every bit of moisture from wherever it could. I thought about trying to make a run for it, but was too weak and too slow, and anyway, they'd shoot me on sight. So, once again, I lay hoping for night but preparing for day, as each approaching sound shot shivers of fear around my system. Embracing them, I stayed alert, as I knew if I drifted off again, I might lose my chance. As I lay still, praying I'd been forgotten about, I tried to interpret each and every sound: the slamming of a door, the ticking of an engine, the now intermittent cries of torture. While all the time, the constant sound of approaching footsteps made me sick.

Finally, the light began to fade. I'd wanted to get through to Dirk, but I couldn't risk the footsteps hearing me. I wondered about Ivan and thought he'd be dead. I hoped not; he was a survivor, and a torturer. I laughed to myself: Dr Black, professional my arse, and I made myself feel better by thinking about Ivan getting a hold of him. He'd show you a real professional. Cunt! I don't know what it was, but after a certain point I knew they'd come, and right on cue the entourage swept through the door like a consultant doing his morning rounds in a ward. 'I'm sorry I left you,' said Dr Black, dabbing his lips after a seemingly fine meal. 'We've been busy.' Then he kicked Dirk before kicking me, which made me wince with pain while I fought the need to fight. This wasn't my chance. 'Anyway,' he carried on. 'We're leaving in the morning, and we have what we want. I'm sorry I mistook you for being part of the other group, but it now seems that you are somebody else, and thus, you couldn't possibly have given me the answers I was requesting.' He started to laugh. 'Anyway, in my business a premature death is a failure by the technician, namely me. So knowing exactly how far you can go, given the political necessity and the tolerance of the subject, is fundamentally important, especially whether or not we have the privilege of letting the subject die, and gentlemen – this evening, we do!' At that moment he bent down to move Dirk aside and clear some space but jolted up as a shout rang out from somewhere else. He paused, then, looking down and into my eyes, said, 'So sorry. I won't be a moment.' And left.

'Dirk! Dirk! Fuck sake, are you there, man?' I said, tapping him while trying to shout my whisper. Nothing. 'Come on, mate. You've got to get it together. Can you hear me? It's Rod.' But still nothing. He was fucked and I knew it. I was enraged. What my mind was reluctant to accept, my body had dictated. The time to act was now! Hope in a future time brings more comfort than knowing you're using your only chance: but that's how some poor bastards procrastinate to death. Not me, though, no fucking way. Every cell in my body was with me, and I'd survive or die trying. That was my ace! I bolted up, but kept my bindings lashed. Then, shaking my head and body to stimulate feeling, I scanned the room to find a tool. Nothing. In the corner, sitting on top of a small luggage carrier, sat the crank telephone, the instrument of hell, but nothing else. Fuck! I looked through the window to a setting sun, but with 'dark out' still minutes away, I held my breath and hoped for time. When I heard screaming and a volley of laughter, my spirits were raised. Like an athlete before a race, I sat trying to stretch and limber up, but with my skin burnt and badly blistered, the pain was all-consuming. Luckily, I thought, I'd only been given the rod; the crank would have killed me! As the moments passed, I began to feel that my granted wish for time had become an unwelcome wait, as, all dressed up, I needed somewhere to go. If nothing else, I was killing Dr Black. That, at least, would be some small victory. I tried Dirk, but again he just moaned and began to spasm. Then, at that moment, I remember having the idea to check the pockets of his trousers, which were still slumped in a corner with the rest of his kit. But as I crawled over and took a hold of his shirt – bang! All fucking hell broke loose. Thump after thump after thump rained down like a giant's footsteps, then rifle fire like I hadn't heard in years, lots of it and sustained. In the dwindling light I glanced through the window to see the .50-cal. bunker destroyed, and the gate totally smashed. Smoke and debris filled the air while the wretched stench of cordite became like a freshener to the damned. I froze for a moment to take it in, but was thrown at the wall by a round which shook the foundations and sunk the roof. With an acrid dust caking my nostrils, I made my move.

I edged through the door and into the corridor. To my left lay the courtyard I recognised, to my right, some yards away, lay an open gable end, so I legged it, but after two steps I stopped dead as tracers darted past like shooting stars. As I took a knee and gulped for breath, I looked to my left. I saw him, Dr fucking Black. Oh, God! Just as I'd left my body when suffering pain, I left my body to inflict it. And while chaos reigned around me, so every ill in the world and every evil I'd endured became focused in my hands as he breathed his last. I was on him. I only dream of what I did – my conscious world has long since forgotten.

As I stood there gasping for air, a familiar face which I couldn't yet place was sat there battered and bruised and smiling straight at me. In the chaos, I'd saved him and I hadn't even noticed. I reached out a hand and pulled him up. He steadied himself and nodded. 'Where's your group?' I shouted. But no sooner had I said it, than I saw them all around me. Christ, what a mess! They'd had their arms broken, their balls cut off and their eyes poked out. I'd eventually learn they'd been killed by having their throats cut and their tongues pulled through the slits.

'Have you seen Ivan, the guy I was with?' I yelled.

'No!' he screamed with an Irish accent. 'What the fuck's happening?'

I shrugged my shoulders. So, keeping low, we staggered from one room to the next, until finally, after seconds which seemed like hours, we stumbled on a ball of bodies tumbling in the fury; one of them was Ivan! Before I could do anything, my new-found friend grabbed a cosh and thumped one of the coons with the same ferocity I'd just spent on Dr Black, while Ivan, already having devoured one, began biting the face of his final foe. I dropped to my knees in pure exhaustion. I fell on my side, to be joined, seconds later, by my revenge-sweetened comrades. For the first time in a long time, we'd created a keep in the castle.

'You all right?' I looked at Ivan. He just nodded. Physically he was broken, but this was his utopia and he was buzzing.

'You?' he replied.

'I'll make it,' I panted. 'Dirk's fucked, though.'

'Dead?'

'Not yet.'

We paused.

'What you want to do?' I said. 'Who's hitting them? If they're no better than these cunts, we'll need to move.'

But as I said that, I looked at the madness outside, then looked at us. We were bruised, battered and hungry. Without sleep and with untold injuries we'd fought like fuck to save our souls, but now, slumped in a darkened room, we were spent.

Knowing we'd have to sit it out, I clambered to my feet and back out to the corridor. The once-thumping insanity had been replaced by a calm, only broken by intermittent bursts of fire, as whoever was outside squeezed the remnants out of whoever was in. Taking a right, and a right again, I found Dirk, still alive but going cold. So, with the last of my strength, I pulled him through and covered him up. Then, slumping down again, I only noticed the Irishman gone when he came back in brandishing an AK47 and a .9 mm he'd fetched from the abattoir next door. He sat beside me and brushed himself down.

'You don't remember me, Roddy, do you?'

I looked straight at him, and although the sense of familiarity was as strong as ever, I struggled to place him. 'Eh – yes. I mean – fuck – where's it from?'

'The Guards, Second Battalion, Kenya.'

Like a bolt from the blue, it came to me.

'That's right, the fucking Guards. But what are you doing here? Lonrho?'

'No, mate!' He shook his head, laughing. 'No, mate, not Lonrho.'

I looked right at him. 'You still in?'

He smiled and shrugged a shoulder. 'You know how it is, Roddy.'

And I did. I'd just met the Fern.

'Who's your boys?'

'It's a long story,' he replied, now cupping an arm, which revealed a fracture. 'They're Provos.'

'Provos? What do you mean?'

'Provisionals! IRA.'

'What, here? What the fuck are they doing here?' I said, as I tried to splint his arm.

'They've been coming here for years, mate!' he laughed. 'They won't be any more, though. Frelimo's put a stop to that, and saved us the bother of keeping tabs on them. We were due to leave, till the fucks hit this place three days ago. Half of our hosts died, the other half scampered. We made as far as some village four miles south, but they caught up with us and slaughtered the village.' I shook my head. I knew that village; I'd heard the slaughter. 'What about you?' he asked.

'Me? I'm just here for a few quid.'

He laughed. 'Same old Roddy?'

'Same old Roddy!' I said.

We remained in our thoughts as the adrenalin numbed our pain, while a silence descended which none of us noticed. Then, from the darkness, came shouts and the sound of screams. We knew that sound well. Then the voices came closer until finally their owners hit the corridor and began booting the doors. As each boot came closer, the tension rose. After a long pause, probably on sight of the abattoir, our door flew in, almost losing its hinges. 'Por favor! Por favor!' I yelled. 'South African – Renamo, boa, Renamo, boa.' Then, gulping for air, we sat waiting on a bullet, which never came. Thank fuck! They left, and closed the door.

If we'd been expecting a rescuing army with food and provisions, we'd have been disappointed. But we hadn't been. They'd killed our captors and let us live. That was enough. Then, as the hours passed and the sun rose, I woke from my shattered doze and, in all sorts of pain, stumbled outside and into a place of death. I'd been here before. Large red patches of sandy dirt lay scattered around me, like mounds of blood-soaked sawdust from a bar-fight floor. The cast-iron gates, once a testament to decay, now lay flattened beside the sandbag bunker, which smoked like an active volcano. Renamo had badly wanted what they'd part-paid us for, and they'd got it. I looked to where the trucks had been, but saw only a line of railway sleepers. Of course, no sooner had I seen it than I realised what it was: our executed men, still lying there from the day before. The place had an eerie silence, one which deafens, but even with no one about, I felt a thousand eyes on me. There probably were. I wandered one way and then another, but when I stood on Larry, I saw I'd wandered enough. We needed out of here, and fast.

I stumbled back to our shattered sanctuary, to find Ivan, beer in hand and puffing away.

'So much for the Muslim north,' he said, as he basked in the sunlight. 'Feels good, doesn't it?'

I looked at him. 'Got to be alive to feel!'

He nodded, then gestured over to our adjacent building. 'Breakfast's served.'

'What?'

'Breakfast,' he repeated, like he'd just been frying eggs. Well, when I looked, it almost was: three lukewarm crates of Castle Lager – better than a kick in the balls.

'At least they left us something,' I said, re-emerging with a crate of breakfast.

'Yup. Nice of them, but that's not all,' he replied, with as much of a smile as you'd ever get out of the man. 'Look round the back! In fact – never mind, take the boys in their breakfast, and get ready to head. I'll be back in a minute.'

And with that, he flicked his spent butt and disappeared, while I hobbled back to our refuge. It stank.

The Fern smiled, though he was starting to go into shock. His arm looked worse by day and, after seeing the rest of his lot, fuck knew what his dreams were like by night. Dirk, on the other hand, still convulsing, just seemed amazed to be alive. Well, I know I was, anyway; I don't think he really knew where he was. I opened the beers, gave one to the Fern and tilted Dirk's head to pour some in, but he just choked. He'd need an IV and fast. But I knew he was fucked; we were all fucked! We were free men who'd just beaten the guards, only to be killed by the swamp. Bastard! But just then came the sound of the swamp draining: it was an engine, Ivan's engine! With total bemusement I looked at the Fern. Then, clambering over timbers from the caved-in roof, I popped my head out of the window and saw Ivan sitting at the wheel of a Mazda pick-up. It was Dr Black's motor and Renamo had obviously missed it. We didn't!

With Dirk lying flat out on the back, as cushioned as we could possibly make him, Ivan took the wheel while we crammed in the front. Ivan's skin was a mess of red welts and blisters, but he'd never answer when I asked what from. So I stopped asking. We thought about what to do as we sat revving at the flattened gates. Go by road, off-road or wait till dark? But fuck it. We needed back to the ship – and fast. So, with fingers crossed and plenty of fuel, Ivan put his foot down and belted forward.

If it was the unknown that bothered me on the way in, then it was the known that petrified me on the way out. Beyond that, I only hoped I'd have a ship to go back to. Otherwise, we'd have crossed a desert to see that the sea was dry. Finally, after several hours of agony, the dirt below us gave way to sand, before, like a mirage for the damned, the *Trader* appeared from behind the undulating dunes. The relief was incredible.

Now I'm not trying to equate our lucky escape from mischievous adventure to anything like what the poor sods at Dunkirk went through, but fuck, it was close. Especially given that we could easily have had nowhere to go, and no means to get there. When we eventually got on board, I saw that Daily, Taff and the Mendes had played a lot of cards, watched a lot of porn and smoked a lot of fags. Fair enough, I'd have done the same. But when they saw the state of us, their jaws nearly hit the floor. We looked bad – really bad. Anyway, as soon as we could, we made south and guess what? When we'd emptied my ship's medic stores, Ivan recognised my jar of 'dead things', and it worked; it actually fought his infection. Personally, I'd rather have taken the infection. But anyway, once within flight range, Ivan radioed for a lift off one of their army choppers. It duly arrived and took us to a military hospital. And while we were well looked after, Taff got his first ever skipper job: bringing the *Trader* to Durban. He did well.

I stayed in for two nights, as did the Fern, and then joined Taff and the *Trader* in Durban. A few weeks later, the Fern invited me to Zimbabwe for a working holiday – well, a long weekend at the Victoria Falls Hotel. It was some place! While there, he filled me in on how he'd been in the thick of it for a long time. For years, the IRA had been sending training units to Mozambique. At first, he told me, it was to give 'fraternal' weapons training on how to turn an African bush war into the kind of guerrilla struggle needed to bring the white nations of Africa to their knees. But later, it was about arms, and Mozambique had plenty. Even as late as 1998, Gerry Kelly, a former bomber and one of Sinn Fein's leading negotiators at the Peace Talks, was allegedly linked to gun-running from Mozambique with a guy I'd later come to know as Robert McBride. Robert, the once commander of Umkhonto we Sizwe, the ANC's military wing and now a South African intelligence officer, was grabbed 'red-handed', according to the Mozambique authorities, after doing a deal for a load of AK47s and grenade launchers at the Polana Canico refugee camp in Maputo. The Fern, fluent in Portuguese and Irish Republicanism, had been in the team's confidence for years. Now, thanks to Frelimo, he was team-less. But, thanks to me, was at least alive.

Anyway, apart from several drinks and a couple of days of doing nothing – well, a couple of days of me telling him all about the inner workings of the then apartheid government – we parted company, but certainly not for the last time. I flew back to Durban and, after sorting my boat and sourcing her work, I made Taff my fully fledged admiral and promoted Daily to his first mate. I also doubled the wages of my Mendes. They deserved it! On leaving, I wanted to say that I was hanging up my gloves, but deep down I knew the truth. I'd lost a lot of money on that deal, but you can't put a price on life, and for that I was content. Besides, my boat had plenty of work lined up, and had already got a contract to move 'army surplus' up to Somalia. As a parting gift, I'd gotten the boys all steaming the night before and, using my new-found wisdom, had nailed 'Rod McLean's ten commandments' to the galley wall. They read:

1. Be courteous to everyone; be friendly to no one.
2. Be aggressive. Be quick.
3. Have a plan.
4. Have another plan, 'cause your first one's piss!
5. Be polite. Be professional. Be ready to kill everyone.
6. Anything worth shooting is worth shooting twice. Bullets are cheap. Life's expensive.

7. Darkness and distance are your friends.

8. Always cheat; always win. The only unfair fight's the one you lose.

9. After a few lagers, nobody will care how – only who; make sure it's you!

10. If you're not shooting, you should be talking!

And with that, I left another battleground to re-enter the 'normal' world in silence. But it was far from golden. And it got worse. Four weeks later, as the wind howled through the freezing darkness of an Edinburgh winter's night, and the branches of the trees tap-tapped against the window to be let in, I sat under the bright, clinical ceiling light, holding my pillow like a shipwrecked mariner clinging to a life-ring. I'd tried but it was no good. If I needed peace, it wouldn't be here.

CHAPTER VI

THE *TRADER* DOWN

Like basic training in the Army, my first time at sea had held few surprises. I'd expected to be treated like shite, and I was. I'd expected it to near break me, and it had. Hell – I even thought I'd enter as a boy and leave as a man. Well, two out of three's not bad. I first started on the 'Old Smokeys' and the steam-powered 'Benidirs', a type of trawler that left from Granton when the harbour still had fishing. In those days my measure of bad weather was simple: crap seas were when the toilet lid fell on you having a piddle, and ultra crap was when you fell over having a shite. But beyond that, immortality and youth went hand in hand.

Joining Salvesen's was different. The Grand Banks, situated off the south-east coast of Newfoundland, are one of the natural world's richest areas, renowned both for fish and oil reserves. The Banks are a series of raised plateaux with a water depth ranging between 36 and 185 yards. The relative shallows teem with life along the bed. For my sins, I was taken on their whaler, the *Fairfree* factory ship, which moored in Leith. It was aboard her that I'd truly come to know the waves.

Like being at war, a ship provides little escape from the weather. Storms can last miles, and miles can take days. Cold becomes a

166

constant, dampness a certainty. And while the continuous gales can blind you, turning your eyes to salt-soaked cavities, the noise, akin to a thousand aircraft, is relentless. But that's not all: what really gets to you is the rolling. In heavy seas it can drive you insane, while in lighter, it's like being in a slow-moving tumbler from which there's no escape. When you drink, it splashes all over you, then, when you swallow, it makes you feel sick. Eating is worse. Your stomach feels like a toiling cement mixer, and your entire body goes green as its motion mimics the sea, while all of the time your cutlery dances and placemats slide. It's shit. But it's better than being up on deck. Up there, the wind only screams, and when you try to shout, your mouth only moves with no sound coming out, while the cumulative miseries – tonne upon tonne of freezing cold water, snow, hail and a blistering sleet – all blow horizontally into your face. It takes some beating.

So with that in mind, if I say I felt undeterred from my next job by a stormy forecast, I hope I'll be forgiven for seeming complacent. Besides, with the kind of gear I was taking to Somalia, the fewer ports of call the better. When I flew back into Durban to relieve Taff of his skippering duties, my arrival, although unexpected, was definitely welcome. Taff had made a good skipper, but he seemed to be relieved when I first walked on board, and I could understand why.

Anyway, it had started out with another fine morning in the Indian Ocean. Like I said, the weather was due for a turn, so I'd spent the early hours with the Mendes checking the rigging, which fastened the containers tight to the deck. Just after breakfast – another one of Daily's now infamous fry-ups – we noticed the sky turning black. Then, within that moment, the light breeze began to stir as the sea birds flocked across our bow and made for land. I took the wheel and increased her speed.

I was still a good day and a half from reaching our port, and at least 10 to 12 miles from shore. I checked the shipping channels to listen for info, but nothing came through. So I gave her to Taff and walked out onto the upper deck. It seemed strange. I looked at the water and the sea was confused, as the darkened humps with their wave tops that broke and blew back on themselves in all directions reminded me of the Pentland Firth with its tides that met. An ominous sign, in hindsight. I walked the deck, then down to the engine room, to where I manhandled several bags of quick-drying cement and, with the help of the Mendes, began placing them about. I told the boys to hold onto their hats. Less than five minutes later, it hit us – a full-on fucking hurricane!

By 0930hrs we were dealing with 70 mph winds and 20-ft waves. By 1000hrs the winds had gone up to 80 mph, while what made it worse was the relative shallowness of the water – probably less than 100 ft – which made the waves mount higher and closer together. Then, as the waves began crashing on the deck and draining through the scuppers, I got Daily on the pumps, in case she started taking on water, but so far she wasn't. The noise was deafening and the fight was on. Now in survival mode, I was barking orders, then, with all my strength, I fought to turn her into the waves, but the wind and seas seemed to push against me, determined to hit us on broadside. Only rapid corrections and hard rudder actions stopped us. But as the gales kept battering down and the waves lashed across, I soon became concerned for the cargo. I knew it was well bolted down, but a moving cargo could mean a capsized ship – and this was a hurricane. Just then, my nightmare was realised, as, with a sharp crack, the port-side cable snapped and began flaying the deck like a cowboy's bullwhip. Fuck!

'Taff!' I shouted, still wrestling the wheel. 'Get it fastened – now!' So with that, he and the two Mendes, like rag dolls in a wind tunnel, began rigging the container. What an ordeal! Ten minutes later they were back, but to our total shock and horror it snapped again, only this time three and a half tonnes of container began moving as the stuff inside came loose. As deck-hands, they were now in all kinds of danger, as each time the bow rose on the crest of a wave it immediately slammed onto another, while the following crest would slam over the deck in a wall of water which engulfed us all. And each time, like soldiers taking cover, the three musketeers would leap into shelter and cling on for life. Sometimes they managed, and sometimes they didn't – at least three times, Taff and the Mendes were knocked for six and swept down the deck, smashing into gear or thrown against the railings, to which they grabbed on like fuck to stop themselves falling overboard.

By now the storm was full on. I tried desperately to push us into deeper water and away from the chop, but I couldn't. I tried to cut a path, but in the confused seas, that seemed impossible too. Then I started hearing some structural creaking, rivets grinding and bolts popping, which drove me mad; then an explosion to my right, where I saw one of the life-rafts getting battered by a wave, exploding open and being whipped away like paper in the wind. Then the popping got worse and, for the first time that morning, I realised just how fucked we were. I shouted for everyone to come up top. There was nothing we could do below, as, if we did tip, I didn't want anyone trapped. I thought back to my trawler days, and tried to comfort myself by saying I'd been in worse, but I hadn't – not even near it. Then I kept saying to myself, 'If the bastard rolls this way, I'm diving that way,' and so on, but then I remembered the time when I was stealing cakes from a shop as a kid, and I said to myself, 'If the cop comes from the right, I'm running to the left, and if he comes from the left, I'm running right.' In the end, he was there before I'd noticed him, and I was nicked. Perhaps this time, I'd be dead!

The *Trader* seemed to groan again. Then, for the third time, the right container of the four broke free and slammed into the left one, sending it careening into the side rail and making her list. I gave Taff the wheel, and, with Daily, I belted down to the galley and grabbed the third life-raft. We struggled with it, then Daily kicked open the side door, which leaned away from the tilt. But to our total horror we saw the next wave. Even with a 10-ft start on the deck, it towered above us, and, if that wasn't enough, there was fuck all between us and the wave but a wide open door. I turned to run for my life, but was hit by a torrent of seawater that threw me down and pinned me hard against the wall. It took me a second to gather myself, but when I did, I realised it was pitch black. I thought that was it, we'd flipped, but we hadn't. The wave had smashed the light and slammed the door tight. It was then I heard Daily. He was screaming. Ankle-deep in water, I fumbled about and grabbed his shoulders, then, with all my strength, manhandled him through to the galley. Poor bastard. What a state. While I had turned, he'd tried to close the door. But he'd been too slow, and the airtight door had been smacked by the wave, which had slammed it shut and left everything from his elbow down on the other side. He was in shock, so I let him be.

As I bolted back up to the bridge, I saw Taff struggling with the wheel while desperately thrashing the throttle to keep the listing ship from tipping. I looked to the skies, but they were as black as they ever were. As another big breaker thumped us side-on, the right-hand container came completely loose and flew down the deck like a ball to skittles. It smacked the galley with a thump like thunder and punched a hole below us. Straight away, I sent out a mayday. I knew that when the water hit the generators and we lost power, we'd be lost in an ocean and nobody would know. When the second container then came loose and slammed into the first, I knew that was it: time to jump.

Racing down the stairs, I grabbed a hold of Daily and brought him to the door. Then, with the other three, we kicked and kicked until finally it opened. With life vests tight, I chucked the raft, which I'd tethered to the door, down into the sea and ushered them out, but nothing. They were all so terrified that no one jumped. So I pushed myself forward and waited. Then, I leapt into a valley between the waves and sunk. Fuck! I waited to rise, but it didn't happen. I tried to swim and almost panicked, as, completely disorientated, I didn't know which way was up. But within that moment, and with my lungs now bursting, I shot to the surface and gulped in air. I summoned the rest as I scrambled for the raft. 'Come on!' I was shouting. 'Fuck sake!' But they didn't move. They didn't seem to realise how fucked we were. Then bang! Another belter broke against the side and they were out, all four of them, like a team of skydivers.

I clambered onto the life-raft, thankful that it was the right way up, then leant out to grab Daily. He was a dead weight. Next came the two Mendes, while Taff, I noticed, was having trouble. It seemed like he was being sucked backwards and under the *Trader*. But finally, after what seemed like a lifetime, he made it over, and we scooped him in before I cut the tether. It was then that the enormity of it all began to hit – but it was far from over. In all my time at sea, I'd never seen anything like this. The waves were vertical walls of angry water and, unlike deeper ocean, these 40-ft monsters were only seconds apart, which made them near impossible to ride, even in our raft! We'd get halfway up, then fall back on ourselves, the five of us tumbling about like pebbles in the swash, only to be held under before popping out to climb again. Soon we realised that we were spending more time submerged than not, and that if we didn't get our breaths in before we went under, we'd be left gasping till the cycle repeated. It was sheer fucking hell.

Anyway, we were soon exhausted and, as we kept colliding with each other, at the total mercy of the sea. Water kept flooding the raft, coming in through the slightest of gaps in the roof, so we removed our shoes in a vain effort to clear it. No use! I looked at Daily and saw his pale white face through our dimly lit tent. We needed out of here – and fast. We wrestled the waves for another hour, then finally the sea eased – slightly. In fact, the wind and waves were still ferocious, but we'd somehow managed to drift to deeper waters, where we could ride the dippers and not be crushed by them. With my badly bruised arms I unfolded the front flaps and took a look out. It seemed like we'd landed on a mass of dark grey sand dunes, except these were moving. My head was in agony, my back was aching and my legs were numb. In reality, we'd suffered more from colliding with each other in the raft than from jumping off the ship. Well, except for Taff. We didn't know it yet, but when he'd jumped and had been sucked back, he'd got flayed against the barnacles under the ship. His shoulders were shredded. Anyway, like five escaped prisoners avoiding the guards, we sat in silence and hoped. I closed my eyes.

Now this wasn't the Navy, and I'd like to have said that in amongst my raft was a survival kit, but there wasn't. On the *Trader* I had three rafts, one on either side of the bridge, and one down below: a spare, if you like, but of spare quality. Well, the two good ones, which included the all-singing, all-dancing survival kits, were fucked. The first had blown away, while the second got smashed by the container. This one didn't even have a repair kit to fix any holes. With my eyes closed, I thought right back to Nampula, to that ill-fated morning when I'd struggled out from the bedlam, and had cursed the irony of surviving the battleground to be killed by the swamp. People could survive at sea – fuck, people could last for months – but without the basics, we'd be dead in a week. And I knew how.

'Water water everywhere, but not a drop to drink,' goes the rhyme. And now we'd be living it. Seawater contains twice as much salt as the human body can hold. So drinking it is madness – and madness it brings. As sailors have gulped it, often knowing the dangers but being unable to resist, their cells would shrink, expand, then explode, as every bit of moisture was released to dilute it. But as the kidneys worked overtime in an attempt to desalinate, the body would enter a vicious circle of self-destruction, with violent fits, rolled-back eyes and foaming mouths. Then, only death was a blessing. I only hoped it wouldn't come to that. For one of us, though, it couldn't.

'Daily's dead!' said Taff, as he slapped his friend's face over and over again. 'Come on, man! Get it together!' he was shouting.

But it was useless. I didn't know how, but his body had probably had enough; still, I'd cry about it later. I looked at my watch and saw it was near five. I knew we'd strayed from our mayday position, and that wasn't so good for being picked up, especially if it was going to be dark. So 'Fuck this!' I shouted, and leapt over to the flap in an attempt to see and, my God – talk of luck! It was like a submarine breaking through the surface, but it wasn't. It was some kind of rusty old tugboat, and was being so swallowed up by each monster wave that it was literally submerged until the swell passed over. But by God, what a sight! By looking at my reaction, the others jumped up like shit off a shovel, and ripped off the front to be immediately swamped by a sheet of foamy water. Two seconds later, and with burning eyes, I waved my arms, but realised he'd already seen me. I tightened my vest and got my boys at the ready, but as the bow of the tug rose as the captain did his best to come alongside, the razor-like hull seemed perilously poised to chop us in half. Fuck! I screamed my head off, and tried to gesture, but 'pissing in the wind' was an understatement. He checked himself, but each time he approached, we, the powerless drifters, seemed ever more determined to slide underneath. Luckily, after three attempts, he managed to come alongside, but within the swell, him being on top of the wave and us being in the trough meant a two-storey height difference. Now, whether by choice or by chance, he'd managed to place himself downwind, so we'd be at a distance from the props as they thrashed away, often exposed by the waves. Constantly wiping my eyes, I looked up and saw a row of tiny black faces; they were shouting something and flapping their arms, but as to what they were saying, I'll never ever know. So I looked along and saw a sequence of fenders thrown over the side, while every yard and a half swung a lorry tyre on the end of an old rust-clad chain, which led onto the deck rail. That was our chance! I grabbed Taff and pointed up. I tried to yell again, but the roar of the engines combined with the screams of the sea made listening impossible. Then, moments later, as the tug rolled our way, the tyres plunged from 20 ft above me to crash in the water before me, and then came back up again to within a yard of my grasp. Fuck it. I jumped and, with as much luck as madness, I clung onto the tyre chain and was whipped up like a catapult boulder and flung against the rail, to where a horde of skinny black hands took a hold of me and wouldn't let go. I hung there like a wet fish.

A second later, and through no merit of my own, they pulled me over and onto the deck. Then, after rubbing my eyes, I jumped up and ran to the rail, to see Taff in mid-flight. This time, though, instead of him grabbing the highest chain, he'd jumped for one further down towards the bow and longer in length. I stood helpless and watched him get flung 20 ft in the air, then slammed another 20 back down. But, like a monkey swinging on a tree, he kept a hold, until finally, after another ducking, we all leaned over and pulled him in, to where he collapsed, exhausted. Minutes later, we'd landed the Mendes.

Well, before we knew it, we were dragged across and put below. We'd been saved. I wondered about Daily, but the dead can't drown, so, with no other option, we left him to wander the ocean. I never heard of him again. Our hosts and lifesavers spoke no English and, although they were nothing short of angels, they seemed totally reluctant to mingle. Instead, they slumped us together in a dark and dampened, rust-covered room no larger than a cell. And even with its low centre of gravity, it soon filled up with vomit. Man, we were sick! Time after time, I'd lie on the floor and close my eyes, but like bed spins when you're totally steaming, I kept jolting up and spewing a fucker. This was the worst weather I'd ever seen, by far. A moment later the skipper walked in, and just stood there being tossed about like he was in the aisle on a speeding train. Instantly, he reminded me of Larry, so much so that I managed a smile. But I knew Larry was dead, and he knew I was ill. Anyway, he was a pleasant enough man: a tall, rake-like figure, unaffected by the storm, who glanced about with a fag hanging from his mouth like it was a rainy day in Brighton. I tried to ask where he was going, but he didn't answer. He wouldn't even speak. I knew it was south, though, that much I gathered. Anyway, he left, then one of his guys brought in a load of water and a relic-like first-aid kit, kept dry in a white metal sandwich box. It did the trick.

The minutes passed, and the hours followed. Then finally, after a full day of anger, the storm subsided. It was over. I looked at my boys and they seemed all right. Apart from the cuts and bruises, and Taff's torn shoulders, our biggest worry seemed to be our spirits. We'd just lost our ship, and our cargo of guns; to me that was a business, but to my crew it was a home. I got to my feet and brushed myself down. We'd been here for hours and the place now stunk. I hobbled to the door and pulled it. For some reason I'd imagined it to be locked, but it wasn't, it was just heavy, and after a tug, it ground open. We may have been prisoners, but our crew weren't our captors. In front of me was a long dark corridor leading to a short dark staircase, while all around me the whine of the engines and the smell of oil coloured my senses like invisible wallpaper. I wandered along, and soon left an area of neglect to find one of transition. From the series of dim, single-bulb lights that swung in the swell like luminous pendulums, I saw two rows of double-decker racks, suspended from dungeon-like chains. It was the crew's quarters. Over each stretched-canvas bunk lay a thin horsehair mattress, while a pillow and blanket only suggested comfort, and seemed ridden with damp. Now, within that mould-scented space, I remembered my youth and the time on the trawlers when I'd busted my knee. At that very moment, I was back.

The trawler had taken an almighty whack when we'd all been on deck tethering the lines. Before I knew it, I was being dragged along, ensnared, towards the deepest darkness of the ocean floor. Well, luckily they caught me, but I'd fucked my knee, so I lay there in that very setting for over four days, with a pain that all but consumed me. In my 14-year-old mind, it was my punishment for being expelled from school after battering the teacher with a T-square, and then being sacked from Martins the Bakers of Grove Street after getting caught pinching their cakes. And shit, I suffered. But all alone and in the dark, something happened that I've never regretted. I lost God, and let go of dogma. How liberating!

I glanced along in the limited light, before walking up the few metallic stairs and coming to a partly opened door, designed as a watertight seal between the galley and the berths. I heard a faint murmur, then a silence, before it started again. I paused for a minute, unsure whether or not I'd be intruding, then, without entering, I poked my head round, to see a row of pushed-up arses, while their owners faced the ground. They were Muslims and they were praying.

I think most people spend a lifetime developing their thoughts regarding the big questions, while others forget about it till life wakes them up. I was lucky: I developed mine at an early age, then spent my lifetime having them proved. It wasn't like I was averse to faith, not like our uncle Charlie who'd worn his atheism like a nametag, after El Alamein. No, quite to the contrary, I'd always wanted to find faith, and I'd always valued the idea of having something to believe in, but it just seemed beyond me. The very same holy man at HMP Leyhill, whom I talked to about evil, had during that conversation looked to the heavens, filled his heart with 'joy' and tried to convince me. He talked about the same things that they normally do: the usual arguments such as there must be a 'first cause' and that everything is so perfectly designed, it couldn't just all be by chance, but must be the work of an all-powerful, all-knowing and all-loving father who judged us all. I wished I could, but I couldn't see it. His 'cause' argument – even if it were true – would only prove a 'first cause'. It wouldn't tell us anything about what that cause was, and it certainly wouldn't prove that the first cause was the all-singing, all-dancing God of the churches. And even if it did, it still wouldn't prove the existence of a designer and of an all-loving being, or, indeed, that any of the other 'proofs' even related to the same being. They could all have been different: now there's a thought! In reality, though, as I stood there watching them pray, I felt their version of God had an easy ride. They'd thank him if they survived the storm yet justify his disinterest as 'will' if they didn't. He couldn't lose!

To me, then, after much suffering, I think it's simple. Because evil and pain exist and our destinies are not given through merit but only by chance, God can never be all-powerful, all-knowing and all-loving. And as someone who's travelled to the ends of the earth and who's seen how religions can differ, it must be that only one, or none of them, is right. For me, it's none. And yes, like my uncle Charlie, who led a life of attrition, I can only say that, as God is invisible, and the world's no different than if he didn't exist, it is simpler to assume that he doesn't. And that's liberating.

When the murmurs had stopped, and the arses stood up, I pushed open the door and was met by a sea of faces. They all smiled. Did God save our lives that day? No, these people did. And did they do that 'good' because they had to? No, they did it because it was the right thing to do, and they were in a position to do so! As far as I'm concerned, that's all the ethics you need.

I walked up to the captain and shook his hand. He offered me a smoke and, by God, I took it. I was never able to ask how they found us, but the more I think about it, the more I feel we got lucky. Within the ocean's expanse, they'd just happened to run by us. I fetched my boys, and while they sat with the crew, sharing their food and drinking their tea, I made myself busy mopping their floor. Well, they'd saved us our skins; I could hardly expect them to mop up our vomit!

Anyway, they say it takes one to know one, so it didn't take me long to figure out that these guys were up to no good. I didn't know what, but I think they were running the coast like us and had detoured to avoid the chop – unlike us. You can't beat local knowledge, although this was a mantra that I'd later come to regret. The next day, they stopped to refuel, then, two days after that, they put ashore at Inhambane Bay, on the muddy Limpopo River mouth, just to the south of Xai Xai. From there we made our way, nautical hitching, if you like, to Durban, from where I made for home and Taff and the Mendes made for another ship.

The loss of the *Trader* was shit – no doubt! I lost a packet of money on the cargo, but at that time I was sure Lloyds would cover me. After all, there was no reason not to; we were downed in an accident, and the manner in which it happened was never disputed. In fact, I later found out that we weren't the only ones sunk during that storm; it was the same weather where one of the big liners, its name escapes me, was deserted by its cowardly crew, who'd fucked off in a lifeboat and left the passengers to sink. No, what got to me was the death of Daily and the breaking of my team. After everything we'd been through, Taff, Daily and the two Mendes were my brothers at best and friends at worst. I'd miss that. And I did.

CHAPTER VII

DANCING WITH DEMONS

Pausing his PlayStation, Kenny leant forward to take the last drag from his boom-stick of a joint. Made with the powder and tobacco spillage from a half-ounce's worth of rolling, it was the only silver lining to running out of hash. After holding it in, he blew it out and sunk back into his increasingly comfortable armchair. The late summer afternoon sun shone brightly through the large bay windows, giving life to the smoke, now thick within his room at the McLean family mansion.

Being often away on business, it helped me to have a bit of extra residential muscle, and with no shortage of rooms to choose from, Kenny was more than satisfied with his temporary accommodation. Zoned out and tuned in, he seemed oblivious to work going on up above him. As the joke went, 'the plaster never sets in Boswall Road', as, since I'd bought the Yacht Club eight years earlier, the interiors were in a constant state of flux. This time, they were ripping out one of the bathrooms to make an extra bedroom. Why, was a mystery to all but me; no one had ever lived up there, and no one ever would. In his dreamy state, Kenny checked his watch – still a couple of hours before I was due back from Paisley where I'd been having a meeting. He felt good.

Just then, there was a shy knock at his door. 'Yes!' he screamed, knowing it wouldn't be Susan or me; he hadn't heard the gates, and neither of the dogs were barking. 'Yes!' he yelled again, but nothing came. His anger at being bothered jolted him to his feet, but this was too quick for his blood – now sedated with Morocco's finest – and he dropped to his knees to avoid falling over. Just then the door opened.

'You all right?' asked a timid teenager to a grown man who, for some reason, was choosing to spend his afternoons kneeling on the floor and facing a wall.

Kenny thought of explaining but, in true hash-head style, couldn't be fucked. 'Never mind, what do you want?'

The teenager, now barely whispering, said, 'Eh, well, we've found something up the stair. I think you'd better come take a look.'

'What is it?'

'I think you better come.'

'It better not be a fucking body!' he joked to the young labourer while righting himself, and with a few more expletives was in tail to the top.

Reaching the works, the tradesman of the duo duly stood aside, while the youth stopped short and pointed to a large hole in the tiling next to the sink. Kenny, still high as a kite, peered through the gap. 'Ah ha!' he said, with a slight air of surprise, but mostly relief. Inside, wrapped up in a clear polythene bag, was a military-style rifle. 'All right, boys,' he said, leaning in and pulling out the dust-covered package. 'I'll just, eh, take this with me. Right. Back to work!' And, with that, marched back to his room.

As there was no one about, Kenny stashed the rifle at the foot of his bed, before sitting back down to his cockpit. Just then, the gates clanged. It was me. By the time he got down to the front, I was on my way back out. I needed off to my lawyers in Palmerston Place and was in all kinds of hurry. 'Hiya, Kenny,' I said. 'I'm just nipping out again. Everything all right?'

'Yeah, great,' he said, seeing I was rushing. I turned my back to leave. 'Oh, wait, there's one thing. One of the laddies found something in the bathroom up the stairs. Behind the wall. You know, next to the sink.'

Initially I looked blank. 'What's that?' I said. I was serious. I was a master of hiding stuff around my houses, and with that much stuff cemented up and partitioned off, I really needed to have a think about it.

'A rifle. A brown rifle!'

'A rifle? Ah, yeah, that one. Ah, right,' I replied, now remembering.

'Well? What do you want me to do with it? It's in my room.'

'Oh, em . . .' I thought about it briefly. 'Och, go down and chuck it in the water, will you?' I said, now pointing to Granton Harbour and the long concrete jetty which surrounded the yacht moorings. 'I tell you what. Take the dog for a walk along the pier and hurl it in at the breakwater. All right?' And with a rhetorical nod, I was gone.

That request had now become a job. 'Fuck!' Kenny said to himself as he saw his relaxing afternoon go down the pan. In his room, he opted to swap the bulky and probably buoyant bubble-wrap packaging for a single bed sheet. Then, not wanting to start fiddling about with it, he left the rifle intact, and looked for a long jacket to conceal it. After having no luck with his own wardrobe, he began searching the store cupboards. The only fruit of his labour was a long number, more akin to a '60s commune than the disposal of a firearm. He looked at his watch. 'Shit! If Rod's back and the job's not done, I'm fucked. Oh well, Pied Piper it is. Now, where's the dog?'

As he descended the steep pathway down to the sea, he looked back up to see McLean Towers, on top of the hill like Dracula's castle. 'Who says crime doesn't pay?' he said to the dog. Moving forward and over the road, they finally made it onto the beach next to the harbour to where the sun scorched down, painting quite the picture. Letting the dog off the leash, it legged it. 'Oh, this is just fucking great,' he said aloud as, being summer, the pier was busy with the usual suspects: ice-cream eating families, seated youths with fishing rods, the odd yacht owner, and of course now, the Pied Piper of McLean. With a slight case of the pot-head-paras setting in, and a realisation that the breakwater was at the end of the L-shaped jetty, still a good ten minutes' walk away, the rifle he was clenching soon began to weigh him down. So, after reaching the halfway point, and clearing most of the pleasure-seekers, he decided that here was as good a place as any.

Removing the sheet, and taking one last recce around him, he slung the rifle as far as he could and shouted, 'Thank fuck!'

But just then, like shit off a shovel, the dog went in after it! In complete disbelief, Kenny made an about-turn, and a beeline for the shore. One minute later, the Pied Piper of Granton was not joined by a rat, but by a firearm-wielding dog. Trying to make an exit while kicking the dog was proving to be a challenge, and the more he kicked, the more the dog, its jaws now tightly clenched around the rifle, enthusiastically grappled with him. I don't fucking believe this, he thought, as he made his way past the spectators lined up on either side of the causeway. 'Max! Max!' he shouted, now turning to the dog. 'What's that you've got, boy? The things they find!' he said, turning to the open-mouthed audience.

Half an hour later I came back to find the sweat-soaked Piper slung over a chair after the K9 battle, while down by his feet lay the evergreen rifle and a well-torn bed sheet.

'What the fuck?' I said, laughing at the sight. 'You need to get off the gear, pal. Why's it still here?'

Out of breath and the sweat pouring off him, he looked at me with all seriousness, like he'd failed at a job. 'Ah had to pretend it was a toy, and that I was a loon! So I've been running about the beach, playing Japs and commandos with a fucking bulldog!'

What a laugh, as he told me this story in detail. That was Kenny – I liked him.

'Right, you useless bastard!' I said, flinging him a dish towel. 'Get your shit together, we've got work to do.'

Ten minutes later he was sitting in the van, drinking coffee. 'Where are we going?' he asked, still trying to get it together.

'Greenock. I've just bought a boat!'

The *Sea Ranger V* was a 1,000-tonne transporter, which Customs had seized in a 1992 drugs bust. I'd originally seen it moored up in Greenock while I was working on another boat of mine, and as luck would have it, it turned out to be for resale. Amongst others I was invited to tender for it and, after having made an offer of £12,000, I got it. Now its estimated resale value to the Exchequer was supposed to be £500,000, which has led some to believe – well, believe whatever they fucking want. But to begin with, it needed a shitload of work done, and, like anyone will tell you when they're trying to sell a car, it's not worth a fuck till somebody buys it. Anyway, I renamed it the *Toto* and registered it in Belize.

Over the next couple of weeks we set about fixing her. The engines needed a service, as did the rest of her parts, but the one thing that really got to us was the tonne after tonne of a thick and toxic oily sludge that lay in her hold and had been used as her ballast. It was disgusting. So, with nothing but shovels, and within compartments where standing was impossible, we poor bastards toiled and spewed with back-breaking pain. It was the worst job ever. Finally, after a month and a half of nothing but graft, she was ready for her maiden voyage; she was coming to Leith.

Two months later, she was painted and polished and ready for sea trials. She'd need them to get her certificates. But a couple of days before she was due to be seen, the harbour master from Forth Ports Authority told me I'd have to move her from Victoria to Albert Dock – only a few hundred yards away, but requiring a bit of manoeuvring. Not a problem, in theory. Victoria Dock is best imagined as a rectangle where, at one end, in line with the short side, lies the access channel. A good way to visualise it is as a snooker table, where the access point is over the yellow pocket running across the baulk, while the *Toto* sat over the left-hand blue pocket facing the yellow. Now, negotiating a 1,000-tonne vessel can be done in various ways, but the *Toto* had a bow thruster, which meant I could propel her forward, keeping her front still, and just swing her arse out for the left-hand turn out of the dock. Then, when she lined up with the exit channel, I'd belt her forward and through the gap. So I did, and to begin with it went well as, unlike the *Trader*, the *Toto* bridged forward of the deck, meaning she fared better at this type of movement. Then, with Kenny on one side of the bridge house, while Sparry was on the other, and my nephew precariously perched on the dockside like a lamb to the slaughter, I waited till the exact moment before launching her full force. But fuck, I blasted her straight into the left-hand wall, demolishing a hundred years of history while my nephew dived for his life in a mass of debris as she bounced to the right-hand side, where – crash! – the same again. With half of Leith now demolished, I had two gaping holes just above the waterline. I couldn't believe it – another delay. Never mind Captain Nemo. I was Captain fucking Birds Eye.

The early 1990s brought a stack of changes. The world as we knew it had changed overnight. The USSR had collapsed and the Cold War had come to an end. To many, it was a velvet revolution. And in some ways they were right. There were no mushroom clouds over London, and South Africa's racial bloodbath failed to materialise. But, for me, that's as far as the flower-waving went. With a collapse in the old world order, there was a rush to build a new one; I liked to call it 'predatory capitalism', or the rush to own resources. Whereas before it was in the name of anti-Communism, now it was in the name of stability; and it was a farce. The new game, which was very British and played by proxy, was in re-colonising, but this time through the back door. How? By creating 'safe zones', almost like World Wildlife Fund game reserves, but in mining areas, which were then heavily protected by private security companies who'd promote them as zones of stability in the midst of continental carnage. In return, the 'grateful governments' handed all sorts of rights and contracts over as kickbacks.

Anyway, this 'new era' spelt new work, and I was dying to get down there. Dirk, after having recuperated with no shortage of gratitude for me, had become involved with the newly formed Executive Outcomes based in Pretoria. Eeben Barlow, its founder in 1989 along with Tony Buckingham and Simon Mann, was another associate of the Civil Cooperation Bureau. And as well as waging a war against change, the CCB had accumulated significant expertise in setting up front-companies to avoid South Africa's many sanctions. So, with the end of apartheid, people like Barlow redirected their skills into the private sector. This meant that Executive Outcomes soon became connected to a web-like structure of multinational mining, oil, security and transport companies that some allege had been created to mask their real function: being guns for hire.

In the end, Executive Outcomes proved decisive in some of the continent's many 'civil wars'. In the case of Sierra Leone, for example, they forced the rebels to the negotiating table, having regained control of the diamond-rich Kono district, which produces two-thirds of the country's diamonds, after only a month of their involvement. Prior to this, in 1994, they'd forced UNITA to accept the Lusaka Protocol after securing Angola's oil and diamond regions for the government. So, all in all – and you can call me a cynic if you wish – Africa was business as usual.

This time, the month-long journey from Edinburgh was pirate-free. And instead of a pit stop in Freetown before a 'diamond coast' delivery, I opted for the easier option of lunch-time in Porto. Since October 1992, Mozambique was in ceasefire. Frelimo had been made to acknowledge Renamo as a political party, while Renamo had to stop butchering folk. Anyway, instead of meddling Afrikaners, the country was flooded with the UN do-gooders, which spelt more opportunity for me. So, after a few backhanders, and a bit of blackmail, I was given a contract to ship aid to the newly stabilised country – the first part of which was coming from Portugal. And with just over 350 square metres of clear deck space and a shallow draught with sealed-keel coolers, allowing her to work in difficult shallows, the *Toto* was well suited to this work. So as soon as I could, I headed for an almost inaccessible inlet near Beira.

It was a hot afternoon when we finally arrived. I'd been up and down this part of the continent more times than a whore's drawers, and could happily navigate the Mozambique Channel with my eyes shut, but this was my first trip to the area near Mozambique's second port. The wharf and the surrounding streets were quiet. Through my salt-water-filled goggles, I discerned a sleepy, almost timeless quality to the place as the distant sea-front dwellings with faded paint jobs and bullet-riddled Coke signs blended effortlessly into the plush green surroundings, broken only by sand-covered roads which led nowhere fast. As I stood on the bridge, I saw a scurry of activity from a distant hovel, then a small army of men – once miserable, now smiling – en route behind a sinewy man in a dirty uniform, a relic from the

Portuguese past. Then, casting my sights further, I saw plumes of thick black diesel smoke billowing like a chimney from the UN crane now tasked with offloading my gear. As I followed its route, past the more industrial area of the now scenic dock, my fantasy was shattered, as for a moment my eyes hit a collection of burned-out Soviet tanks. The scars of war ran deep, I thought. But although I was right, I soon saw I'd got the wrong idea about these tanks. In fact, a few intrepid South African scrap merchants had decided to get in early for the spoils of war. Only problem was that these spoils were still surrounded by land mines – three million of the bastards, to be precise. And one of them had just lost his legs.

Elsewhere, there was plenty of tension. The war was over and the multinational forces were in, but thousands were still to be demobbed, and thousands more were pissed off, hungry and full of scores to settle. Beyond that, I was still nobody's fool, and no sooner had I discharged my cargo to the local UNOMOZ commander, an Italian captain from Albatross Battalion who enforced his stability from behind a mass of razor wire, than I was off. Two days later, I was back in Durban and into the thick of it.

I'd like to say that seeing Dirk again was a happy experience, but it wasn't, as with him came the demons. Together we'd shared an intimacy that went beyond others; together we'd shared torture, and torture's unique. While our cuts and bruises healed over time, the deeper trauma sat like an open wound, which festered away beyond its days. Depression, insomnia, nightmares, anxiety, irritability, affective numbing, flashbacks, shame, mistrust, the permanent notion of injury and a host of other bastard problems that jumped up when you were least expecting them were only some of the symptoms that plagued our existence as time went by. But even living with those afflictions seemed negligible compared to – what, for me, sets it even beyond war – the subtle erosion of our humanity as our minds struggled to rationalise the untold humiliation inflicted upon us from behind closed doors. They say rape isn't a crime of sex, it's a crime of power. So is torture. Like the 'fucking' bit of rape, or terrorism as a means and not an ideology, so the extraction of information is really superseded by torture's true virtue, the breaking down of personal identity.

Over the years I'd often wondered how I'd managed. How had I got through it when so many hadn't? Then, when I saw Dirk had made it too, I wondered even more. I have the answer now, and it's pretty simple. We'd both managed but for different reasons. For me, well, I'd killed the bastard who'd done it, and so had had my revenge. But for Dirk, it was because he'd managed to tie it in with the greater struggle: the quest for his great Boer nation. And now, like a martyr, his bodily sacrifice had changed him from disciple to apostle, as every time he suffered, his spirit gave him strength. What a guy!

Anyway, it didn't take me long to see that his relative survival had come at a price. Just before the 1994 elections, the first since apartheid, Dirk and several thousand of his AWB pals had invaded the homeland of Bophuthatswana, a small state within a state. Eventually they were escorted back by South African troops, but not before they'd killed 30-odd blacks, most of them in drive-by shootings. As Dirk then explained, the white right wing, which had so far posed a serious threat to the elections, was now split down the middle, as moderates and hardliners scrapped for direction. The result? The start of a right-wing bombing campaign, which culminated in a series of massive blasts that left over 20 people dead and scores more injured. And although Dirk wouldn't say it at first, I knew he was up to his neck in it as, over the next few days, 34 of his mates were lifted and charged with murder. I knew then that he felt it was only a matter of time for him.

'Rod,' he said, smiling, as he gave me a list of working options. 'There's no government, no law and no hope, just a rampant wild frontier in which anything can be had for a price. This is the future.'

He was right.

Three days later we were set to sail. For the first time in a long time every piece of cargo was legit, and it kind of felt good. I was heading back up to Beira, and hoped to chance on something for my return. I'd been unable to get anything from my agent in Durban, which was unusual. Still, time was with me, and with my next run over two weeks away, I could afford to relax. That afternoon, and literally minutes away from casting off, I saw a Mazda pick-up scream along the wharf, and an excited Dirk jump out, brandishing a scrawny black lad like he was a trophy. In some ways he was. Fidel was a former Renamo commander and long-term fighter with Giraffe Platoon, one of their infamous units. Renamo, according to Dirk, had been hiding its weapons throughout 1993, and now Fidel and others were trying to sell them – recycling at its most efficient. Fidel, along with a few of his pals, knew the location of scores of weapons caches dotted from Massingir to Machado in South Africa, most of them simply buried in the sand. Now, like Long John Silver, Dirk wanted us to scour the shallow coastline in a bid to reclaim them. Only thing, he then pointed out, was that others were already at it: kind of rivals, who were entering South Africa through the Red Cross camps or across the desolate reaches of the Kruger National Park. Having said that, to our advantage was that these guys only operated in teams of five or six, so could only deliver small shipments every few days, and were still in the business of bribing long-haul truckers to ferry them between the northern Transvaal and the PWV (Pretoria–Witwatersrand–Vereeniging). We, on the other hand, could take their entire lot in a 'one-er' – and for free. Well, we'd have to sling Fidel and his pals a few quid, but certainly next to nothing. Dirk even knew where to get rid of them, though it didn't take me long to figure it out for myself.

Anyway, talk about 'right place, right time'. By the time we got them, I felt a bit like a Durex trader when Aids hit. Political conflict, growing crime and a perceived need for self-protection meant that South Africa's demand for shooters went through the roof. Even the criminal networks, who needed arming themselves, began to trade with the mass population as, by that time, murders had shot up over 60 per cent, armed robberies 100-odd, and rapes sky-rocketed by more than 80 – and believe me, if there was one thing that put the wind up the white folks, it was the thought of their women getting shagged by a black man.

As the weeks became months, I soon became part of the scene and was constantly in contact with other networks. Any criminal fraternity worth a fuck was down here and doing business, and I was in amongst it. Some smuggled guns, others did drugs, others concentrated on vehicles, gems and precious metals. Fuck, some even did ivory and rhino horns, which really pissed me off. Anyway, after initially saying no, it was only a matter of time before I did my first drug run – with a substance called Mandrax, much of it coming from Pakistan but transited through Mozambique en route to South Africa. When Dirk first asked me, I thought he'd said anthrax. Then, after telling him to get fucked, he clarified Mandrax, so I told him to fuck off again!

Although most traffickers tend to concentrate on one drug, or one commodity, there's those who'll transport anything. In the old days it was less common, but then that was before the networks. In all, given opportunity, capability and a profit, there's now little that specialist transporters won't handle. Personally, I'd always shied away from drugs. If I'm honest, I was still trying to retain an air of nobility; namely, the 'noble warrior'. Now I know that logically, that's a load of piss, taking into account the fucking misery the arms trade causes, but that was then and this is now. In reality, though, I'd never been a drug user so knew little about it. But I had been a soldier, and that was my game. Anyway, one thing for sure was that it was always going to be a matter of time. And that time had come.

About a week after he first asked me, I got news about my bank account in Pretoria. When the ANC came to power, they set about dismantling the instruments of apartheid. The CCB was disbanded and hounded, and along with it, every bit of juice that came with it, which included finances. Luckily, I'd seen this coming, and to a large extent had put it into something else, which I'll come on to later, but I still had a chunk of cash and a safety box full of gold, which simply went missing. I was obviously gutted because, on top of this, I'd just found out that Lloyds had refused to pay out on the *Trader* after losing £8 billion in four years. So, all in all, I was down about four hundred grand – not exactly small change.

Anyway, Mandrax, as I soon found out, was a synthetic drug pressed into a tablet form. The active ingredient, Methaqualone, was prescribed in sleeping tablets and used for high blood pressure during the '60s and early '70s. Folk even reckoned it was going to be a miracle cure for all the world's ailments, so that softened the blow for me. The problem was, though, that serious side effects soon began to surface, including dependency. So when most of the world banned it, the rest became drug prohibition history. No sooner had the pharmacies walked out than the crime syndicates stepped in. It was perfect. With a hooked market already established, it was always a winner.

Packaged by the 1,000 at source, before being exported in bulk, it seemed nothing in size compared to the equivalent in arms. And with still a few years before crack cocaine began to squeeze it out of the market, it didn't take me long to see its merits. After a few successful runs, and having completed the last of my UN jobs up the coast, I decided on a trip back home.

When I returned to South Africa, I was met at the airport by an over-excited Dirk and, to my surprise, none other than the man himself, Ivan. My stomach turned. While I'd been away, they'd got together and had been busy. I thought I was coming back to do a job with Executive Outcomes, which in part, and to the best of my knowledge, was still available; but before doing that, they wanted to do a deal – the last 'big one', they said. Had I not learnt my lesson?

The rain pelted down with anger, while the torrents of floodwater cascaded along the cracks of the unmaintained tarmac and forks of lightning struck all around us. The smell of dampness and the lack of air did little to rest my nerves as we sat in Dirk's sky-blue Datsun, awaiting our man. From my back-seat view, the rows of all-white houses – probably spectacular in the usual sunlight – looked depressing, reminding me of Florida when cloudy: a real cultural abyss. Beyond the yards of pristine white security fencing ran the primitive street drains; nothing more than open irrigation ditches like you'd see on most farms, and now a symbol of just how close poverty and wealth were entwined in this country. As I began to daydream, I saw Ivan as he sat patiently, his left hand gripping the overhead handle, while his short-sleeved shirt revealed the lasting legacy of a time we never spoke about. The full length of his arm was dotted with large scars, the result, he'd eventually told me, of them burning plastic bags and pressing them onto his skin to form big raw welts, which were then 'washed' with salt water, causing him to pass out. Now, I'd want to say that, like Dirk, he carried them as trophies, but in reality he saw them as little more than birthmarks. He was fearless!

Finally, after 20 minutes, a distant ball of spray revealed an oncoming pick-up, while a moment later the automatic gate began to grind as its rusty mechanics struggled under the weight of its obvious reinforcements. I held my breath. Under the relentless rain, the pick-up stopped dead in front of us, to reveal a large bearded man and a dog, while on the open-air back, clinging on for dear life, sat a boiler-suited black man, struggling to stay alive. This was his servant.

'Are you well?' he shouted, followed by something in Afrikaans, before he gestured us in and out of the rain. He looked kind of familiar, but I couldn't place him. When we got inside, I couldn't believe it. Fucking Joost De Vries: that fat cunt from Namibia! I looked at Ivan and Dirk, but thought better than making a childish face. They'd known that had they told me it was him, I'd probably have told them to get fucked. So they hadn't. Anyway, I was here now and there was nothing I could do. So, swallowing my anger, I sat down in his white-tiled and white-walled temple of kitsch and began to listen. He was an angry man.

Throwing round his Madison Reds, a strong cigarette, before placing them back on a wooden zebra, seemingly designed for the job, he muttered in Afrikaans till his servant boy had left to pour the drinks. Then, with a quick squint to the now closed doors, he said in a lowered voice, 'You won't have heard of Project Coast, will you?' And looked to Dirk and Ivan as they sat there shaking their heads for me.

'No,' I said. 'Should I of?'

'No, not really. It was our way of bringing South Africa's CBW programme up to date.'

'Chemical – biological – weapons?'

'That's it. I worked closely with Dr Basson, the project officer and head of the CBW group. Our aim was to conduct secretive research, namely conventional and covert support of CBW production and technology for warfare. During the 1980s we hired Dr Basson, who supplied us with lethal CBW to use against any possible threats to our regime, and we had plenty,' he said, laughing, which then turned into a fit of coughing. 'Anyway,' he continued with a red face, 'then came that bastard de Klerk, who was hell-bent on giving our country away. First he lifted the ban on the ANC, then he ordered a stop on the CBW programme, which obviously threatened Project Coast.' He looked down, as if biting his lip. 'So what did we do?'

'Kept on?' I said, half-arsed.

He smiled. 'In a manner. You see, our focus with Basson turned to a different area; that of non-lethal substances. Namely . . .' he smiled even more at the boys who were already grinning, 'Mandrax, Ecstasy, CR – a riot-control agent, and BZ – a psychoactive incapacitant. And, man, I tell you, we've really done it! Two years ago Dr Basson got $2.4 million from the Surgeon General, Neils Knobel, to import half a tonne of Ecstasy from Croatia. And last year alone, we made nearly a tonne of crystalline ourselves. And that's not all,' he said proudly. 'We import as well – especially the kind of stuff you've been running.' He looked straight at me. 'Mandrax.'

As I sat staring him out and holding his gaze, I felt contempt; as the more he said, the less I felt able to say no. I was back in a bad place and I knew it. And whatever it was, I was going to hate it. Sometimes I have these flashes; they're visions of the person in front of me lying bludgeoned to death as a result of my hand. Sometimes my urge becomes a compulsion and it's difficult to control – there's even been times when I couldn't! And now, within that space, I fought my need to batter that fat fuck to death with the wooden zebra which sat beside him. I felt my heart begin to race.

'Why? Why bother?' I belted out.

He laughed out loud. 'Why? So we can get the fucking Kaffirs hooked, that's why! The Americans have been at it for years. I just can't believe it's taken us that long to start.' He turned to Dirk. 'Tell him, who takes Mandrax?'

'Coloureds and Indians!'

'That's right, fucking goffles, places like Merebank and Wentworth are full of them.'

191

I shook my head; this was always a by-product of dealing with these people. But like water off a duck's back, I'd never paid any attention. As I thought about it, he obviously read my mind.

'Oh, don't worry about it, you Kaffir lover. Even those days have passed – that's not why you're here. You see, Dr Basson was given a year to wind up the remnants of Project Coast, as de Klerk eventually ordered all CBW research destroyed. Now, when that finally happened, Basson and some of his chums made a fortune from the privatisation of their front companies. While others, like me, were simply paid off.' He shook his head. 'And that's simply not good enough!' He sparked another smoke. 'Anyway, I'd always felt something like this might happen, so when it came to declaring our inventory, some of us were less than honest about what was where, and, in particular, the stuff that we had in transit. I like to see it as my pension: a replacement Rolex for my years of loyal service.'

I was beginning to see what he was getting at. I smirked. 'So where is it?'

He paused. Then, after a deep drag, he looked through the smoke and whispered, 'Quelimane.'

'Mozambique Quelimane?'

'The very place,' he replied. 'All you need to do is get it, and bring it back. We'll do the rest.'

I said nothing, but leaned forward and poured another drink. To be honest, regardless of his underlying threats, this was the kind of job that interested me. And provided we weren't dealing with fuckwits at the other end, there was little reason to say no. Besides, I knew Quelimane. It was a small fishing port along the Rio dos Bons Sinais, 'River of Good Signs', in the Muslim north, about 16 miles in from the Indian Ocean. So I was about to start negotiating the deal, when, to my total fucking amazement, his arrogance got the better of him.

'You know, Rod,' he said. 'We've been very good to you, what with all the work we gave you during the '80s, and, of course,' he stopped to look at Dirk, 'that bit of property we helped you get, just before the Kaffirs took your dough. I'm sure they'd still want it, and we've not even concluded the papers – yet.'

I couldn't believe it. 'Are you fucking kidding, you fat cunt?' I screamed as I jumped to my feet and reached for my blade to slash him to fuck.

'No, don't!' shouted Dirk and Ivan like a chorus, as they hurdled the table to stop me.

'He didn't mean it that way! He's just saying,' spluttered Dirk, seeing his last chance at riches fly down the shitter. 'Come on, Roddy, calm down. He's not threatening. He's just saying.'

But he was, and I knew it. I knew exactly what the fat bastard was saying: help us out or we'll grass you! I stopped, took a deep breath, then, after much thought, sat down. I'd fucking have him. One way or another, I'd fucking have him.

'I see now why these boys think so highly of you!' he said with a laugh, as he tried to diffuse the tension. 'Look, all I'm saying is that our nest egg's got a shelf-life. Whether it's the Kaffirs up there or the Kaffirs down here, someone's going to take it if we don't act fast.'

I finished my drink to calm my nerves. I was still raging. 'It's got an airport, hasn't it? Why don't you just fly it out?'

'In the old days, we did. That's why it's there. The ships would come in from Pakistan, and we'd fly it over. But we can't now. We don't work for the government anymore and UNOMOZ has the airport. Besides, we're average Joes – just like you. Which is another reason why we want you. This is what you do – and do well.' Then he leant in again and lowered his voice. 'Listen, I'm not alone in this deal and I'm not even in charge. Apart from the four of us, there's another two whom I'm not going to mention, suffice to say that they're from the political class – and we don't want to cross them. We've thought about every bloody way to do this: the 91 miles along the rail line to Mocuba, or by road somehow up to Nampula. Fuck, even by getting one of the shrimping boats to bring it out to you in the ocean. But we can't – we just can't. For one, there's too much of it, and when it's out, it's out. We've only got one shot at moving this, and we've got to avoid them all: the government, the UN and any other Kaffir who wants to put his nose in. No, there's only one way to do this, and that's right down the middle, through the front door.'

I wished he hadn't, but the prick had got my attention. 'How much are we talking?'

'Well, the whole deal's got to be worth a million US. That's not street value, of course, but for that we'll give you a fifth. Two hundred grand. Oh, and your house is a done deal. What do you think?'

I paused. 'So let me get this straight. You want me to sail up a river in broad daylight with a 1,000-tonne vessel, bright red, and moor up to load a million quid's worth of Mandrax like it's a few crates of bevy? Are you fucking mental?' I started laughing. 'Sorry. Am I fucking mental?'

He paused. 'Are you?'

They all looked at me.

I started to shake my head while feeling a burst of excitement. Then, after a long silence, I looked up. 'Aye, I am!'

Like a hammer falling on glass, the tension shattered and the smiles broke out, apart from on Ivan, that was. 'Good,' he just kept saying. 'Good.'

'What are we picking up, anyway? I mean, what are we *supposed* to be picking up?' I asked.

Fat Balls laughed. 'Coconuts.'

'What?'

'Coconuts – lots of them – and maybe the odd shrimp if you fancy!'

That day I left Fat Balls as a slave. Not to him and his gang of wanks, but to the demons of my very own impulses. We all have liberty; we come and go and do as we please. But like me that rainy day in Durban, few of us have freedom. Now, within my cell, deprived of either, I see that at that moment my life became rudderless, bouncing me down the rapids as, for the first time ever, I switched from pro-action to reaction. I was now on the back foot. Since I could remember, I'd always had discipline; it's what got me through. But beyond that, I had willpower. And willpower makes you smart because it comes from the head and not from the heart. It brings you wisdom, which lets you forge the life you imagine rather than the life you have to live. My need for adventure and making good on my losses had allowed that willpower to partially slip, and I would eventually pay the price. Two days later, we sailed past Maputo for the River of Good Signs. Looking back now, I seemed to have missed them all!

'What's wrong with you, boss?' said Taff as he saw me wipe my brow and throw on a jacket in the midday sun.

'Na, nothing, pal. I must have caught something the other day, from all that fucking rain.' To be honest, I was starting to shiver, but like a sick kid on match day, I was determined to play.

Soon the open sea gave way to the muddy water of the Rio dos Bons Sinais estuary. To the north lay the beach of Praia de Zalala, with its endless white sand, lined by a dense foliage of casuarina trees – the kind of place most of us only dream about. While Quelimane itself, another colonial relic founded in the fifteenth century as a Swahili trading city, had seen everything from gold and ivory to David Livingstone passing through on its waters, now it would see me.

Now, ships aren't exactly seagoing 'artics', so entering a harbour is nothing like driving a HGV through an unfamiliar city. In a harbour, things change, often suddenly and without warning. Sandbars can suddenly appear, as can the wrecks of stricken ships. Navigational aids can move, or even disappear, while shipping channels, narrow and often tricky to negotiate, can soon become a nightmare if the wind gusts up or a fog sets in. For that, then, you need a pilot, an experienced guide who knows the waters and who can draw an accurate chart, with all its shoals and buoys, from nothing but memory.

At 1400hrs we hit the 'precautionary area', the place where you'd normally expect to meet the pilot before heading up the channel. But by 1500hrs we were still waiting, and by 1600hrs I was raging. So while Taff was busy in the engine room, I sat with Dirk and Ivan on the bridge and tried to figure out what we'd do. We'd obviously been let down by the man who'd guide us, but we'd already heard that the stash had been moved from its hiding place on the outskirts of the town, and now sat at the harbour with nothing to protect it but a pile of coconuts and a few tonnes of shrimp. No fucking good at all! So, after some arsing about, we agreed that being there by dark to load up and leave by the next morning was a priority. Any longer and we'd probably get grabbed. So, reluctantly, we did what we had to, and I got on the VHF-FM radio and asked for a pilot. Now, the problem is that pilots on rivers and canals aren't always professionals. In fact, they're more likely to be regular crewmembers, like mates, who've been running the river for years. Combining this inexperience with the conditions of war-torn Africa, I got a vision of even more red flags than I'd normally see on a winter's day on Portobello beach. Anyway, when the bastard turned up – promptly and with a smile – I let him be and gave him the wheel. Then, after watching him negotiate a sequence of channels without a hitch, I relaxed a bit. But then my fever soared.

'You better take a lie down, Roddy,' said Dirk, after taking a look at me. 'What have you got?'

'I don't know, mate. I don't fucking know.' I tried to play it down, and lit a smoke, but I felt my stomach go and I spewed a fucker, while moments later I began to shit like it was going out of fashion.

'Go lie down, man! I'll grab Ivan!'

And with that, I slumped onto my bunk as the *Toto* made the last mile towards the port. I always remember being sick and vowing to appreciate good health when I got it back. That normally lasted as long as the first smoke; but as I began to fade into delirium, I swore on my grave that I'd give up my vices if my flu would pass. But it didn't.

A minute later Ivan walked through the door, took one look at me and said, 'You've got malaria, mate!' He then disappeared, to return with two bottles of water, a bucket and a pack of chloroquine. 'Let's hope it's benign,' he whispered. Then, as there was little else he could do for me, he went off to do a drug deal, and left me to shit in a bucket to the sounds of the muezzins calling the faithful to prayer.

Well, as it turned out, the gang that brought the gear only brought us half, because they were worried about getting bumped for money. Then it turned out that on top of the Mandrax they had a load of crystallines as well. Looking back, I think that they really had a clandestine lab set up, which they were shutting down, meaning I was more like a removal man than a courier. But anyway, that all took an extra couple of days, which was lucky for me, because I was out of it. As my temperature soared to 40°C, I swear I've never felt so ill or so alone, as within my own inferno I was living a nightmare, where my only comfort was a call five times a day, reminding me I was alive: 'Allah u Akbar, Allah u Akbar – Ash-hadu al-la Ilaha ill Allah, Ash-hadu al-la Ilaha ill Allah', and so on. Bizarrely enough, though, it was beautiful and it kept me going.

On the morning of the third day, I stepped outside to a rapturous welcome and a crystal-clear morning. Had I been home, I'd have stayed in bed for a week, but thanks to the chloroquine and helping hand from Ivan, the worst had passed. So, still feeling weak, I took my first food in days, and thankfully my energy rose; but as soon as I inspected my cargo of coconuts, a sudden surge of adrenalin took over and shoved me back to reality. We needed to go.

'Right! Have we got everything?' I shouted to Dirk.

'Yeah. It's all here.'

'Any problems?' I asked, as I started to get myself together. There was a pause. 'What?'

'Na – it's nothing,' said Ivan, walking over after hearing my conversation. 'Just the usual fuzzies wanting to go thieving.' He stared at me. 'But put it this way, it's time to go.'

I wanted more of an explanation, but I'd rather have had it back on the move. 'Have we got a pilot?' I shouted down from the bridge, to where Dirk pointed at a scrawny old black man, now propping his clattered old bike against the crumbling harbour wall.

'Who's that?'

'That's the first ever guy who didn't make it,' he answered.

'What?'

'It's all right; he's a good man. We've been using him for years. He was sick, or so he said.' Then Dirk looked at me with an air of uncertainty. Well, any other time I would have told the old guy to get fucked, but as it was, I felt a certain empathy for the lame. So he jumped on board and we were off.

Call me super-paranoid, but ever since Freetown, all those years before, I'd always made a note of checking every boat around us as soon as we were under way, so if it popped up again, I'd let fucking rip if it came anywhere near me. Well, a lot of the shrimpers looked the same, and we'd become quite the occasion in the big red ship, although in hindsight it was probably more to do with the steady stream of hookers who'd lined up for Taff. But anyway, as we left the port and cruised the river, I couldn't help but harbour a really bad feeling. I was sure we'd get hit and here seemed perfect for doing it. So while Taff stood at the wheel with our alleged pilot, I made my rounds to search for stowaways. I checked the berths, I checked the cabins, then I walked the length of the deck and down the side-stairs into the engine room, where I had a good forage about, but nothing. Oh, well, I thought, as long as the pilot's not a plant, we should be fine. But no sooner had I said that than crash! This massive wall of noise ripped through the ship and shook everything from the rivets to my bones.

'Oh, no!' I shouted, 'cause straight away I knew exactly what had happened. We'd run aground. 'Stop! Fucking stop!' I screamed, as I tried to run, but as soon as I made the stairs, I felt the engines stir and, again, this long fucking grind. 'No – stop – fucking stop!' But no, he grinded one way, then the other, and before long the dim fuck had wedged us in solid.

They say there's three kinds of skippers: those who have, those who will, and those who have but won't admit it. And that's fine, 'cause it's what you do next that counts. So when I got to the bridge and saw him thrashing the controls like a fucking prick, I hooked him a fucker and sent him flying. Bastard! Unless you're totally sure there's deeper water ahead, you do not apply power and push your way through. He did, and we stuck in harder. The second most stupid thing to do is to then shift into reverse, power-up and back out; that only sucks up mud and vegetation, while fucking up the propellers. The bastard had done that as well! So now we were fucked – and it was about to get worse.

After half an hour's cursing there was only one thing for it – on with the suit and over I went. Being in a rubber suit with malaria is a sentence. There's no way round that. But as the only one who knew what to look for, it had to be me. When I got down and adjusted to the murky water, I saw that the hull was wedged tight and, worse still, the propellers were thick with vegetation, and buckled. Bastard! So, sick as a dog, and with the sea snakes now biting my heels, as lethal as the saltwater crocodiles they shared the river with, I struggled to fix my boat while knowing I was fucked. And I was. After two hours of coming up and going down, and almost passing out with dehydration, I began to entertain an old friend I'd long since banished – my very own self-doubt. We were marooned in broad daylight!

I'd been sitting on the deck and staring at nothing for ten minutes before Ivan said something. I tried to pretend that I'd been thinking, but I hadn't. My body was all but broken and now, mentally exhausted and plagued by the absurdity of it all, I was enjoying the nothingness. I unzipped my suit and tried to fall out, but, like running in mud, my movements were hampered. Instead of thinking about how to get my drug-laden ship away from these hell-riddled shores, my entire being was consumed by a lamenting for my family.

'Rod. Roddy!' It was Ivan. 'I'm sorry to say, mate, but I think we've got trouble.'

I looked up, but already knew what he was saying. Being marooned in this part of the world was like being an injured animal while the vultures circled; it was only a matter of time. I climbed to my feet, stuck my jeans back on and lit a smoke. 'Come on, mate,' I said to Ivan. 'We've been in worse.' And we had, but we'd been in worse in better shape, and that was the difference. I'd lost my feelings of immortality years before, probably in the Congo, but I'd replaced that with a calm acceptance of death which served like a shield, and that had seen me through. Now, though, for the first time ever, I felt vulnerable. Maybe I'd aged.

'Have you seen something?' I said to Ivan. He just looked at me. Just then there was a crack; then another, this time followed by a whizzing noise that we knew only too well. So we hit the deck like sniper victims and crawled the length to the bridge. On entering the galley, I saw Dirk, R4 in hand, clambering up the stairs and onto the bridge.

'What the fuck is it?' I shouted.

'Man, fucking moonts on the bank,' he answered, pointing to an area some 200 yards off. Two seconds later we were up behind him.

'See anything?' I shouted to Taff as he scanned with binoculars.

'Yeah – a few bodies. No boats though.'

'Where's that fucking pilot?' I said, starting to turn the place over. They looked at me. 'I've not seen him,' said Dirk.

'Oh, fucking great. Just great. Now they'll know who we are and what we've been doing.' We're completely fucked, I thought, but never said. 'What's he done – jumped the side and swam for shore?'

'Probably. I've not seen him for the last hour,' said Taff. 'But let me check anyway.' And with that he left, leaving the three amigos to plot our fate. So I grabbed a bottle of rum and four half-washed tumblers, and divvied up a grog ration like it was the Battle of Trafalgar.

'Right! What have we got?' I asked, with the sweat pouring off me.

Ivan removed his metal-framed sunglasses, wet them with his breath, then looked up as he polished them on his well-soiled shirt. 'I think they'll hit us tonight – and in force!'

'How many?' I asked.

'Fuck,' answered Dirk, standing up at the window. 'Could be scores. It depends who gets here first. The word's out that we're grounded, and as soon as that Kaffir makes shore, they'll know it's more than coconuts we've got.'

'How's that?'

Dirk hesitated to answer, but then Ivan gestured him on. 'Because, well, he's the bastard that's been looking after it, and he knows we're out on a limb!'

'If we lose this, that fat cunt's not going to be happy!' They just looked at me. 'There's going to be trouble, right?'

'Right,' said Ivan.

Just then we heard another burst, then a ricochet that smashed against the deck rail and nicked across the window. We hit the ground, before Dirk, taking it upon himself, slowly eased an eye up to the bottom of the window and tried to look out.

'You look like you're trying to avoid your landlord!' I said. 'How many times have I seen that?'

We all started laughing – but not for long.

'Oh, fuck!' yelled Dirk when he finally made it. 'Taff! He's down.'

We bolted down and onto the deck, to where, only 5 yards away from the door, lay a twitching Taff over a pool of blood.

'Fuck!' I screamed, running over, but as I did, the fuzzies opened up from the bank, too far off to aim, but 'spray and pray' can still kill. So, grabbing a hold of his shoulders while Dirk took his legs, we dragged him back and onto the galley table, my makeshift theatre.

'Right, Dirk!' I shouted as I stripped off his shirt and fumbled with the light. 'Up on the bridge. Anything comes over, kill them! Ivan, on me! I need the med-kit.'

Looking down, Taff had a classic 'sucking chest wound' from an AK47 round which had gone in through the upper right side of his chest. The blood was bright red and foamy and I could smell the wound as I watched the steam escape with every breath that he struggled to make. I took a hold of his head and supported his body while I squeezed him tight to lift him forward, and when I did, I could see the exit wound, a carbon copy of the front but with a bit less foam. So, with Ivan still away, I sealed it with the cellophane from my smokes packet and taped it up, while suction from the front sealed it nicely. Just then, Ivan thrashed back fumbling with the zip to grab an IV, which we started immediately. Then, as Ivan held it up, I cellophaned the front, which wouldn't seal as well as the back, but still stuck as we struggled to keep its pressure.

Then, to my horror, the pandemonium increased as we heard Dirk from the bridge, and the R4 ripping away. It was on! Ivan looked at me, then shook his head.

'Fuck this!' I screamed, but more out of frustration as I fought to keep the pressure. With my left hand, I tipped the kit upside down and grabbed a load of field dressings. I knew one wasn't enough, and folded a first one in half to push it against the cellophane before taking another to fasten it down. Then, almost instinctively, I flipped him onto his bad side, with his legs in the air, and tried to get some colour back. But just then it hit me – probably what had already hit Ivan, but he didn't want to say. What now? What the fuck was I going to do now?

Without thinking, I'd packaged him up for an ambulance that was never going to come. And within that moment I felt jealous, as for the first time ever I envied the dead, whose fate was already written. I looked up at Ivan, who'd entertained my performance, to see him staring right through me, not an emotion in sight. Slowly I let go, and when I did, I saw that Taff was long since dead. His last breath had passed and I hadn't even noticed, as once again I'd lost myself within a process to escape reality.

'Come on, Rod,' he said. 'Let's go fight some Kaffirs, eh?' And with that, he stopped humouring me and turned back towards his berth and grabbed his rifle. But I stayed, frozen in time. To me, this was hell. Today, in my world, hell was like this: my floating opportunity now a grounded coffin, while everything I'd done, and everything I would do, had been left at the mercy of a faceless enemy who'd trapped us by chance and would kill us by their numbers. Somehow, I'd fallen down a rabbit's hole where, like my upturned boat, everything that was up was down, and what was left was right! And now, like so many times before in my life, the harder I pushed, the further backwards I went. I was now moments away from losing all. So, instead of reaching for my rifle, I walked to the bridge, to where Butch and Sundance stood waiting for the onslaught, and picked up the phone. I phoned home.

My youngest son answered. It was a portal to the real world. And while he waited for his mum to come back from Tesco's, I waited on something which no doubt would be terrible. But when he asked after me, I didn't have the heart to tell him. How ironic. As he tried to make his life sound more exciting, I tried to play mine down. How it touched me. I was never very good with goodbyes, anyway; I hated the finality of it. I'd always preferred to slip out the back door and let time do the separating. And now, faced with 'the end', I could only say that I loved them. There was nothing ever beyond that!

I put the phone down, poured the last of my rum and lit a smoke. It was approaching 1800hrs. Now, half-dazed with chloroquine, booze and a healthy burst of adrenalin, I made my way back to the deck and sat down, back against the galley, and took comfort from my disassociation. I thought back to my time with Dr Black, and of how I'd got through it by almost letting go, and so now, faced with little alternative, I put my face to the red glowing sun and accepted my fate. It felt warm. It felt good!

If sunrises are a privilege, then sunsets are a reminder. And as I sat looking down on myself, on what I'd become, it suddenly hit me. And I began to laugh! Yes, like a total fucking nutcase, I began laughing – loud! Had I lost it? No – I'd just got it. Like before the Granton seagull had shat in my eye, I was taking comfort from the fact that nothing could get worse, and so now, here I was, bewildered and aspiring to be broken. But I wasn't, and I knew it, and now I saw it with clarity. My body was weak, but my spirit was strong and was refusing to die. My spirit was my ace. And my ace was my wisdom. So, like those who only pray when times get bad, I'd only acknowledged my ace when it was do or die. But it was always there, and now I felt it.

'Right, you bastards!' I screamed as I tore back up the stair at a rate of knots. 'Fuck the gear. It's going over.'

They laughed and looked at me.

'I'm serious!' I shouted. 'They don't want the ship, they want the gear. Well, they might want the ship,' I corrected myself, 'but if they're willing to die trying, then it's got to be for the gear. Otherwise, what's the rush? And as for that fucking pilot – cunt's stuck us in it, and by the way,' I stared right at Dirk, 'he's done this deliberately! This was no fucking accident! And as for your bunch of fat fucks down the road, I'm not dying for them, nor for anybody else, and if they've got a problem with it, they'll fucking get this!' I pulled out my cut-throat and held it up. 'I'll slice that fat fuck's ball off and stuff it up his arse! Now, mayday; channel 16! Ivan – with me!'

So with the last half-hour of daylight, and under sporadic fire, we set about chucking a million quid's worth of Mandrax over the side, while a stunned audience sat in disbelief. Was it hard to do? Was it fuck! What's all the tea in China if you've not got your life? And although, later on, that kind of thinking would come to bite me on the arse, it bought us the night we needed; it seemed nobody wanted to die for coconuts!

The next morning, a small shrimper returning to port picked us up and took us to Quelimane. One day later, and with a heavy heart, I left the *Toto* and flew back to Durban. Of course, like my route back from the Congo, I'd returned with a war debt. And this time it wasn't just the lack of money earned, but the amount of money now owed. The fat fuck had taken my house; the new government my bank money; and now, my last remaining asset lay at the mercy of the river and the speed of the salvagers, though even that would carry a price! Anyway, although I'd again done so much and gained so little, and what little I'd got had been taken away, I was far from down, and was far from out. And while the shit had hit the fan, I'd managed out, alive and in one piece. So, as I made my way back home, I couldn't help feeling like I'd gone full circle; as, for the first time in a long time, whatever I'd do would be out of necessity. That was a change for me, and I liked it. It was perhaps my only silver lining!

Anyway, the Mozambique I left behind was soon to become a cornerstone for the world's drug trade, with an estimated $50 million a month passing through its waters. Since the end of the war, those who'd made their money through arms automatically turned to drugs, while Mozambique's rebuilding aided their distribution. With no navy, Mozambique's score of islands, coupled with incessant corruption, meant it was nothing short of a paradise for traffickers. Heroin coming from Pakistan and Afghanistan still passes through Dubai and Tanzania before reaching Mozambique, from where it's redistributed to Europe. Cocaine from Colombia passes through Brazil to reach Maputo, before heading to Europe and South-east Asia. Hash and Mandrax are transited down to South Africa. And that's only half of it, because where there's drugs, there's cash, and lots of it. As soon as the money's in, it's laundered on a massive scale through operations which centre around property deals and an ever-developing market for tourism. And, of course, who's still right in the middle of it all? My very good friends, Dirk and Ivan.

For the first time in a long time, being back home with nothing to do was great. My boats were fucked and my ambition in tatters, but somehow I didn't care. We'd moved from Boswall Road back up to Inverleith Row, where I'd press-ganged the top two floors of number

31. Well, I'd actually done that before heading off with the *Toto*. It wasn't that Susan was going to have any trouble while she was on her own, but with 30 and 31 being an old folk's home, I liked the idea that there was always someone about. To be honest, I wanted to sell Boswall. I'd even rented it out to 'Taste', a night at the Honeycomb in Blair Street, which by all accounts was some party, but it was always a one-off, and I knew that. So, with the market in a tumble, I had to hang onto it, and ended up renting it to Kiwis who just wanted rooms for a few months. And that was all fine, for a while. But then it got shit.

I loved home. I loved my family. But I just wasn't the sit-about type; and when I ended up having to smash some bastard to bits in Pilton after his bird, who we used to employ in the Home, had been all threatening when we'd sacked her, I realised that I'd gone full circle with nothing to show for it. Fuck that! I hadn't been fighting the Zulus just for the privilege of slashing a Piltonite – no offence, Pilton! So, two phone calls later, and the odd favour due, I was back in the game.

The European scene in which I found myself was a head fuck from start to finish. Instead of the odd adventurer, there now came the rise of Italian-style crime groups like never before. These 'clans' had developed agreements with other groups and operated from country to country, taking advantage of drug-price differentials, logistics and local knowledge. And if Mozambique had become a cornerstone, then Europe was a crossroads. From the west, Colombian cartels brought in cocaine, helped by the Galicians in Spain and the Mafia in Italy. From the south, Nigerian 'clans' gave their expertise in fraud while other groups from the Maghreb area of North Africa brought in the hash. From the east, Chinese Triads came with drug- and people-smuggling, local extortion, illegal gambling and prostitution rackets, while the Turks and Pakistani groups brought in heroin from the Middle East and Central Asia, with sometimes the odd bit of hash as well. Then, on top of all that, came the Eastern Europeans with pretty much the same as above, but with a strong preference for stolen cars.

Anyway, for my sins I ended up in southern Spain, and, in amongst all this action, I tried to carve out a slice. Now, I've got to be careful because these guys are still at it, but initially I started dealing with the 'Winston Boys', and their 'cigarette boats' – though I soon termed them the 'Banana Bunch'. And these guys were fucking mad! They were drug and tobacco smugglers who thrashed between Morocco and Spain using super-charged speedboats, while using Gibraltar as a base. Picking up a tonne or a half-tonne at a time, they'd cross the Straits in a matter of minutes, while the authorities would try to catch them using everything from helicopters to fucking naval vessels. And let me say, neither side had any qualms about letting loose with whatever they had, normally automatics of some sort. I'm telling you, this place was high-speed bedlam, but was always just a temporary measure, as the crazy fuckers would hoover a massive line of coke, then batter across with their music blaring! Well, as fate would have it, my hand was soon forced, when first of all a helicopter was taken down in a pursuit, killing the crew and focusing attention on the practice; and secondly, when riots seemed inevitable on the streets of Gibraltar after Mr Bassano, the then first minister, under pressure from the UK, hinted at a banning of the boats. So, two weeks after the crash, I was back in Edinburgh and onto a job of my own, and this one was a beauty! Again, without saying exactly what I was doing and with whom, my time in Spain had introduced me to the network I wanted and had given me the few quid I'd needed. Now it was time for 'Operation Snowgoose' – intended to be my finest hour!

CHAPTER VIII

THE 'SET-UP'

Waif-like bodies litter the ground while others, propped up and frozen in time, are waiting for something long since gone. Their numbers are endless but their lives seem short. I hesitate to call them living; I hesitate to call them dead. Instead, to me they're an anonymous mass now stranded by circumstance, a cabbaged crop from a dividend of peace. In disbelief I walk one way, and then another. Then, with my senses dulled, I clamber over a knot of legs and into an ice-cold air. There's danger here! From inside my frying pan, I look at a map and check for the fire – it's close. I walk a bit further, but soon check my stride, as from nowhere a tram flies past me unable to stop or alter its course. I'm approached by a repugnant man who's speaking. He's white, early 20s and on crutches – but even though it's English he's talking, I can't seem to listen. I hate him. I hate him so much that nothing he'd say could ever be of interest. I don't even know him, but I know I never will. I take another step, and curse his stench, but within an instant am almost killed, as another tram rumbles past and into the bustle that lies ahead. I stop, light a smoke and throw the spent match over the side and into the half-frozen canal. 'Fucking trams,' I moan, and, 'Fuck the junkies too!' I look at my watch; it's late, but I'm not. I've still half an hour to get there. I think I'll walk.

I leave Central Station and head for Dam Square. It's Saturday night and mobbed. I've been here before, but only during the day and with the family after coming by yacht when the boys were young. I loved those times. To my left was the famous Grasshopper, well known for being the first coffee shop you see when leaving the station, but more famous, so I was later told by someone who cared, for being open all night and handing out shite deals. It's also a signal to the Red Light district; a handy staging point for many a yob. I walked on, and after narrowly missing death by a Turkish moped, I cursed the fucking streets.

The Dam's a mad place. On the right of the roads you've got hawkers and muggers, then the cycle tracks, followed by the bus lanes, which are in turn followed by car lanes and tram lines. On the other side you've got exactly the same thing, except instead of getting a doing, you can drown in the canal. In fact, you've really only got about a yard and a half of concrete to call safe, and in some spaces, even that's shared with the trams. Thank fuck I didn't smoke! Though I pondered the chances of those that did.

I hit Dam Square bang on time. It's beautiful. Amsterdam, like the rest of the Netherlands, is amazing. And although Central Station's got more in common with a Burmese railway than a European city, saying that this area is the city is like saying Las Vegas is America – it's not! I took a seat in one of the bars, ordered a strong beer in a small glass, which was all head and no body, and watched the world go by. I was here to arrange 'Operation Snowgoose', my second attempt at bringing in hash to the UK. The first had ended in tears – not mine – near Rotterdam the month before, when things went from bad to worse, and for the first time I learnt the merits of a metal bar over a handgun, when I took one across a bastard's 'home-permed' head as he stood there still fumbling at his belt.

This time, my plan was to buy a boat somewhere and sail it down to the Azores, where I'd meet the big hash ships coming in from Pakistan. Originally I was in a consortium, in part with those from the Gibraltar job, and we'd wanted to bring in at least 15 tonnes of gear, which is a staggering amount. But, as ever, some people backed out and others fucked around, so cut a long story short, it got down to a 3-tonne deal, with about half of it belonging to me and the other half belonging to, well, let me call him Ben.

Ben was a 'heavy', and I mean a proper 'heavy', not just some jumped-up yob covered in gold; there's plenty of them. As a major trafficker who had real global connections, he always settled his scores, often through the hiring of Polish hitmen. I know of at least four killings, one in Britain, where the gunman would catch the red-eye from Warsaw, do the job and be back home for tea before anyone twigged it was done. That was power!

Just as I finished my drink, a Mercedes taxi pulled up and a Turkish-looking man walked over to the window and waved me out. So I followed. Now, there's a reason why I went, and a reason I was travelling alone, but I can't go into it; suffice it to say that I'd met Ben before and trusted him as much as he trusted me. Ben's house was impressive, but understated. He was well educated, came from old Dutch money and, unlike his rivals, preferred to display his wealth on the inside. 'When I see a man in a Ferrari, I laugh,' he once said. 'I prefer to know that I could buy ten, rather than drive one.' That was Ben, and that's why we did business.

Over dinner and a few bottles of Leffe Blonde, his favourite beer, I explained my plan to him, at which he laughed uncontrollably until it almost choked him. When he started to breathe again, he was in. Essentially I'd give him a bundle of money; I won't say how much, but enough to be a deposit of intention. He, in turn, would put me in contact with his man in the Azores, who'd be paid a second stack of money on transfer, while the rest he'd front me until I'd sold it on – pretty ideal. But with all that said, I knew one thing for sure. There were no second chances, and no excuses – that was the risk in dealing with Ben. And I knew it.

So, a few months later, 'Operation Snowgoose' swung into action, and I adopted the nickname of 'Popeye' to remain relatively incognito. During the summer of 1995 I bought an old Icelandic trawler, the *Dansk*, for £55,000 in the port of Esbjerg, Denmark. She was never the *Queen Mary* but the team and me soon gave her a sound going over, while the other members of my gang in Edinburgh were getting busy on the clever bit. An Edinburgh blacksmith, in his innocence, was making eight large, metal-framed, heavy-duty plastic containers. To his knowledge he was making chemical storage tanks, the cover story for when they were moved or talked about. At about 5 ft by 5 ft, each container had a sequence of hooks and eyes so they could be chained together, but easily separated.

When they were sorted, the containers plus diving equipment were driven by four members of the gang – two in a 7-tonne lorry and two in a Luton, both from Ryder van hire – to Harwich in England, where they then boarded an overnight DFDS passenger ferry to Esbjerg. After laying low until darkness fell, the lorries were backed up on the dock's edge and their contents manhandled onto the deck of the *Dansk*, where they were carefully slotted down a specially cut hole, one member of the gang losing part of his finger in the process – which is a story in itself. Anyway, the next day the Edinburgh team returned home on a DFDS freight ferry, while the Danish crew and I headed down to the Azores, after sorting out a bit of engine trouble. Without saying anything about the network, the buy went well, and no sooner had we arrived than we were off again, back up to Scottish waters. Now, en route, we took a hold of each tonne, split it evenly and packed it into the airtight and waterproof containers. They were then brought on deck, near the shore, and slung overboard, where they sank in sufficiently shallow water to be retrieved at a later date. The *Dansk* then proceeded to dock in the Spanish port of Huelva, home of Christopher Columbus and many an English smuggler, where it was then searched by Spanish Customs as a potential smuggling vessel, and although one of their search dogs took a bite out of my arse, nothing was found!

About a week later, we were all set to head back to the dumping ground, where, with a diver, some electronics and a couple of air balloons, we'd start floating the gear to the surface and bringing it ashore, just one or two bails at a time. Well, as ever, the wind of shit blew in my direction and, to my total shock and horror, my engine went on fire. The *Dansk* was fucked! I couldn't believe it. It never rains but it pours, and now, like so many times before, all my efforts lay wasted. After the drama was over, I stood alone, and now in isolation sat against the wheel, trying to assess the pieces of my shattered dreams. I could think of nothing – my mind was blank. I tried to feel angry but I couldn't. I tried to feel sad but I couldn't. I even tried to feel sorry for myself, but I failed there too. I was, for the first time ever, without feeling, but even that felt like nothing. I lit a smoke and dreamed within my locked-up cabin, but the pictures flashed by like someone else's photos – stirring no emotions. Then, within a breath, I realised I was laughing. Again, like the time on the *Toto*, I was laughing out loud. How prophetic. On my CD player, stuck on repeat from an earlier time, was my favourite Simon and Garfunkel album. 'Hello darkness my old friend; I've come to talk with you again . . .' And I had. Bastard! Now, with my James Bond dreams in tatters, a third boat fucked and the sound of Dutch war clogs being sharpened on the horizon, that darkness all around soon descended and became me. I had entered hell!

The Japanese word for hell, written with two characters meaning 'the lowest' and 'to be bound or imprisoned', is *jigoku*, and doesn't describe a particular place, but rather a state of suffering we project onto the outside world which reduces everything to that one point of agony. Now, like so many times before, be it the Congo, Southern Africa or right home in Edinburgh, my inner turmoil had projected hell onto the outside world, and now, within it, my battle wasn't to survive, but to think, and think clearly. As soon as I realised my struggle was on, that awareness, that understanding of my lack of freedom drove me deeper still, until, like a voyage through the inferno, I became rage. This time, though, I raged from hell, and that was different! Mutilating Steve Gilmore came from a rage of anger, which I'd directed at the outside world as I attempted to enforce my superiority. But now, my rage of hell was directed at myself, and it was a dangerous rage, full of frustration and potential self-destruction. My blood had been spilled and the vultures were beginning to circle. And it didn't take them too long to close in!

With my hash stuck on the seabed, and my debts sky-rocketing, one disaster after another had left me out on a limb with nowhere to go. Now, like a gambler chasing his losses, I was hurtling towards a financial precipice without the power to stop. I hated it. Well, for every action there's a reaction, and there's been no shortage of press coverage over what I did to resolve it; but before I go into my doomed adventure, it's probably best to cite what the Crown alleged happened because, believe me, nothing's what it seems.

During May 1996 I planned to import a large quantity of cannabis into Scotland, and as part of this a transfer was to be made by the Dutch-crewed ketch *Isolda*, sailing from Cadiz in southern Spain, to the British-crewed *Ocean Jubilee*, en route to Inverness. The skipper and leader at the UK end was me, or 'Popeye' for the purpose of these events, while Jan van Rijs, an alleged leader of Octopus, the Dutch mafia, and a major global player in the trafficking of drugs, skippered the *Isolda*.

Following the purchase of the *Ocean Jubilee* on 12 June in Milford Haven, Wales, my on-board deck-hand, Gary Hunter, and I sailed the vessel to Ullapool and then on to Scrabster only a few days later. While she was lying at Scrabster, I apparently obtained coordinates of a meeting point in the North Sea, and made arrangements for the use of a shed in Kirkcaldy where the cannabis would be stored. On 23 July 1996 we returned to Scrabster. Two days later we sailed into the North Sea and to the intended rendezvous, in what the Crown later referred to as the 'practice run', thereafter returning to Edinburgh.

On 28 July we returned north, initially to Inverness and then on to Wick, where bottles, a hose and some white spirit were seen to be loaded onto the *Ocean Jubilee*. Later that day, the vessel set sail. The Crown states that in the early hours of 29 July, the two vessels came together and the transfer took place. Later, in the afternoon of that day, officers of Her Majesty's Customs and Excise, arriving on the cutter HMS *Sentinel*, dispatched an inflatable boarding party and attempted to board the *Ocean Jubilee* in 'British territorial waters'. In part, they succeeded. The Crown alleged that, on their arrival, I set fire to the vessel and in particular the bales of cannabis now booby-trapped with a flammable substance. It's also alleged that I placed the throttle on full, giving her a speed of 7 to 8 knots, which made her veer to port in heavy seas. This, it was maintained, further endangered the lives of the Customs officers. At that point, Gary fell off. So, while the inflatable went to retrieve him, the master of the cutter made the decision to come alongside the burning *Ocean Jubilee* with the intention of taking his two remaining men off. The first of the two, a Mr Townsend, was taken by surprise but managed to stay out of danger, while the second, Alistair Soutar, not a seaman but a regular Customs and Excise officer, was sitting against the *Ocean Jubilee*'s deckhouse and didn't. The starboard side of the cutter's bow overrode and came into contact with the *Ocean Jubilee*, striking Mr Soutar and killing him.

The vessel was brought back to the Scottish mainland and seized. The Crown maintained that, had the boat been allowed to continue, it would have put in at Inverness, where the cannabis would have been unloaded into a waiting van, driven there by one of the land-based co-accused. It would have then made its way to the shed in Kirkcaldy, where all, or some, of it would have been driven to London. The *Isolda* was stopped in a separate operation as she headed for Makkum in the Netherlands.

This sequence of events was to bring to a climax 'Operation Balvenie', one of the longest and most complex Customs and Excise surveillance operations ever. In all, a total of nine were arrested: four at sea, on board the ketch *Isolda*, two on the *Ocean Jubilee* and three on land in Scotland. I, the suspected mastermind and now-publicised Mr Big, was charged with contravening section 170(2)(b) of the Customs and Excise Management Act 1979, namely the charge of drug importation, and secondly, with attempting to defeat the ends of justice, namely trying to destroy the cannabis and sink the boat. In all, Customs recovered 3 tonnes of the drug, with a value of over £10 million, and, on the face of it, had smashed one of the biggest cartels in the country, catching us red-handed, in an open-and-shut case. That, however, was on the face of it, and as for the open-and-shut? My arse!

Alf had a proper English accent, and, to begin with, he gave me the impression of being quite a sophisticated type. After taking me out for a meal and a few drinks, he convinced me that my only option was to smuggle for him, which by the sounds of it was an everyday occurrence. I was in a real predicament, and he knew it. For the first time in a long time, I was financially fucked. One catastrophe after another had left me broke, and now, with the *Dansk* going on fire, I was caught over a barrel with nowhere to go. Being in debt to the banks is one thing. You can ignore letters, hide behind the couch or bury your head in the sand. But between the South Africans after my scalp, the salvagers wanting paid and the financial backers of Dr No's failed underwater adventure, which included Ben, my feelings of impending death now seemed stronger than ever. And whereas normally I'd take the fight to them, this wasn't Africa, they weren't tinkers, and I was never fucking Rambo!

I was introduced to Alf by members of the Dr No team in Huelva. This was about four months before my arrest. He seemed to know my situation and was able to provide the answers. First of all, he'd keep Ben off my back by slinging him a few quid. Secondly, he'd buy me a boat and thirdly, I'd get a cut of whatever I'd be taking. In my state of bedlam it seemed like a godsend, as, once we'd finished, I'd be free to pick up my underwater treasure. As for the boat, he'd either deduct it from my cut or I could sell it on and pay him back – whatever I wanted! So, after we'd ironed out a few other bits and pieces, he gave me a mobile number to call, which I did when I got back to Britain.

On 11 June 1996 I arrived with my son at London King's Cross on an InterCity express from Edinburgh Waverley. We flagged down a black cab and made our way to Bethnal Green – a 20-minute ride through the sun-soaked streets of London. On arrival at Bethnal Green Park, it was a short walk to the Salmon and Ball pub on Bethnal Green Road. Standing outside the pub, the ten minutes now passing seemed like an eternity as the sweat, at first a drip, began to flow. This, though, had fuck all to do with nerves and a lot to do with our attire. While the rest of London was dressed for the beach, we were dressed for the birch. Sporting steel-toecap boots, heavy jeans and other cosh-compatible clothing in case the deal went wrong and became a pagger, our inherent need for padding was soon melting away.

'This is a fucking waste of time. It's just no goanna happen. This wanker's ten minutes late!' said my eldest, now starting to feel the sunshine.

'Listen,' I said. 'It's fine, not a problem, this Alfie's the real deal; a real cockney rebel. This boy's goanna turn up.'

And he did. Five minutes later, a small man, about 5 ft 8 in., brown hair, brown eyes, wearing a baggy shirt, shorts and sandals, walks over, and with a thick cockney accent says, 'All right, mate? How'ya doing, Popeye?'

This was Jeff, and he shook our hands.

'Alfy's in the motor, do you want to go for a wander?'

So we did; but on walking across busy Bethnal Green Road, I couldn't believe my fucking eyes. There, parked across the road, Mr Incognito de Huelva, was Alf, dressed in the Paul Smith summer collection, leaning back on his sapphire blue M3 convertible BMW with roof down, white leather piped in blue, music blaring, 15-grand, diamond-encrusted Rolex watch on his wrist and Gucci sunglasses, diamond-studded at the side! I shook my head. This man was a total fucking knob!

As the introductions were made, we got into the car, but Alf started to act even stranger by shouting at some man on the opposite pavement. He didn't seem to be doing anything other than just standing about. Looking back, Alf was trying to draw this man's attention, and I now believe he was a second Customs officer who had missed us going over. I later saw the same man at a phone box I was using in Edinburgh and, of course, he was eventually to give evidence at my trial.

Anyway, not to draw any attention to ourselves whatsoever, Alf sped off, cutting up the number 73 bus on its way to Crystal Palace, just about causing a major incident on the street. Then, at 80 miles an hour, skidding round one corner, skidding round the next, parking the car and jumping out, lo and behold, we were at Bethnal Green. We were now in the fucking park! Now, to those who know, the best place to have a secure meeting is while walking down the busiest street possible. So Oxford Street at lunch-time is an obvious choice. It's difficult for body-strapped devices to separate your voice from the surrounding noise, and long-range equipment will find it difficult to zone in. The antithesis of that is a quiet park in summer.

As we walked through the park, Alf started to act normal again. To be honest, my first thought was that he'd just come down from a line of coke – it was never my thing, but I'd seen enough folk on it. Anyway, I gave him the benefit of the doubt as we discussed the deal. I would arrange everything on UK soil, while he would finance it and get it moving via Jan van Rijs. It was Alf who introduced me to the Dutch. One thing he did insist on, though, was that the delivery be made as far north as possible, as it was too dangerous down south. I now know this was a load of piss. Every boat coming into a harbour in the north of Scotland is far more likely to attract attention than the busier places down south. Five minutes later we ended it with me agreeing to call him in a few days, when he'd have the money for me to buy the boat. Alf and his sidekick then sped off in their £50,000 BMW, this time pausing to put the roof up. Now, I'm not stupid, and something wasn't sitting right. I'm no fashion guru, but all that kit and that kind of car spells one thing and one thing alone – knob cheese! Whether he's then one thing or another is beside the point – being a prick is reason enough to take a walk. So here's the revelation. I used an old friend, who'd been helping me out every now and then since our reunion back in Mozambique, to check out whether Alf and his job were a safe bet. He said leave it with him, and two days later he got in touch saying all go! So I did, for that reason and that reason alone.

The next day I phoned Alf. He said the money for the boat was ready, but that he was busy so a friend of his would meet me instead at the same pub, the Salmon and Ball. Looking back, I now realise that had Alf been 'genuine', this meeting would never have happened in the same place as before, but anyway. When I got there, a saloon car pulled up and I was given a plastic bag containing £30,000. I never saw the driver again. It was on! Customs later claimed not to have been able to find the number plate of the BMW, nor the owner, but do admit to being present at the meeting.

Anyway, smuggling gear onto land isn't in itself too much of a challenge. What is, is delivering it and getting paid, which, as a sequence of events, needs to fall in line like a row of dominoes. For the benefit of the average citizen, the bulk look of each tonne is roughly the area of a large dining-room table, so 6 ft long by 4 ft wide by 2 ft high. Each kilo is packed within a 10-kilo package, and the 10s are then wrapped in a hessian fabric bag, each with its own handle. A hundred of these bags make the tonne. As soon as we could, we began to scope out a suitable landing spot. So for over a week we travelled the length of the east coast looking at the pros and cons of various sites, including Wick, Scrabster, Inverness, St Andrews, Kirkcaldy, Kinghorn, even down to Granton Harbour and Leith Docks in Edinburgh. In the end we agreed on Inverness. Logistically it had the right roads to and from the harbour, while the A9 down to Edinburgh was well traversed by heavy lorries and other traffic. From there it was easy access to the M8 and Glasgow. This would be the first drop-off. At a Govan industrial site, a member of the gang would take one tonne and enter it into the Glasgow market. From there it was an easy ride down the M1 into England and, ultimately, London. At the job's end, the loaded truck would finish in another industrial area near City Airport on the north-easterly side of the city. On delivery of the cannabis, a representative of one of north London's notorious crime families would have made a payment of £1 million. The cash would then be returned to Edinburgh by car the same evening, while the lorry, as a one-way hire, would stay.

The harbour itself was suited for easy boat access. Neither too busy nor too quiet, we could slip in and out with relative ease. A 7½-tonne Ryder self-drive lorry with a tail-lift was hired, to ensure that the gear was exposed for the bare minimum of time. Once loaded, the lorry would set off in convoy with two cars for Glasgow. The first car would travel approximately two miles in front, while the second approximately two to three behind. All vehicles would be in contact by walkie-talkie, but not by mobile phone, as the authorities could listen in to them. The first car was the scout. Any problems ahead, such as accidents, police checks or road closures, could be radioed back for the driver to take action; anything from diverting onto another road, as already mapped out, to turning around and heading back to the harbour. The car behind was there to ensure that the driver was covered. If the lorry was involved in an accident or if it simply broke down, the car could pick him up. The driver's story, on the off-chance he'd be stopped by traffic police, was that he was hired by a London company to transport asbestos material, now sealed in the back. It was hoped that this would deter any suspicious officer. We laughed at that idea then, and I'm still laughing now!

The next piece of kit was, of course, the boat. At this point I didn't know where the rendezvous would be, so my choice of boat would have to take in all eventualities. It had to be reliable enough to handle a pounding, have the engine power to carry the tonnage and, most importantly, be able to carry the diesel fuel reserves in case the meeting point was further out than expected. After searching about I found the perfect boat in Wales: a retired 36-ft lifeboat with a Turner engine, which meant that it was virtually unsinkable and had the capacity to sustain itself in any conditions. The deal was agreed on by phone, and the next day Gary and myself travelled down to Milford Haven by car, where we handed over £28,000 before sailing her up the Irish Channel and round to the port of Scrabster on the north tip of Scotland, where she sat from 20 June.

Now here's where the fun starts. A month later, while the *Ocean Jubilee* was lying at Scrabster, I apparently obtained the coordinates of a meeting point in the North Sea. It was alleged, by the Crown, that Jan van Rijs of the *Isolda* communicated these to me, and that we sailed out to the intended rendezvous, in what was referred to as the 'practice run'. That was 25 July. Three days later, on 28 July, we set out to meet the *Isolda* for real, and the transfer was made the following morning. And the rest is Crown history – but not mine!

On 25 July, I was given coordinates and times by Alf to meet a French fishing boat. He said that he'd arranged another cargo, but one of his skippers had let him down. So, since I was set, would I take it?

My first reaction was to say no. It wasn't like I was picking up a few packs of fags! But then he got all adamant, and in no uncertain terms threatened me into it, by basically saying that if I didn't take this job on then the whole fucking deal was off. Of course, had he threatened me in any other way, I'd have chopped his fucking hands off. So anyway, three nights before I met Jani, I sailed from Wick to meet the French boat just off the Scottish coast. Initially, contact was made by radio, then when I saw her she turned out to be a standard-looking Breton type. It had no number or name on its bow and was in a work-weary condition. At first I couldn't make out what was being said, as the person speaking had a really heavy accent, made worse by the radio. But this mysteriously and dramatically improved when I said I couldn't understand any of his instructions and wanted to cancel out. Eventually, we tied together; he had large fenders and car tyres along his side. On doing so, I saw his five crewmen, who all bizarrely spoke English to each other; one of them even had a Scottish east-coast accent. I expected the bales to be passed over, but, for some reason, no sooner had I tied up than something appeared on the horizon which spooked them, causing them to bolt. So, unsure what to make of it all, we sailed back to Wick, to wait on Jani in a few days' time. When I managed to touch base with Alf, he seemed quite blasé about the whole deal and told me not to worry – a far cry from the aggressive persuasion of two nights before.

When the big day came, 29 July, we were set, and yes, I did load up with flammables. Well, your boat's your evidence – but the only reason I did it was because of that fucking fiasco three nights before, which had left me with a case of the paras. I'd tried to figure out the best way of rigging them up. Originally, I'd even wanted to use a couple of Calor gas-holders, a length of copper wire and a car battery. I'll refrain from further details in the interests of health and safety, but anyway, I decided against it; I wanted her to sink, not blow up. After some hours we finally reached our mark, and within minutes Jani had made his. Everything from our side seemed well and, apart from the heavy swell, there was nothing to give me the shits. That, though, was just me. As soon as I heard Jani's voice, I could sense his apprehension. There was a lot of sea traffic that morning and, in hindsight, also the kind of aircraft that, at our position, should have been at cruising altitude, instead of just above the clouds. I told him to come in towards us, but he initially refused. Then, after a few more exchanges, he did, and we took the bales. The transfer was a lot quicker than we'd anticipated, not forgetting that this was the first time we'd done it. So no sooner than we'd tied up, we were away, and heading back to Inverness. But then it happened!

I'd like to paint a picture of sudden chaos – of an SAS strike with exploding windows and hundreds of 'flash bangs', as kitted-out commandos screamed their heads off while we, the villains, bit carpet, face down in the broken glass and flying debris. But it wasn't and, although that's what they'd want to portray, this was never going to happen. Why? Because we were at fucking sea! And apart from commando raids on the beaches, nothing at sea ever happens in a hurry. At first I wasn't so sure, as the grey dot on the greyer horizon seemed to cut a path towards me. But as soon as I saw the dot become the *Sentinel*, a 34-metre Island Class cutter, and the largest craft in the Customs fleet, I knew we'd been had. Bastards!

Still, though, I waited. I waited until she came to within 100 yards and stopped. Then I realised what they were up to, and I couldn't fucking believe it. Carried by a hydraulic davit, mounted on the aft deck, was a 6-metre Avon Searider inflatable, and they were starting to board it. When I saw that, I doused the *Jubilee* in spirits and set her alight. We were already making 8 knots and had at no point altered our speed. Within minutes they were upon us and had partly boarded when, just then, she veered violently to port in a heavy swell, and Gary fell off. Well, the rest was as it happened. The inflatable sped off for Gary, while the cutter's skipper decided to come alongside, whereupon he hit the *Jubilee*, and one of his men was killed.

Now, before I go into it, let me say one thing. For the death of Alistair Soutar, I am sorry. I am truly sorry that he died on that day, and if I could change anything it would be that. All I ever wanted to do was to bring a bit of hash into the country to clear my debts and salvage my other ship – that's it! And, believe me, I could have easily opted for harder drugs, which were way more profitable and a sight fucking easier, but I didn't. In the end I was set up and fucked over by Customs from start to finish. Even the *Ocean Jubilee*, the boat on which their man died, was bought with Customs money.

Anyway, I was grabbed along with Gary and taken to Wick, where the fun and games were about to start. There were about 1½ tonnes in the forward section and 1½ tonnes in the aft. The aft section of the boat was completely destroyed by fire, meaning that 1½ tonnes must have been consumed. But somehow, Customs and Excise produced 3 tonnes for inspection. It seems clear to me that they produced another 1½ tonnes to make up the load and report a significant find, to further their own ends. I even remember one Customs officer saying there were 3 tonnes on board the *Ocean Jubilee* before she'd even been brought into harbour. Drugs have to be weighed to find their weight. How the fuck could Customs know what was on board that day? Even with intercepts, announcements can't be made before verification. How did they know? I'll tell you – because they put it there! And as for the burnt tonnage in the aft, the pictures submitted to court were testament to just how severely gutted that section was; something entirely substantiated by the surveillance video taken both before and during the event, which I'll come to in a moment.

Anyway, the man in charge of the video, Nicholas Ernest Jones, an ex-RAF Nimrod captain and, at the time, a systems operator with a private company which carried out secret operations for the MOD, was also in charge of tracking. To begin with, whoever placed the device that tracked the *Isolda* did so while she was moored in Spain, and consequently without lawful authority, as British operatives have no jurisdiction. As for the *Ocean Jubilee*, she was broken into by Customs while she sat in Thurso, and was fitted with a device while no cargo was on board. When asked in court about how many tracking devices his plane was detecting that day, Ernest Jones replied he'd seen up to 40. Apart from that being a shitload of plants, it has to mean that each device is unique, and so, once they had a fix on the *Jubilee*, she wasn't going to get away. After meeting the *Isolda*, I made my way to Inverness, to where the van was waiting. My vessel's speed was 8 knots at all times, the boat's top speed. I was in a situation where my only destination was the sea lochs at Inverness. Customs knew the boat was making for the hire van, as they were watching it on land; something which they later stated in court. So, putting it simple, there was absolutely no need for a 'high-speed' chase at sea. We were in a trap, with no way out. But recklessly, to suit their own purpose, they engineered a dramatic incident, namely the boarding of a burning vessel against all MCA and sea-safety rules, using men untrained in the way of boats, one officer admitting it was his first time ever. I mean, why? With all that surveillance, at sea and on land, why not allow the *Ocean Jubilee* to dock before seizing her? Surely that was the obvious thing to do? Not only would that have ensured the safe recovery of people and drugs, but it would have cemented the case against the land-based gang members, one of whom was to be later found 'not proven'; quite rightly so, as he was just delivering a van. At the time, though, that never seemed to bother them. Besides, why not tail the gear the full length of the country? Surely that amount was enough to implicate those in Glasgow and London, especially when the buyers at the other end were as notorious as they were? Fuck, talk about a wasted opportunity!

In all, the whole fucking show was at best ill conceived, and at worst negligent. The 'elite' NIS, the Customs branch responsible for Operation Balvenie, operates throughout the entire world and can call on the services of the SAS, Special Boat Service, MI5 and MI6, as well as countless specialist police teams. Of these, the Special Boat Service, elite Royal Marine commandos, will be the first to say that the boarding of a vessel under these conditions, in such heavy seas, regardless of the fact it was on fire and under way at 8 knots, is both insane and unnecessary. If this type of intercept was so important, so fundamental to my capture, why didn't Customs request their services? And even though the Crown had chosen not to charge me with murder or culpable homicide (manslaughter), no inquiry was ever held, while the courts, press and prosecuting agencies were all happy to lay the blame for Mr Soutar's death firmly at my feet. I mean, as the Crown had decided it was an accident, shouldn't that accident have at least been investigated?

THE 'SET-UP'

In Scotland there's a system for investigating fatal accidents governed by the Fatal Accidents and Sudden Deaths Inquiry (Scotland) Act 1976. This Act states that a fatal accident inquiry (FAI) is mandatory if 'it appears that the death has resulted from an accident occurring in Scotland while the person who has died was in the course of his employment'. This would appear to indicate that an FAI would be mandatory in this case. The Lord Advocate, however, the man who has the final say in these matters, and who, incidentally, is also the head of the prosecution in Scotland as Her Majesty's Advocate – a potential conflict of interest – decided that an FAI wouldn't be required. Justifying his decision, he cited the section of the Act which says that an FAI isn't required 'in a case where criminal proceedings have been concluded against any person in respect of the death or any accident from which the death resulted, and that the Lord Advocate is satisfied that the circumstances of the death have been sufficiently established in the course of such proceedings'. But again, no charges were ever brought 'in respect of the death' or 'any accident from which the death resulted'. People were charged, but with drug smuggling and of 'defeating the ends of justice'.

Secondly, the UK has another agency, the Marine Accident Investigation Branch (MAIB), whose 'fundamental role is to determine the circumstances of an accident and its causes'. Their aim is 'to improve safety at sea and prevent accidents in the future'. However, the MAIB also refused to hold an investigation into this accident. They cited two reasons: that the circumstances did not fall within their remit because the regulations don't apply to Customs and Excise vessels – a liberal interpretation of their own regulations, taking into account the deceased was on board a civilian-registered vessel; and secondly, that the fire on board the *Ocean Jubilee* was started deliberately and therefore everything from that point on was as the result of a criminal act. But again, there was no doubt that we planned to torch the gear if caught, and that accelerants were put on board for this reason, so the link between the fire and the death is tenuous; something verified by three High Court judges.

Why then does an inquiry matter? Well, there are two simple

reasons. The first is why it matters to me and my co-accuseds. At my trial, Lord Dawson's sentence was meted out as if I'd been charged with Alistair Soutar's death. This was made pretty fucking obvious when he said, 'Had you been charged and convicted of his homicide, I would have had no hesitation in sentencing you to life imprisonment.' Well, he did anyway! Then, later, in a written report, he writes, 'but for his selfish action in trying to desert the burning vessel, the Customs cutter would not have required to approach the *Ocean Jubilee* and the Customs officer would not have lost his life'. Not only does this indicate what was in the judge's 'mind', namely that I was wholly guilty of Alistair Soutar's death, but it's also inconsistent with the facts. The inflatable launch was never an attempt to rescue or approach as a result of the fire, but an unnecessary attempt at seizing drugs, which rapidly went pear-shaped. I mean, let's be clear: had the Crown thought that there was even the slimmest possibility that I could be tried for murder, or manslaughter, believe me, they'd have done it. But they didn't!

At the very least, then, had an inquiry been allowed, our subsequent appeals would have answered, or at least posed, the following questions: why board at sea in the first place?; what were the qualifications and experience of each member of the boarding party?; why did the captain of the *Sentinel* not issue the correct order to abandon the burning vessel?; why was Mr Soutar the only member of the boarding party not wearing a dry immersion suit?; and why did the captain manoeuvre his vessel, five times larger than the *Ocean Jubilee*, alongside a vessel which was under way, unmanned, and on fire with a risk of explosion?

The second reason, though, for me, is why it mattered to those in Customs and Excise not to have an inquiry, as, in whatever light this episode is seen, it's far from perfect. For the Dutch, their arrest in international waters, without 'reasonable grounds', breached international law. No drugs, guns or money were ever found on board the *Isolda*. This, they claim, was substantiated by the lack of evidence against them. And while I don't want to go into anyone else's circumstances, for obvious reasons, while we Britons had more than a hundred witnesses arrayed against us, only four were ever brought against the Dutchmen. Anyway, as far as I'm concerned, we were both victims of the same plot, entrapment, which is: 'The inducement, by law enforcement officers or their agents, of another person to commit a crime for the purposes of bringing charges for the commission of that artificially provoked crime.' And under British law, it's illegal, as, apart from artificially provoking a crime, it ultimately involves officers abetting the commission of a crime, which, in turn, is a crime itself! Now, although in Scotland entrapment isn't a recognised defence, the test is whether or not the conviction has been achieved 'fairly'. But considering that the whole deal was run by Customs from start to finish, I fail to see how that was ever going to be the case. And apart from that, what really gets me mad is how it ties into the bigger picture, and how that's then been tied in with me.

It's been suggested, by subsequent newspaper allegations and ultimately the Crown itself, that this incident was one of the many cases of entrapment being run by specific divisions of Customs and Excise during that period. It's probably safe to assume then, that the investigation into the accidental death of Alistair Soutar was bound to bring this up. But would that be all? In focusing the investigation away from the crime and the accused, what else could an inquest unwittingly uncover? Indeed, how deep does the 'set-up' run?

Some have suggested, right from the start, that somehow I was a Customs and Excise plant myself. One of my co-accused has even suggested, along with others, that the whole plot, from start to finish, had been arranged with the authorities in order to catch four major Dutch drug-traffickers, who were all members of Octopus. Another gang member has even said I'd participated in previous 'sting operations', which were run by Customs at the time, and further stated that a meeting at Harthill, a service stop between Edinburgh and Glasgow on the M8 motorway, between me and Customs involved setting up a sting to catch two men, Thomas Porter and John Smith. Both of them were subsequently found guilty of smuggling £20 million worth of cannabis into Troon, on the west coast of Scotland, and sentenced to 14 years in jail. Well, that's a load of utter shit! Just take a look at what happened and tell me if it doesn't sound familiar. Their case revolved around a Customs operative, Baird MacKenzie, who subsequently admitted receiving £20,000 for his efforts and a relocation package of £100,000. He initiated a deal for the accused to sail an 80-ft vessel, which was owned by Customs, to the Moroccan coast, where they picked up 100 bales of hash. On their return to Troon, they were all arrested. In all, it meant that MacKenzie was nothing more than an agent provocateur.

Yes, agent provocateur – but in my case, I wasn't the agent! It was Alf. My co-accused said in a statement, 'Rod had told us not to worry, everything would be all right because we were working for the government . . . but the problem being that the Customs officer dying meant that the whole deal was off.'

What fucking deal? I'm hardly going to draw a swashbuckling bust on myself. How would I get out of that, especially with 3 tonnes of gear on board? And even if I was, it would only make sense if Customs were going to tail the stash to London. Otherwise, why just grab your agent? And again, let me spell it out, grasses don't get 28 years! If they did, why bother being a grass?

Anyway, let's put it all into some kind of perspective. Believe me, I've had time to do it. Customs have long been accused of organising drug runs into Britain to boost arrest rates. And as a result, West Midlands police spent four years running 'Operation Brandfield' – an inquiry into their crooked practices. Throughout the period of 1998–2003, police investigating illegal sting operations held and questioned various members of the NIS. In some cases it was shown that Customs officers encouraged guys to send shipments of drugs to Britain, where the recipients were then swooped upon. These shipments were called 'controlled deliveries'. In other cases, the officers were an integral part of the dealing process. Sound familiar?

All of these occurrences fly in the face of Customs' own professional guidelines, which prohibit officers from 'counselling, inciting or procuring the commission of a crime'. As a result, NIS tactics have been criticised by judges who have been steadily quashing convictions or ordering retrials, so much so that even some defendants who have pleaded guilty are being fed back into the loop. At my time of writing this, West Midlands police have since reviewed 92 separate operations in both Scotland and England dating back to the mid-1980s, resulting in a quarter being sent to the Criminal Cases Review Commission.

Following 'Operation Brandfield' came 'Operation Gestalt', a 10-month Scotland Yard inquiry in 2003 which listed a further 16 Customs officers suspected of widespread malpractice and impropriety. This investigation concerned a further two-dozen trials and related to officers, both middle-ranked and senior, committing perjury in court, perverting the course of justice and malfeasance in a public office. Beyond that, though, it stated that, within these trials, crucial evidence wasn't disclosed to the defence – a necessity in law – and that much of that evidence was supplied to Customs by supergrasses who were themselves involved in illegal activities, albeit supervised by Customs. And Customs' chosen method was to present the supergrasses in court as innocent victims, when they were, in fact, integral components of the crime. How the fuck, then, was I ever going to be presented as an innocent victim, when I had 3 tonnes of hash on board?

Well, as you'd expect, these were massive blows to an organisation that traded on its squeaky-clean image during the headline-grabbing tales of police corruption in the 1970s and 1980s. And while I'm no expert, having a vested interest has led me to a couple of brief conclusions as to why Customs wanted to stitch me up, along with people like me. For some, it's been difficult to notice the decay within an under-funded and under-supervised Customs throughout the 1990s. The Gower and Hammond report of 2001 (a QC inquiry into the role of Customs and Excise as a prosecuting authority) identified cutbacks in the Customs' solicitor's office and a massive increase in its workload as one of the reasons for the cracks beginning to show. It also mentioned a 'tendency of investigators to bypass' lawyers and the identification of an 'investigators' culture of secrecy' that caused them to 'withhold important information from their lawyers'. At the same time, Customs had to become more business-friendly following the Maastricht Treaty and a dismantling of the EU's internal trade borders. As such, Customs officers were pulled back from the ports and warehouses and staff were cut, meaning that the organisation became ever more reliant on investigations to catch criminals. So, like any organisation competing for survival, they needed headlines and justification. They needed me – high-profile and, under my circumstances at the time, easy pickings!

Serving to increase this downward spiral was that even the usual independent monitors, the press, found it difficult to keep an eye on developments. More proactive investigations, as opposed to the traditional reactive finds, were going through the courts with accompanying reporting restrictions. Much of this was due to the 'sensitive' nature of their work; namely the use of informants and agents. In this culture, then, is it any wonder that 'Operation Balvenie' was anything other than a 'set-up'?

For me, the case of Amjad Bashir, a Customs man who'd hung himself during a 'Brandfield' investigation after fearing he was about to be made a scapegoat, typifies their practices. Five years earlier, he'd sat in a van in Leeds while his agent, Mark, handed over a plastic bag containing 2 kg of heroin to three Bradford dealers. Mark, a Pakistani known to Customs as a participating informant, or PI, was one of their top operatives who regularly delivered heads, and so had collected a fortune in rewards, estimated at half a million pounds.

The heroin in the bag belonged to Customs and was part of a 35 kg consignment sitting in one of their warehouses, which Customs had arranged to be shipped in from Pakistan in another 'controlled delivery'. The Customs version was later to be that the three dealers had demanded test samples, and when they finally took delivery of the full amount, they were arrested in 'Operation Serin' and presented by NIS as a headline-grabbing victory.

But the true story's far different. What actually happened was that Mark told the dealers he needed £40,000 up-front, before he could get his hands on the cheaper heroin, so that night in the van, he gave them the drugs to sell to raise the money, but lo and behold, both the heroin and the cash took a walk. Now there's a thing! So, apart from being a total fucking shambles, the principle of large chunks of cash being paid out to would-be criminals, i.e. in relation to the £30,000 to buy the *Ocean Jubilee*, is well established. And again, I say, who the fuck was Alf? Just another Mr Bashir, or, indeed, another 'Mark'? And who the fuck was the man at my trial, Mr 'Standing on the Pavement' down in London? And I'm the grass; the man doing 28 years?

Anyway, I understand that, for some, it's difficult to see how Customs officers, and in particular those of the NIS, can so easily misrepresent themselves when necessary. At the 16-week trial of Thomas Porter and John Smith at the High Court in Kilmarnock in May 1997, a Customs officer known only as 'Frank' testified that they were tipped off about the gang 11 months before the eventual sting. But Judge Lord Abernethy said Customs had produced a 'diary of events' which showed they'd been watching the men for four years. And I'm the one who'd supposedly grassed them. I was in fucking Mozambique at the time! Still, as 'luck' would have it, the same outfit from NIS in Paisley were to testify at the High Court in Dunfermline relating to my case. They stated that Customs were first alerted by a phone call from my shop in Edinburgh, a bugged phone call. But it can be proven that no phone calls were made from the shop for some months prior to this incident taking place. The premises were closed and the phone bill was available to back this up. But neither this nor any warrants were either challenged or seen by my counsel. Why not?

In all, the story of 'Operation Balvenie' is best described as a story with layers. Certain events happened – these are facts. But like layers of acetate being placed across an overhead projector, each sheet adds an insight, not altering the structure, but complementing it. Each layer is a key, a key that makes sense of the previous slide. The question is, then, how many slides exist and, ultimately, who knows when the last slide is on? I don't – but I know who does.

Two years later I had my appeal. During the hearing before Lord Justice Clerk, Lord Kirkwood and Lord Hamilton, Neil Murray QC, the QC who had represented me during the original trial, submitted that my two sentences of fourteen years were excessive. Yet, for some reason, he took no objection to the fact that they were made consecutive to each other. I couldn't for the life of me understand why.

For the first charge, he accepted that I was the organiser of the British end, but stated that there was always a person beyond me in the background, outside the jurisdiction of the British courts. He was referred to in the trial as 'Alf'. Alf, of course, was a Customs and Excise man, so consequently I was far from being the instigator or the principal. And lo and behold, they accepted that I wasn't at the top of the pyramid, but instead an organiser putting into effect the plans of others, which I'd engaged in at a time of financial difficulty.

In relation to the second charge of 'defeating the ends of justice', my QC pointed out that the trial judge Lord Dawson had stated my culpability to be no less than that of the first charge, and so had imposed the same: the maximum. This view we firmly disputed. Lord Dawson's observation, that setting fire to the cannabis would endanger not only the vessel but both Gary's life and my own, as well as the officers attempting to seize its cargo, was a serious cause for concern. Dawson had stated, 'Nevertheless, you put this deadly plan into operation, endangering the lives of a number of officers of Her Majesty's Customs and Excise bravely going about their duty and, indeed, causing the death of one such gallant officer. Had you been, as your counsel envisaged, charged and convicted of his homicide, I would have had no hesitation in sentencing you to a life imprisonment.'

My QC chose not to dispute that danger arose from the fire. But within the context of the original charge sheet, and for good reason, the Crown had chosen not to charge me with manslaughter. So in this case it was improper for the trial judge to treat me as if I had been responsible for causing the death. Then he referred to my original attempt at pleading guilty to both charges, and how Lord Dawson had been informed of this prior to the trial, but that the Crown was unwilling to accept it in the absence of guilty pleas from my co-accused; something which was never going to happen.

I even did them a favour, though I regret it now. You see, during the trial there was a lot of doubt over the identification of the *Isolda*. In terms of the video evidence, Nicholas Ernest Jones, who'd never given evidence in a court before and who refused to answer certain questions, while seeking guidance from the gallery when faced with others, stated that the material was never intended to be used in evidence, but was for internal debriefing purposes only. And to cause more confusion, it was suggested that this aerial surveillance video, used at the trial to show the Dutch yacht *Isolda* coming alongside the *Ocean Jubilee*, may, in fact, have shown a completely different vessel. A crucial element in substantiating this claim was a report from BMT Offshore Aberdeen, a leading multidisciplinary engineering and technology consultancy and the official assessors called in to examine the *Isolda*. BMT says it would have been an operation 'of some difficulty' to bring the *Isolda* and the *Ocean Jubilee* together to transfer the cannabis. The examination found 'no evidence of damage to the deck-edge fenders on *Isolda* as could be expected to be inflicted by the steel-hulled *Ocean Jubilee*'. After comparing the surveillance video with a later film of the *Isolda* under tow in Aberdeen Harbour, BMT said that the tow video 'gives further backing to the opinion that the vessel appearing at the start of the surveillance video was not the *Isolda* at all'.

But beyond this, there was also a healthy doubt over the authenticity of the tape itself. Two further independent video experts, one of whom was called in by the judicial pressure group 'Justice For All', claimed that there were certain irregularities, which meant that the film fell far short of the necessary standards demanded in court. It was said by the Crown that the drugs were transferred from the *Isolda* to the *Ocean Jubilee* in 23 minutes. However, both experts cited gaps in the footage, including the crucial 23 minutes.

> There is an accepted standard when engaging in this type of evidence-gathering exercise . . . and the first rule is that the tape be authenticated at the point where recording has started and again before uninterrupted recording is stopped. The moment you have a break that is not authenticated the material becomes useless as evidence.

Indeed, at 1.58 a.m. on 29 July a voice on the tape is heard saying the boats are 5 to 6 miles apart. At 2.24 a.m. they are said to be together, but the camera is switched off. When the camera comes back on at 2.47 a.m., the boats are as far apart as 1 mile. Assuming the film was shot at the same height throughout and the boats separated at the same speed with which they came together, the time the vessels were side by side must have been considerably less than twenty-three minutes – possibly just one minute. So in defence, they claimed that, as the boats weren't together for more than two minutes, it was impossible for 3 tonnes of cannabis to be transferred. Well, sorry, but it was, and I told the court so. Anyway, in mitigation of my sentence, my QC drew these matters to Dawson's attention, but he didn't seem to think they were of any merit.

As for Gary Hunter, his treatment pretty much sums up the whole affair. At his appeal, his QC took a similar approach to his sentence, in that, for much the same reasons, 14 years was excessive. He referred to a number of instances where sentences had been given in comparable cases, and stated that Brian Silverman, a co-accused in the original trial in charge of the London end, who was regarded by Lord Dawson as being a 'major player', had received ten years at retrial, following his original sentence being quashed. He pointed out that Gary never had the same level of involvement as me – an understatment, to say the least. And as he wasn't a 'player', there should have been a real difference between our sentences. You see, Gary was never a criminal. In fact, he never had a criminal background and I only recruited him for his technical skills, as he'd received useful training while working at Ferranti. When I bought the *Ocean Jubilee* in Milford Haven, Gary was mainly busy in the engine room and was never part of the deal by which she was acquired. This was a deliberate move on my part. I wanted a worker, not a partner! And although there was a load of evidence at the trial relating to phone calls, none of them involved him, while any other evidence linking Gary to the crime only related to his movements with me, and not to him acting alone. So much so that, while the *Ocean Jubilee* lay at Scrabster for the weeks before the job, he was in Leeds, getting on with his own business. Hardly the actions of a major criminal!

In relation to the second charge, his QC supported mine in his criticism of the trial judge's reference to the cause of the Customs man's death. He said that if the Crown had considered us responsible for causing the cutter to come into contact with the *Ocean Jubilee*, they would have charged us with culpable homicide – but they didn't! He pointed out that, when the boarding of another vessel was carried out, it was always done by inflatable. And that, in sentencing Gary, Dawson had said to him that much of what he had said to me should also be directed at him – a load of piss, I say! Dawson added: 'Throughout your evidence you displayed a purely callous attitude to the officers of Customs and Excise, some of whom risked their lives in saving yours.' But Gary's QC challenged this reference to a 'callous attitude' as incomprehensible. The same could also be said when Dawson stated: 'But for his selfish action in trying to desert the burning vessel, the Customs cutter would not have required to approach the *Ocean Jubilee* and the Customs officer would not have lost his life.' The reality, though, was that it was inconceivable that Gary would have voluntarily jumped into the sea, or have set fire to the cargo with a view to abandoning ship. He had no lifejacket, and the sea was heavy and freezing. It was a miracle that he'd survived. He'd simply been directed to get off the boat, had put his foot down, and fallen. At the trial no one had accused him of deserting, let alone causing the death. So in other words, if my sentence was a travesty, then Gary's was a tragedy!

Anyway, in considering our appeals, the three Justices gave their decision. They agreed that Lord Dawson, in my case, was right to lay down a long sentence for such an 'elaborate' enterprise. And although not at the top of the pyramid – 'Alf' being at the top – I was still the organiser at the British end. However, I'd aided the court by pleading guilty at the outset and hadn't contested, and had assisted in the leading of evidence, which had brought out my role before the jury. These considerations were of distinct significance, but Lord Dawson, for some reason, seemed to have attached no importance to them. For this, the appeal judges concluded that the 14 years originally imposed were excessive.

As regards the second charge, Lord Justice Clerk simply wrote:

We find the trial judge's reference to the causation of the death of the Customs and Excise Officer disturbing. We have come to the conclusion that he misdirected himself in this respect, and on that basis we propose to consider the appropriate sentence for that charge *de novo*. There is no doubt that there was a contingency plan for setting fire to the cargo of cannabis resin which was hatched on the mainland, and that suitable accelerants were put on board for this purpose. To set fire to a cargo on the high seas plainly carries with it a special degree of danger to the lives of those who may become involved. McLean compounded the danger by setting the throttle of the vessel in the way in which he did.

He continued:

In considering what sentences to impose on these charges, we have in mind not only the individual sentences but also their combined effect. The suitability of disposal by way of consecutive sentences is not in question. We will quash the sentences imposed on McLean by the trial judge and substitute 12 years imprisonment on charge 1, and 9 years on charge 2, to be served consecutively, making a total of 21 years, which will be dated, as before, from 29 July 1996.

As for Gary, they stated:

As for the appellant Hunter. The remarks which we have made as to the magnitude and elaborate nature of the enterprise apply here also. He was active from an early stage, so far as the evidence discloses. However, he was not in any sense an organiser, but a technical assistant to McLean. In convicting him, the jury was plainly satisfied that he was aware from the outset of the nature of the enterprise from which he was playing his part. In relation to the second charge we are also satisfied that the trial judge misdirected himself, not only by inference by remarks which he addressed to McLean, but also from those which he directed to Hunter himself. We will accordingly consider what was the appropriate sentence for this charge *de novo*. Having regard to the circumstances put before us and through the submissions which we have heard, we will quash the sentences imposed on Hunter by the trial judge and substitute a sentence of 10 years imprisonment in respect of charge 1, and 7 years imprisonment on charge 2, to be served consecutively, making a total of 17 years, dated, as before, from 29 July 1996.

As a result I got 21 years while Gary got 17. Was justice served? My arse. Somebody was determined to keep us away. The average term served by someone convicted of the worst offence in the criminal spectrum is 10 to 12 years. The recommended custody period to be served by Abdelbaset ali Mohmed al-Megrahi, the Libyan convicted in 2000 by the Scottish court for the murder of 270 persons by blowing up Pan Am Flight 103 over Lockerbie, is 20 years. Something isn't right!

For me, the problem relates to two as yet unanswered questions: why the sentences were given as consecutive and not concurrent, and why neither QCs on appeal or the original trial chose not to argue against this. The appeal judges wrote in their summation, 'Mr Murray submitted that the two sentences of 14 years were excessive, individually and cumulatively. He took no objection to the fact that they were made consecutive with each other.' They further said, 'The suitability of disposal by way of consecutive sentences is not in question.' But this begs the question for me, why the fuck not?

The basis on which the consecutive sentence was imposed after the original trial, and not argued against at the appeal hearing, is that a person can receive a consecutive sentence for each charge where the separate charges are different crimes and rely on different facts and circumstances. So the charge in relation to the drug-smuggling took evidence from a number of different sources, not necessarily from the day that the Customs cutter intercepted me. Quite separate was the attempt to pervert the course of justice. However, Lord Dawson and the appeal judges seemed to have completely forgotten something I later came to know as the 'totality principle'. The Criminal Justice Act 1991, s. 28(2)(b) is clear: 'A court which passes a number of consecutive sentences should review the aggregate of the sentences and consider whether the aggregate sentence is just and appropriate taking the offences as a whole.' It's then the court's duty to review any case which carries consecutive sentences with this principle in mind. Why not mine? In particular, there are three instances where it's mandatory. The first of which, and with specific relevance here, is 'where the offender has committed a series of offences of moderate gravity and has received an aggregate sentence equivalent to the sentences which would have been imposed for an offence of a much more serious nature'. So, once again, the Lockerbie bomber gets 20 years for the murder of 270 people, and I get 28 reduced to 21 for importing cannabis, bought from Customs in the first place, and for subsequently setting fire to it in a bid to evade capture, a capture which was shown to be wholly unnecessary.

Anyway, enough said! I'm here now and that's that. And while I might be moaning, I'm far from complaining. 'Always cheat, always win. The only unfair fight's the one you lose,' was the eighth commandment I'd left on the ill-fated *Trader*. So to live under any other mantra would make me a hypocrite, and a hypocrite I'm not! But I am under no illusions as to how the world works, and that's a comfort. It's conditioned, and our country, although great, is a conditioner of it. And it's simple. There's one basic concept which underpins the lot: the idea of our society's own basic benevolence. That we, on the balance of things, are inherently good, and as a nation only limit our criticisms to whether our agencies' strategies are the right ones for achieving their always-noble objectives. Piss! Take our tabloids: champions of the people, yet they branded me a grass like it was a bad thing. Grasses prevent crimes, don't they? Aren't appeals for information really appeals for grasses? So where's their benevolence? Or are they really the champions of the criminal classes? No – in reality, they're neither. They're just the vendors of papers, and flag-waving sells. And as for the Crown, they're not daft either. It's like the Hutton Inquiry into Dr David Kelly's death. By focusing on one thing, they avoid the bigger picture: going to war in the first place under their own false pretences! Still, I'm not egocentric enough to claim a platform with the government, but it's the same old means. Brand me evil and label me a grass, while focusing on the how and forgetting about the why.

Prison, on the other hand, is shit! In fact it's appalling. It deprives you of everyone you love, and of everything you own. It renders you a hollow man, reduced to suffering and needs while the regimentation that you first despise soon becomes the very thing you rely on for sanity. And if, that day in Huelva, I thought I'd entered *jigoku*, now, looking back, it makes me laugh. The two Japanese characters are 'the lowest' and 'to be imprisoned'. I wasn't then, but I am now, because with your freedom and liberty, you've always got choices, and choices are hope. As soon as Dawson's hammer came down, he thought he'd smashed me, but never! I've lived a hundred lives, and within each one I've lived a hundred more. I was born on borrowed time, and lived within its debt. And like a con's view of regimentation, my lifelong aversion to hope soon became a longing to feel it again. And, in time, I did. My fight was on!

After your conviction and sentence, the powers that be are quick to categorise you. So whether you're Category A, B, C or D is based on your supposed potential for escaping, based on various pieces of info that the authorities put together. To do this they make risk assessments, which include your custodial records, details of previous offences, details of the charges, pleas, findings and sentences, and really anything else that the Prison Service has, such as medical and psychological reports, in case you're a nut. Once all that's available, prisoners are categorised according to the likelihood of their escape and the threat that they'd pose to the public should they succeed in doing it.

From there, you're allocated a suitable jail, and move through the system by a process of recategorisation. It's supposed to determine whether the risks posed at the previous assessment have changed, and, if so, by how much. Like everything else, risk levels can rise or fall during a sentence, so your category and allocation has to reflect it. And so, if you ever do get considered for an open jail, it's essential for your risk levels to be totally reduced, just like me, who poses no risk at all!

When I was remanded in custody on 29 July 1996, and sentenced on 13 March 1997, I was initially deemed a Category A prisoner and a so-called 'strict escapee', which basically meant I was glued to the walls. But soon, with a bit of sense and a helping hand, I was downgraded to Category B on 10 June 1998 and lost my strict-escapee status on 23 March 1999. I was subsequently recategorised as Category C at HMP Shotts, just outside Glasgow, before being transferred to the English prison system on 13 March 2001. Now, here's another revelation: it's a simple fact that on the English circuit you get to an open nick quicker!

Anyway, I was received at HMP Bristol, a local prison, on 23 March 2001. Then, on 20 August of that year, I was allocated to HMP Erlestoke, which is a Category C prison, before arriving at HMP Leyhill on 4 September 2002, where I'm an exemplary prisoner and have maintained perfect behaviour and timekeeping on all of my temporary releases. I've gone from Cat A, 'strict escapee', to Cat D, 'major fucking trustee', in what, six and a bit years? That's got to be a first! Anyway, now I've not only got hope, but I'm full of it!

Well, as an open nick means unsupervised day trips to Bristol, it's amazing who comes to visit when your visits aren't noted. Amongst others, I've met Ivan; it had been a few years and was damn good to see him, and in his typical fashion, he appeared from nowhere. He said he was in London on business, and seemed well determined to see me. When we met in a coffee bar, he told me he had HIV, and that he didn't have too long to go. I searched for emotion within him, but good old Ivan, he couldn't give a fuck! But as we talked for hours, we spoke about me, and when we did, he got a look in his eyes that I'd only seen once before. Then he stared right at me and said, 'Roddy, you're my only family, and what's happened to you keeps me awake at night. There's wrongs needing righted.'

I nodded. 'You're fucking right on that one,' I said. 'But it's all right. Things are happening. They'll never beat me!' But I knew what he was really getting at – this was Ivan. He shook his head and wouldn't speak, and although I tried to skip around it, he just kept on staring. Soon, our silence seemed cold.

'I'm not leaving without them,' he said. Then, without breaking my gaze, he slid over a paper napkin, followed by a pen. 'Wrongs are needing righted!'

I thought long and hard about it, but what I did then, I don't regret. Like that morning in the Congo, all those years before, this was war and people died. So I picked up the pen and wrote them down. 'On one condition,' I said. He nodded up. 'Only if something happens to me, all right?'

'All right!'

And with that we finished our 20 deck of Marlboro, then said goodbye like two mates after a weekend. Neither of us were very good at farewells. All the best, my friend!

Anyway, back to now. Who knows what the future will hold? Who even knows when it starts? As you'll appreciate, writing about 'the now' is more difficult than my past – for obvious reasons. But even with back then, I've had to change some names, alter some times and move some places. Well, to quote my favourite film, 'no need to give the Zulus the present of fire'! Anyway, along the way I've had some laughs, some of which I've not had a chance to write about. Such as me putting a human skull in the window of 363 and hanging a fag out of its mouth. Or the hippy and the broken watch, where, in a fit of anger at him having gotten away after being cheeky, I threw it at him, and, like a hole in one, it smacked into his head and knocked him flat. Or the circling panda car, where I held up a sign saying 'Come in 23' like it was a boat on a lake. Or 'gimpy Ross', the one-legged thief who I'd caught in the side lane at night, next to Inverleith, when I was wearing nothing but cordless 'jammy bottoms', so when the police arrived, they found me bare-arsed, battering fuck out of a man with his own wooden leg.

But beyond that, I've had some sad times as well – no doubt! I've lost some really close friends; something I got used to at too early an age. And yes, I've got my regrets, and if I could, I would change them all in an instant. They may be part of what makes us, but they're fundamental to what breaks us. And that's a shame. And then, of course, there's my family, which is my life! We've long gotten used to being separated by distance – but never by loss of liberty. Enough said.

So, in the end, what can I say of myself? Like that firefight in the Congo when Mark, my mate, dropped down dead, I've had so many chances to prove to myself who I am, and I always did. But like I said then, you don't need a bloodbath to know yourself; it's just about stretching your comfort pocket and pushing your boundaries, and when you're on the edge, just about to snap, take a picture of yourself and have a good look. What will you see? What I saw defined me for the rest of my life. I invited pain in, and it became my friend, and when I welcomed its arrival it became me and I became it. For that, I survived when I should have died – that's resilience! In my split definition of humanity, I'd become the second type of person, the type who sees his own blood but tastes it, and, like a wounded animal, attacks. In the face of almost certain death, Mark, the crazy bastard, had attacked. It was because he enjoyed the taste. So now, like Mark, after having lost it all, but with a new dawn breaking, what can I say? I seem to enjoy it too!

POSTSCRIPT

Oh – and by the way. Remember my treasure, abandoned when the *Dansk* went on fire? Well, it's still there, and I'm the only bugger who knows where it is! But even though it's pretty accessible, I can't ever touch it. So, as a gift to humanity, and for a fair bit of humour, here's what I've done. I'm giving it to you, and there's a clue in the book. Find it, and you'll have 3 tonnes of Morocco's finest, perfectly preserved. Enjoy!

CHAPTER IX

OUT WITH THE LAUNDRY!

Like the 'gentleman and a scholar' he was, Rod McLean waved to the guards and left the nick. It was 10.00 a.m. on Saturday, 8 November 2003. As a man who kept impeccable time and whose behaviour inside and out was exemplary, there was no reason to suspect that his 21st day release should be any different from the 20 before. Planning to get the bus, he was pleasantly surprised by a fellow detainee's offer of a lift. When you've only got eight hours a week to live your life, an extra half-hour, not on a bus, is like a day. On arriving, he thanked his ride, and with what seemed like all the time in the world, made his way through the centre of Bristol, stopping for a cooked breakfast and a read of the morning papers. Lasting until lunch-time, his bottomless cup of coffee finally bottomed out, and he then spent an hour wandering the shops. At two on the nose, like the changing of the guard, Rod McLean absconded from prison. Thanks to the 20 visits before, he knew exactly where he was going and how long it would take. On rounding the corner from Woodland Road onto Elton Road, in the university district of Bristol, he found the 'firm'.

As he approached the blue hire van, a stocky man with a shaved head leaned out and ushered him round to the passenger's seat. But before he could reach it, the side door slid open and a voice inside called him in. It was a voice he recognised, the voice of an old friend. As soon as he sat down, the man issued him with a change of clothes, a baseball cap and, most importantly, his new identity. From that moment, John Nicholson was born. The time was now 2.45 p.m.

All secure, the inconspicuous troika left town and sped for the M5 North to join the A5 to Holyhead in Wales. At some point, probably around 5.00 p.m., Rod telephoned HMP Leyhill to say he would be late. As his lateness was completely uncharacteristic, and perhaps due to the fact that the prison was operating with a shortage of staff – around 12 officers, while a further 50 inmates were still away – allowances were made. At 6.00 p.m., the exact time he was due to return, Rod McLean as John Nicholson boarded the Stenaline Catamaran Explorer from the port of Holyhead, en route to Dun Laoghaire in the Republic of Ireland. When he failed to return by 8.10 p.m., over two hours late for his curfew, the staff notified Avon and Somerset Constabulary. By that time, Rod McLean had escaped from prison, gained a new identity, made it to another country on a 99-minute ferry crossing and, more incredibly than that, was no longer a man on the run, but a man who was now actively back in business.

They call it the secret island. Take the N11 south from Dublin and you'll hit Wexford: the first soil touched by the Normans when they invaded Ireland in 1169, and now home to Rod McLean. Serviced by two major rivers, the Slaney and the Barrow, and with beaches spanning 200 km of coastline intermittently breached by scenic villages and picturesque harbours, the setting provided an ideal backdrop for Popeye's return.

The next morning, on the outskirts of Wexford Town, Rod knocked on a door. It was Billy's. Billy, a former soldier with the King's Own Scottish Borderers, was one of the many faces that fell in and out of Rod's life over the years. As a man who trusted no one, he was a great believer in 'skeleton crews', groups put together for one job at a time. Billy was a leading skeleton. He had done time while Rod was in HMP Shotts and, as 'luck' would have it, was now working within the Wexford syndicate. A small world indeed!

OUT WITH THE LAUNDRY!

'Are you fucking kidding?' said Billy, in shock. Stood before him was Rod McLean. 'Get in here, you arse!' he said, frantically grabbing him with a laugh. 'You bastard!'

'I've done a runner, went out with the laundry, know what I mean?'

'Fuck me! C'mon, quick, through to the kitchen. You want a drink, mate?'

And with that, Rod McLean set about explaining the version of reality Billy needed to hear. What he didn't explain was that he'd just come from meeting the firm. He'd never had any intention of staying with them any longer than was necessary and that necessity had passed with the first night. He showed Billy his new identity, a set of the usual documents including a passport.

'Fuck, they're well made,' he said, looking at them from various angles with the expertise of a lifetime of fraud. 'Who did them, someone inside?'

Rod winked. 'Yes, someone inside.'

That morning, the firm had taken him to see the boat they could offer him. Rod wasn't impressed. Of the three handouts on offer – money, a boat and somewhere to stay – Rod had chosen the bundle of cash. That was sure to piss off the firm, but he knew that, in reality, they'd have expected nothing less; something that clicked as he stood over the Vivacity 20 motor yacht on display. In the car world, a Ferrari will attract as much attention as a clapped-out Lada, albeit for opposite reasons; he'd just been offered the Lada.

'All right then, John,' said Billy, after hearing his plight. 'You need a job?'

Rod laughed. 'Yes, I do, mate. Why not?'

BACK TO WORK

A few breakfast rums and 20 Silk Cuts later, they were en route to Kilmore Quay, a typical fishing village. On entering, he was instantly struck by the blaze of yellow thatch and whitewash that ran the length of the road. 'Things you miss from inside a jail,' he said, turning to Billy. The Green Flag Marina, with its picturesque lobster pots and shark-fishing tackle, was an unobvious cog in a larger wheel, operated to supply two million UK cannabis users with the tools of their leisure.

'There she is,' said Billy, proudly standing aside his vessel. 'It's an aft-cabin Colvic Watson 26. Built in 1984.'

Rod paused and looked the boat up and down, before jumping on board to make himself busy. Like a mechanic buying a second-hand car, he looked in all the right places. Any structure is only as strong as its weakest point, none more so than boats.

'First run's tonight. You up for it?'

'Yes,' said Rod, still head-down in the dark spaces.

'Right, we'd better get you introduced to the other three.'

'No need; I've met them!'

'You have?' said Billy, who wanted to press, but stopped short. Rod looked at him like a parent to a guilty child. He'd met them the night before, when he'd arrived. Of the three, the third was the firm man, one was Spanish – although you'd never have suspected it – and the other was local. The boss was the local man. As drug dealers go in that part of the world, the chances are that somewhere along the line a paramilitary connection will pop up. But, for whatever reason, it seems that this was the exception. Whether it was because most of the cannabis was for UK consumption, and Wexford was just a safer place to operate from – like the Winston Boys used Gibraltar – or whether the man had just got 'lucky', is unclear. However, Rod cared little for luck, especially when it stretched for sustained periods of time.

Right from the beginning, Rod had felt like he was part of a well-oiled process. In his suspicious mind, he wondered how many in his position had passed through the Wexford criminal-laundering plant, or how many schemes like it were operating around the British Isles or Europe. Even regarding Billy, it all seemed a bit too perfect. In all, the shape of anything depends on the perspective it's viewed from. It reminded him of his old gun-running days in Africa, when the people he recognised would pop up in the unlikeliest of places. He would think of Occam's Razor, useless trivia learnt from his long days at sea: 'Don't make more assumptions than the minimum needed to explain an occurrence.' In other words, when you're explaining a coincidence, keep it simple!

That evening, just 24 hours after his escape, Rod as John Nicholson and now-relegated-to-first-mate Billy went out to rendezvous with a Spanish fishing boat somewhere off the southern Irish coast. The boats came alongside, and within minutes had parted company, with Rod and Billy heading back to Wexford to hand over their cargo to the Irish local. Two nights later Rod made the same journey, but this time sailed to England, where he met a smaller fishing boat one mile off the coast of Cornwall. The night after that, four days after gaining his freedom, his firm contact announced he was leaving, and gave him a number to call the following day at 12. It would be his old friend.

For the next week and a half, Rod made three more trips to and from Wexford, each time taking his cargo to England, and each time being met by the same boat. Around 23 or 24 November, Rod made his first trip back to British soil. This time he offloaded the cargo, and, courtesy of the small fishing vessel he had been rendezvousing with, made his way back ashore, where he followed the cannabis by car en route to London. On arrival he was taken to a flat in Clapham, south of the river, where he was welcomed by a man named Sonnar.

The Clapham flat had a 'red flag' on it. That is, it was known by both the local police and Scotland Yard for being a place frequented by the higher echelons of the drug trade. Drugs were never on the site, and it made better viewing for the police from a distance than up close and inside. Sonnar, who lived in the flat, was more of a resident caretaker than a homeowner. He, and others like him, only let the apartments, and never stayed longer than six months. That way, they hoped to stay, if not ahead, then at least on a par with the authorities. Sonnar himself was a well-spoken man in his early 30s. A Turkish Kurd from the south of the country, he'd been given asylum with the rest of his family in the early 1990s. He had a scar down his face like a half-moon from the top of his forehead to the base of his chin; a souvenir from his old life in a north London kebab shop, the night when Arsenal played Galatasaray at home.

After spending two nights in London, Rod had achieved his

objectives. The first was to arrange a meeting with a notorious Turkish crime clan for the following week; the second was to instigate the start of a cannabis deal through Sonnar. He then returned to Wexford the same way he'd come, courtesy of Billy's water taxi.

The following morning they were back at Billy's.

'What's your plan?' Billy asked in a rhetorical manner, pouring another breakfast rum after a night on the seas.

To his surprise, Rod answered him. 'I'm trying to put a deal together with the Turks.'

'Where from?'

'Spain. Well, Morocco or Spain, the usual place.'

'Just hash?'

'Oh, yeah, you know me. Just the hash, but loads of it.'

'You should ask the "local" to see if he'll put you through to the source. You're not dealing with the same Turks as us, are you? Is it the "clan"?'

Rod smiled.

'Do they know you? I mean, do they know who you are?'

'Yes, I'm John, John the smuggler from Scotland, working on the Wexford job. Cut my teeth in East Africa after the Army. A good man that does what he says, when he says he'll do it. You know, a man you can do business with,' he said, standing up and walking over to the cooker, brandishing a pack of Irish-recipe sausages. What Rod wasn't saying, was that he actually knew the clan. Well, nobody, not even the firm, knew this. They knew who he was, and would more than likely have known that he should have been inside. Again, he'd gotten to know them in the old days, and, although they were as ruthless as you could get, they'd never had any reason to cross swords.

Rod was under no illusions as to what the firm were after. They wanted the clan on a plate, at best, or at worst, some insight into their routes for both drugs in and money out. The clan were the biggest for the heroin trade, and although knowledge of their trafficking routes from source countries into Europe and the UK had been improving, due to the gang's flexibility, the firm was short on details. In practice, consignments rarely travelled the whole way from Afghanistan to

OUT WITH THE LAUNDRY!

Europe in a single journey. Normally they'd be bought and sold by different gangs along the route, while the modes of transport changed, and the loads split or merged. All of this meant that the details varied according to the capabilities and preferences of whoever had control at the time.

Rod, however, was nobody's fool. Right from the beginning he had no intentions of handing them the clan. Yes, he had taken the firm's help in getting out, but even they would have known that this was a long shot. Instead, Rod was to offer them apples in place of oranges. After all, something is better than nothing, especially when that something is truly something. Besides, Rod had a trick up his sleeve and he was working towards it. Like anything, including boats, an organisation is only as strong as its weakest link. In the case of the firm, it was their 'accountability'.

By early December he had left Wexford and headed back to London. Sonnar had arranged another Turkish buyer for what Rod had said he could offer, approximately 2 tonnes of cannabis, with the inference that it would be the first of many from a regular source on a secure network. (Rod's buried treasure, meanwhile, would be remaining untouched beneath the sea, as going anywhere near it would have been suicidal.) The buyer, a large fish within one of the Turkish crime clans, was prepared to pay the money provided Rod made a goodwill deposit of £30,000 to be held by a mutually trusted third party until the goods arrived. The firm obliged with the cash, but only after Rod had tried to secure it himself by withdrawing the amount from a building society and been refused by a meticulous manager.

After some delicate negotiations, and the odd empty promise, Rod managed to extract the details of the Wexford source and a sound recommendation from the local. So, for a cut beyond what he'd normally receive for several of his own runs, the local agreed to stump up the necessary 'front' money needed to buy the 2 tonnes directly at source. This time, instead of rendezvousing for small amounts off the Irish coast, Rod would sail directly down to the port of Cadiz on the southern tip of Spain and moor up in one of the sports basins, either

Puerto America or the Nautical Club. Between them, there were 231 mooring points — a substantial number for blending in unnoticed. Whilst there, he'd wait for word before heading to a designated spot where the transfer would be made. He would then return to England, where it would be passed on to the Turks. In the meantime, while waiting on a meeting with the clan, Rod as John Nicholson moved into a hostel at 22 Streatham Place in SW2 London, owned by another Turkish Cypriot, Savas Stavrou. The clan meeting was then postponed for a week for unknown reasons.

Being a highly intelligent man, Rod knew not to arouse suspicion. For him, you either had to be working, or be on the dole. Well, for obvious reasons, he could never sign on, so when the job of a part-time helper came up at the hostel — for free board and a few pounds in his pocket — he jumped at it. There's nothing to suggest that Savas Stavrou knew anything about who he was or what he was doing. While he busied himself rejoining the land of the inconspicuous, his on-duty hours were spent scouring the contents of endless yachting trade magazines, looking for the perfect boat to head south in.

It had now been a month since Rod had absconded. To date, he'd felt quite safe. The only people who knew where he was could either be trusted, or had a vested interest in keeping him on the outside. And, due to the quality of his new identity, there was no reason for any of his trails to be flagged up. The one and only possibility that could spook him was having his face on the cover of every newspaper. For 'some reason', this never happened. As such, one of the most wanted men in Britain was just another of London's eight million faces.

TIME FOR TURKEY

One week before Christmas, word finally came through that the meeting was on. At a time and a place set by the clan, Rod called the firm to say it was on. The day after, one of their men arrived at the Streatham guest house with a hire car, already taken in the name of John Nicholson. The car was necessary for Rod to make his own way to the meeting, which turned out to be in the Muswell Hill area of north London. Both the contents of the meeting and the people present are unclear; however, a second meeting was set for the beginning of the year, indicating that, on the face of it, the clan was interested in doing business. As soon as he returned, he contacted the firm. A meeting was arranged for 23 December between Rod and one of their men, but it passed with a no-show, as did Christmas Eve, Christmas Day and Boxing Day. Rod could smell a rat.

By the afternoon of Saturday, 27 December 2003, when there was still no contact, he knew something was seriously up. At the very least, contact should have been made; silence was never an option. As a result he made a few phone calls, including one to Billy in Wexford to say that all was well and that he was going ahead with the cannabis deal as planned. The next day, Sunday, 28 December, the story broke. 'Cover-up fury as evil drugs baron flees jail,' was the *Mail on Sunday* 'exclusive'. That was the first of hundreds to come. From the television to the radio, the entire show was unfolding like a virtual matinée, journalists scrambling to 'one-up' their rivals on the developing plot. To many there was astonishment at how a man who had served a relatively short period of such a long custodial sentence, with all the intelligence about his background, resources, contacts and foreign connections, could have found himself quietly transferred to an open prison more than four years before he was even eligible to apply for release on parole, and with over a decade of his sentence left to serve. And why hadn't the Prison Service or the police announced he had checked out of HMP Leyhill for almost two months until the story broke?

For those concerned, the playing field had just evened out. On the face of it, no one knew where the leak to the press had come from. Whether deliberate or by chance, everyone's first reaction was to consolidate their positions and to see who or what was making a move. While the rest of the world was after Rod McLean, John Nicholson went about his business in the knowledge that the firm would be watching him closely. It seems that this eventuality was integral to his plan from the outset. As long as he did what they'd expected him to do before the news ever broke, they'd probably stand off and bide their time.

On 6 January 2004, the second clan meeting took place. This time, however, and unknown to the firm, the topic was not of bringing drugs in, but of getting Rod out – his exit plan all along. As he'd always thought, the firm did continue to hold off in the hope of salvaging something from the media-imposed wreckage and, to this end, seeing him with the clan could only have raised their interest. To keep their attention, he also decided to go ahead and buy the boat that he'd been looking for. In keeping with the drug-smuggling plan, he needed something that would suit a Spanish marina, but also something he could sink if he had to. For that, a 30-ft yacht moored in the south-coast port of Hamble caught his eye. All he needed to do was to find a way of buying it.

Two days later he called Billy. On 10 January Billy arrived at the Streatham guest house.

'We all set for the deal?' Rod asked.

'It's all off. The local doesn't want to know. And I can't see the Turks wanting to play now that they know who you really are. Mate, you won't even get through Sonnar's front door. What about the clan?'

Rod didn't answer, but sat down in the one chair of his bedsit accommodation.

'Look,' said Billy, tossing over a copy of that day's *Daily Record*. 'I picked it up this morning at Leicester Square Tube station. Pages four and five!'

Rod opened it up, and with an expressionless face began to read:

MI5 Riddle of the Run Away Drug Baron – Secret Service helped con escape to Africa.

An escaped drug baron who helped cause a Customs man's death has been spirited out of Britain by the secret service, police believe. Sources say cannabis smuggler Roddy McLean is hiding in Africa after walking to freedom. And detectives and Customs men believe MI5 helped him escape so he could carry on his role as one of their informers. It's thought the Security Services are particularly interested in his contacts in Mozambique.

'Is it true, Roddy?' asked Billy, now seeming unsure of himself.

Rod looked blankly at him.

'It's a lot of pish,' he moaned, before throwing the paper back and lighting a smoke.

'Rod, they're branding you a grass. The Turks will fucking kill you if you set a foot near them. They're going to think you're a plant. Last time I knew, the local just thought you were on the run, but he's likely to shut up shop when he sees this shit.'

Rod laughed. 'The local. That guy's something else. Don't worry about him; he's probably the safest trafficker in Ireland.' He paused. 'In any case, it makes no difference, that was never my endgame anyway, just one of the many ways of doing it. Besides, this is what I'm really up to. I'm going to buy the boat I was to use for picking up the gear in Cadiz, and instead, I'm going to use it to fuck off. Simple as that.'

'Simple as that?'

'Yes, simple as that! But I need one last favour from you, my friend. I need you to come down with me and do the buying from the guy that owns it. If he recognises me from the papers, I've had it.'

Billy thought long and hard, but in the end there was always going to be one answer – yes. 'Rod, I know you say you're not. But if MI5 did have something to do with your exit from Leyhill, now that it's out, they could bang you back up any time.'

'Listen, I've got fuck all to do with them, right? But if this happened to someone else, the last thing they'd want is him going back to jail, where he'd sing like a bird. If I was them, I'd want to make sure he'd "escaped" for ever. Know what I mean?'

Billy stopped pressing.

So, later that day, the duo drove down to the river Hamble estuary, sandwiched between Bournemouth and Portsmouth, and Billy gave the owner £3,000 in cash. After checking it over for seaworthiness, he explained to the proprietors of MDL Marinas that he would be back again the next week, when he would remove it to another port.

On arrival back in London, Rod drove Billy to Clapham Junction station.

'Rod, what the fuck's going on?' he said timidly, shaking his hand with one foot out of the car.

'Billy, the wood from the trees, mate, the wood from the fucking trees!'

And with that cryptic message, Billy closed the door. It was the last time he was to see his friend.

For Rod, this was all just a grand diversion. He had no intentions of ever setting foot on the boat he had just bought. Like a giant white elephant, it would sit there taking up time and resources from those who would plot to 'off' him. The prospect of a fleeing convict disappearing on a 30-ft yacht in the middle of the Channel would be an opportunity too good to miss. Instead, Rod was leaving for Northern Cyprus courtesy of the clan. Even if he was ever located, the country still had no extradition treaty with Britain. And as for the firm, it was hoped that Cyprus was 'out of sight, out of mind'.

The date was Tuesday, 13 January 2004. Following an early afternoon trip to the yacht, Rod drove back to London, where he had a third and final meeting with the clan. He parted with the first third of a significant amount of money, with the second part to be paid on arrival in Cyprus, and the third some months later. The exit date was set for the next day, 14 January 2004. Things were now beginning to heat up. David Blunkett MP, the Home Secretary, was being pressured into investigating the circumstances of his disappearance at the highest level. Avon and Somerset police had finally issued an arrest warrant and informed Interpol, while every day the tabloid and broadsheet revelations were whipping the story into a frenzy.

On the face of it, Rod had left prison courtesy of the firm, smuggled drugs courtesy of the Wexford gang, infiltrated the clan courtesy of himself, and made leaps and bounds towards his own permanent freedom. On the other side of the coin, the firm had pulled the rug from under his feet and the media had been informed, forcing him into seeking help from the very people he was ousted to spy on in the first place. In all, it seemed like the plan and the alliance had fallen to bits. But had it?

Just what had he meant when he said 'the wood from the trees'?

Indeed, what had Rod in fact delivered? The firm had wanted him as close to the clan as possible. Forget north London, he was now on his way to Turkish Cyprus. The firm had wanted him inside their network by being one of their traffickers. He was so close that the clan were now trafficking him. The firm had wanted information on heroin trafficking. Rod was about to live at its epicentre and associate with its leaders on a daily basis. In all, Rod had made more progress inwards in two months than anyone had ever done in two years.

And of Rod, what had he delivered for himself? He wanted out of jail. He was out. He had needed both financial support and legitimacy. He got it. He needed the police, the Prison Service and, indeed, the law off his back. He had managed to negotiate that too. But beyond that, he had a future. He would live in Cyprus in the house of his dreams, have money in his pocket and would soon be able to access the shipping world of East Africa, the seas he loved the most. One way or another, he had engineered the whole thing way beyond anyone's expectations, and while the dogs fought over the scraps, he was running away with the meat. That is to say, with a helping hand from an 'old friend'.

Sitting in the pub with his old friend, on the eve of another spectacular coup in the making, there's no doubt that Rod's rum, a long glass of OVD, would have tasted better than ever. They'd had to overcome some serious obstacles to get to this point, but they'd managed it, and all in perfect time. For some reason, the firm had decided against proceeding with the arrangement, but somehow, within a 'firewall' almost, the arrangement lived. Who knows, that may have even been a play on behalf of his old friend to disassociate the firm from him. For Rod, he had always known that while his old friend could be trusted, the firm could not, and for that, when he had to, he had pulled his trump card, which cloaked him like a protective blanket. He had informed the media of his own escape.

At the meeting's end, final arrangements in check, he made his way back to the seedy guest house he called home. He'd always hoped to enjoy a retirement, but once again it would have to be shelved. The next morning, Rod McLean was to embark on another chapter of his epic life — a life that would, as always, serve both himself and his country in equal measure. His planned route out is unknown, although there is some evidence to suggest that most of it would be over land, probably by truck. In any event, it wouldn't have mattered, as he was soon to be back on the road, and back with his wanderlust. But that was not to be. That evening, Roddy McLean, the reluctant legend, was to breathe his last.

On 12 February 2004, 29 days after his death, a statement from the Metropolitan police read: 'At 10.35 a.m. on Wednesday, January 14, the body of a man was found at Streatham Place, SW2. A post-mortem examination was held at Greenwich mortuary and the cause of death was ruled to be natural causes (heart failure).' They would not explain why it took so long to make the announcement. Nor why Avon and Somerset police, the force still trying to recapture him, were kept in the dark for that period.

The *Daily Record* front page read:

> An escaped drug baron, suspected of being an MI5 grass, has been found dead in a London flat. Roddy McLean's body was discovered four days after the *Daily Record* told of fears that Secret Service officers had helped him escape from jail. Police sources are convinced that McLean was an MI5 informer. Some even believe he may have been murdered. A Scots police insider said, 'This may even have been made to look like a natural death before the body was found.'

A week after the announcement, Rod's body was taken back home to Scotland, where his family were making the necessary arrangements. Media scrutiny and speculation were at fever pitch. The government was demanding explanations and MPs were demanding explanations from the government. Some, such as Annabelle Ewing, the SNP Home Affairs spokeswoman at Westminster, demanded, 'We really need a public inquiry, as the authorities must not be allowed to get away with a cover-up.'

On 22 February, as the family prepared for the funeral service, detectives from Avon and Somerset requested a second post-mortem. The force, under strict instructions from the top, later known to be the Home Secretary David Blunkett, wanted toxicology tests carried out on his organs to find out whether the 'heart attack' was caused by noxious substances, as, to many, it was bewildering that this was never checked first time round. However, this did little to stem the mystery. As a senior Lothian and Borders police officer said at the time: 'If there had been a cover-up, it's possible McLean's organs could have been swapped before his body left the coroner's office in London – making the second post-mortem useless. Given the publicity this case attracted, it is simply unbelievable that toxicology tests were never carried out the first time round. Just what were they frightened of finding?'

VERITAS

What actually happened to Rod in his final hours can only be speculated on by most, and verified by a few. And until those few start talking, the mystery will remain. Rod used to say 'it's better to live one day as a wolf than a thousand as a sheep', and it was this ethos which meant that, although he'd lost the battle, he had won the war. And he did win, as in reality true victory comes from beating the demons inside yourself, and not in those around you. Some day, perhaps, when the time is right, those few who know what happened will be forced to consider their actions, and the truth shall set them free. But until then, they will carry their burden like the sword of Damocles. Only this time, it doesn't hang above them; it's within them.